TRUTH IN TRANSLATION

Accuracy and Bias in English Translations of the New Testament

Jason David BeDuhn

University Press of America,® Inc.
Lanham · New York · Oxford

Copyright © 2003 by
University Press of America,® Inc.
4501 Forbes Boulevard
Suite 200
Lanham, Maryland 20706
UPA Acquisitions Department (301) 459-3366

PO Box 317
Oxford
OX2 9RU, UK

All rights reserved
Printed in the United States of America
British Library Cataloging in Publication Information Available

ISBN 0-7618-2555-X (clothbound : alk. ppr.)
ISBN 0-7618-2556-8 (paperback : alk. ppr.)
ISBN: 978-0-7618-2556-2

For my Bible ladies:
my mother and grandmothers

CONTENTS

Preface	vii
Acknowledgments	xi
Introduction	xiii
The Origins of Modern English Bibles	1
The Work of Translation	11
Major English Translations	27
Bowing to Bias	41
Grasping at Accuracy	51
When is a Man not a Man?	63
Probing the Implicit Meaning	75
Words Together and Apart	89
An Uncertain Throne	97
Tampering with Tenses	103
And the Word was . . . What?	113
The Spirit Writ Large	135
A Final Word	161
Appendix: The Use of "Jehovah" in the NW	169
Bibliography	183
Index	189

PREFACE

This book is written to provide you with a foundation for understanding the New Testament in the form in which it comes to you today -- English translations of texts written about two-thousand years ago in Greek. There are many different English translations of the Bible, and no two read alike. If you have noticed this, you may have been alarmed. Since Christians believe that their salvation to some degree depends upon understanding the truths found in the Bible, the idea that Bibles differ in what they say can be very disturbing.

In my experience, people want to know which translation is the best, which is the most reliable, which has the least bias. Priests, ministers, and teachers like myself are often asked for their opinion and advice on this subject, and we all freely give it. We recommend particular Bibles and warn people away from others. Some people are content to take our advice simply on our authority, but others would like to know why we hold our opinion, and on what basis we have reached it. This book is for all those who ask why -- and everyone should ask why.

The general public can see for itself that Bible translations differ, but it possesses no criteria for judging those differences, or even clear information on why those differences exist. As a result, a great deal of misinformation and accusation can be found in the public discussion of the differences between Bibles. Of course there are reasons for the differences between Bibles, some good reasons and some bad reasons. To tell the difference between them, though, you need information on how

Bibles are made, who makes them, and what sort of things influence the choices made by Bible makers. This book is designed to be a starting point for exploring such information about the Bibles most widely in use in the English-speaking world.

Since all Christians agree on the great importance of the Bible as a source of religious truth, there is no more important subject for them to be informed about than the accuracy and reliability of the book they turn to repeatedly for answers and guidance in their lives. Yet, surprisingly, while an enormous amount of energy is spent on the interpretation of the English words of modern Bibles, very little attention is given in public to assessing the quality of the translations themselves. Only a handful of books have been published on this subject, and their own reliability is, unfortunately, very poor.

It may come as a shock to intellectuals, theologians, and religious philosophers to discover that the face of modern Christianity is being shaped not by them, but by the Bible. The democratization of Christianity over the last several centuries has instilled in the ordinary believer a passion for direct encounter with the Christian scriptures. The motto of the Protestant Reformation -- *sola scriptura* ("the Bible alone") -- remains the dominant voice in Christian reasoning and argument today, powerfully felt even in non-Protestant forms of Christianity. We can see a tremendous hunger to know the Bible especially in the large amount of best selling support literature churned out year after year in the form of books with titles such as, "How to Read the Bible," "What the Bible Really Says," and "The Biblical View of Marriage," "of Angels," "of what-have-you." Equally telling is the large variety of "study Bibles," which integrate such guidance into a Bible itself.

When the public turns to a Bible translation, or to a book that claims merely to summarize biblical teachings on particular subjects, it relies heavily on the principle of "truth in advertising." The public trusts that those who translate have done what they claim to have done, namely, accurately supply the meaning of the Bible in English. The public counts on "truth in translation."

One can scarcely blame the individual Christian for relying on the training and expertise of others to help make sense of the Bible. The Bible is a difficult book. It is nearly two thousand years old. Its thought world is very different from that of modernity. The biblical text assumes familiarity with the religious and social environment of the ancient Mediterranean region, rather than the highways and byways of Middle

America. Credit the people for their instinct that they cannot simply read the words on the page and have it make immediate sense to them. They are right.

The problem, then, that Christians face in their passion for, and reliance on, the Bible as the shaper of their faith is that they must rely on experts to guide them to its meaning. The average Christian may be unaware to what degree he or she depends upon the knowledge and intellectual integrity of papyrologists, translators, commentators, historians, and ministers to accurately and honestly convey what the Bible really says, as difficult as that may be in modern times -- uncertainties, contradictions, and all. And in that dependence, modern Christians have been let down terribly. There is no system of control, or of editorial oversight, in the market of popular biblical "scholarship." Anyone can write a book about the Bible, claiming to explain it. In a free society, we wouldn't want it any other way. But the sensible advice of "buyer beware" seems to be forgotten in this market. Even people with the best of intentions can be led by their commitments and biases to produce inaccurate or careless books on the Bible.

So I am writing to clear up a number of misconceptions about the Bible, and about the claims made by those who are listened to when they speak about the Bible. I am not writing to support any denomination or sect of Christianity, but simply to inform -- to add information to a debate that has been conducted mostly in the shadow of ignorance. I am writing because I am a biblical scholar, not by assertion or by the approval of authorities, but by training -- I know the language in which the New Testament was originally written, as well as the social, political, and cultural environment that shaped how the New Testament expresses itself.

I was moved to write because of my shock at the lack of the most basic facts about the Bible in the modern popular debate over its accurate translation and meaning. I was greatly disappointed to find that the few well-trained scholars who have participated in the debate, for reasons known only to themselves, have chosen to reinforce rather than alleviate the burden of misinformation and wanton bias in the debate. I am writing because I understand how to take on the role of a neutral investigator, with a stake not in any predetermined outcome, but only in hearing what a two-thousand-year-old book says in the terms of its own time and place. I personally know dozens of other biblical scholars with the training and self-discipline to do what I am doing, but they are detached from the public debate (just as I was until now), engaged in their own very specialized and arcane researches, and perhaps unaware (as I was until rudely shaken out of my ignorance) of the debate raging around us.

Modern Christians can determine for themselves how to use the Bible, to take it literally or figuratively, what parts are the most important, how to weave all of its ideas into a whole. This book is not about this process of interpretation and application. It is focused only on translation. It is essential first that we have the most accurate translations upon which all of the other questions can be worked out. Since Christians regard the Bible as Truth, with a capital T, and this Truth was first communicated in languages other than English, we need "Truth in translation" first of all, before anyone can test this Truth, explore it, apply it. I have written this book to help you explore the issue of accuracy in Bible translation.

ACKNOWLEDGMENTS

This book took me by surprise. It grew out of extensive correspondence I have had over the last seven years with a large number of earnest, serious students of the Bible who approached me with the questions I attempt to answer in the pages that follow. As I gave my initial answers, these were copied and spread around (often through the internet), and I received several challenges to my statements, requiring me to be more careful and systematic in explaining the basis for my assessments. As a result, the book practically wrote itself, with the help of my many correspondents. So to them all I wish to express my deep appreciation for their inspiration and aggressive pursuit of the truth.

Conditioned as I am to academic prose, the hardest thing about writing this book was making its expression suitable for a wider readership. For help with this I turned to my wife and partner in all things, Zsuzsanna Gulácsi who, although herself an academic, has the best ear I know for crisp, clear communication of ideas to non-experts. I have seen her do it time and again in the classroom and public lectures, and I knew she could help me do it with this book. For those many exciting, creative evenings together sharpening and focusing my prose, I wish to express my gratitude and admiration. The rest she knows.

Scripture quotations marked (AB) are taken from *The Amplified New Testament*. Copyright © 1954, 1958, 1987 by The Lockman Foundation. Used by permission.

Scripture quotations marked (LB) are taken from *The Living Bible*, copyright © 1971. Used by permission of Tyndale House Publishers, Inc., Wheaton, IL 60189 USA. All rights reserved.

Scripture quotations marked (NAB) are taken from the *New American Bible with Revised New Testament* © 1986, 1970 Confraternity of Christian Doctrine, Washington, D.C. and are used by permission of the copyright owner. All Rights Reserved. No part of the *New American Bible* may be reproduced in any form without permission in writing from the copyright owner.

Scripture quotations marked (NASB) are taken from *THE NEW AMERICAN STANDARD BIBLE*. Copyright © The Lockman Foundation 1960, 1962, 1963, 1968, 1971, 1972, 1973, 1975, 1977. Used by permissio

Scripture quotations marked (NIV) are taken from the *HOLY BIBLE, NEW INTERNATONAL VERSION®. NIV®*. Copyright © 1973, 1978, 1984 by Internatonal Bible Society. Used by permission of Zondervan Publishing House. All rights reserved. The "NIV" and "New International Version" are trademarks registered in the United States Patent and Trademark Office by Internatonal Bible Society. Use of either trademark requires permission of the International Bible Society.

Scripture quotations marked (NRSV) are from the *New Revised Standard Version Bible*, copyright © 1989 by the Division of Christian Education of the National Council of the Churches of Christ in the U.S.A., and are used by permission. All rights reserved.

Scripture quotations marked (NW) are taken from the *New World Translation of the Holy Scriptures*, Copyright © 1984 by Watch Tower Bible and Tract Society of Pennsylvania.

Scripture quotations marked (TEV) are taken from the *Good News Bible in Today's English Version*, copyright © 1976 by American Bible Society. Used by permission.

INTRODUCTION

What do I mean by the words "accuracy" and "bias" used in this book's title? By writing this book, I am involving myself in debates that have been going on for a long time before me and no doubt will continue long after me. People have already been throwing around the words "accuracy" and "bias" quite freely, and I am merely taking up this rhetoric and focusing it on solid reasons and criteria for judging the applicability of the words to particular cases.

People are quick to charge inaccuracy and bias in someone else's Bible. On what basis do they make such charges? Charges of inaccuracy and bias are based upon the fact that a translation has deviated from some norm of what the translation should be. So what is the norm? It seems that for many the norm is the King James Version of the Bible. If a new translation varies very far from that norm, it is criticized as inaccurate and erroneous, and its translators are suspected of ulterior motives in producing a different translation, a hidden bias that perverts the truth of the KJV. You hear it all the time: someone has "changed" the Bible by offering a new translation. The "change" is from the standard of the King James Version, which was, after all, presented as the "standard" translation. If a translation differs from the "standard," clearly it must be wrong.

Unfortunately, this view of things is based on ignorance of the most basic facts about the Bible. The King James Version was not the first Bible (not even the first English Bible); it was itself a translation. It just happened to be a translation that was used by many people for a long time. Age adds a certain sanctity to things. It starts to seem that it has always been that way, and any change is a dangerous innovation. When a new translation is made, it is, of course, different from the long-established KJV, and people fault it for that. But what else can people do? The only thing they have to compare a new translation to is the old translation. They have no means to assess real accuracy and bias because they do not have a valid norm by which to compare translations.

But the fact that the general public does not have access to a valid norm does not mean that one does not exist. In fact there is such a norm that is available to anyone who is willing to take the trouble to learn how to use it: the original Greek New Testament.

Truth in advertising in the realm of Bible translation centers on the word "translation." By claiming to be a "translation," an English Bible is being put forward as an accurate communication of the meaning of the original text, in the case of the New Testament, the original Greek text. If a translation freely departs from the meaning of the Greek, and rewrites the Bible, leaving some things out and adding other things in, it must be judged very poor in its accuracy. Notice that I said "sticks to the *meaning* of the original Greek text." Accuracy does not require following the Greek in a hyper-literal, word-for-word way. Such a "translation" is what we call an "interlinear translation," and it is not really a "translation" at all, as you can see if you ever try to read an interlinear. An interlinear is a stage on the way to a translation, correctly identifying the basic meaning and function of each Greek word, but not yet assembling that information into coherent English sentences.

The important thing in judgments of accuracy is that the translators have found English words and phrases that correspond to the known meaning of the Greek, and put them together into English sentences that dutifully follow what the Greek syntax communicates. If a translator chooses rare or otherwise unattested meanings for Greek words, and constructs English sentences which do not straightforwardly communicate the most likely sense of the original, then he or she is producing an inaccurate translation. Comparison to the original Greek is absolutely necessary to make judgments of accuracy or inaccuracy. Without the Greek as a factor in the comparison, no valid judgment can be passed.

Bias comes into the picture when we try to identify why a translation shows inaccuracy in its handling of the original Greek text. So first we have to demonstrate deviation from the meaning of the Greek, and only then can we see if bias is the cause. After all, everyone makes mistakes. Furthermore, in any translation there are several ways to convey the meaning of the original. There is a very good and untroubling reason why Bible translations differ among themselves. Put simply, Greek is not English. Greek words do not have a one-to-one correspondence with English words in terms of their meaning. Greek sentence structure and patterns of style differ radically from the English structure and stylistics that would be used to get the same idea across. So there is room for legitimate variation in translation. Bias does not necessarily enter into it.

Bias is involved when differences in translation cannot be explained by reasons based in the likely meaning of the original Greek. When a translation seems to come out of nowhere, we are likely to find that it involves certain ideas that the translator would like to see in the Bible. Most people interested enough to undertake the arduous work of making a Bible translation have an investment in a particular understanding of Christianity, and this investment can affect their objectivity.

Since there are many different forms of Christianity, bias in New Testament translation can be in various directions. Sometimes, translators make their biases explicit, by identifying themselves with certain denominations or interpretive agendas. The New American Bible was prepared by Catholics, for example. The New World Translation was produced by Jehovah's Witnesses. The New International Version translators confessed explicitly their commitment to "evangelical" Christian doctrines and biblical harmony. And so forth. But even translations made by broad inter-denominational committees can be subject to the collective, "mainstream Christian" bias of the translators. The hardest bias to catch is one that is widely shared, and it is quite understandable that the common views shared by modern Christians of many denominations would influence how the Bible is translated. Understandable, but not acceptable. The success of numbers or of time does not guarantee truth.

Accuracy in Bible translation has nothing to do with majority votes; it has to do with letting the biblical authors speak, regardless of where their words might lead. It has to do with strictly excluding bias towards later developments of Christian thought. Avoiding bias involves obeying probable meaning rather than wished-for meaning. The first choice when faced with options of how best to translate the original Greek usually should be the most obvious, straightforward, unspecialized understanding of the word or phrase. Any other choice needs to be justified by strong evidence from the literary context or historical and cultural environment. Such evidence can sometimes make a less obvious meaning possible, even probable; but it cannot rule out the other possible meanings allowed by the known rules of the Greek language.

When there is no way to resolve rival possible meanings, we really can't blame translators for following the one that corresponds with their beliefs. But they owe it to their readers to make a note of the uncertainty. In passing judgment on how well or poorly translators have done in avoiding bias, we have to give them the benefit of the doubt. If the translation given is at least within the realm of possibility for the meaning of the Greek, we must grant that fact and not be too hard on the translators for preferring one possible meaning over another. But if they stretch beyond that rather generous range and reach for the truly novel, rare, or unlikely sense of the Greek, we must be very suspicious of their motives. We have to wonder why they couldn't let the Bible say what it has to say, why they had to put some other idea there in place of the more likely, obvious meaning of the original biblical text.

Accurate, unbiased translations are based on (1) linguistic content, (2) literary context, and (3) historical and cultural environment. The very same three things are consulted to assess a translation once it is done. We use these three bases for making and assessing New Testament translations because we presume certain things about how the New Testament was written by its authors. Our reliance on linguistic content presupposes that an author used Greek correctly, in line with the linguistic conventions of his or her time. If he or she didn't, we really have no way to know what might be meant. Our use of literary context assumes that an author was relatively consistent and non-contradictory in what he or she said. If the author has not assembled a coherent piece of writing, we would be unable to judge our ability to understand it. Our attention to the historical and cultural environment presumes that an author worked with images and ideas available in his or her world (even if working to redefine or transform them), and that a contemporaneous audience was the intended readership. If the books of the New Testament were written in a way that was incomprehensible to the earliest Christians, they never would have been valued, preserved, and collected into scripture.

Having identified (1) linguistic content, (2) literary context, and

(3) historical and cultural environment, as the basis for valid assessment of Bible translation, it follows that the person qualified to assess Bible translations is the person who knows these three things. Let's consider these credentials more closely.

In order to have any ability to make a judgement about the accuracy of a translation of the New Testament from its original Greek into modern English, you have to know how to read Greek, and the particular kind of Greek in which the New Testament was originally written (something known as *Koine*, or "common" Greek). I am sure this seems obvious to you. Yet, amazingly, the majority of individuals who publicly pass judgement on Bible translations -- in print, on television and radio, on the internet, and in letters they send to me -- do not know how to read Greek.

The obvious question to be asked here is: then how can they tell what is a good translation and what is not? The fact is that they cannot. Their opinions are based not on the accuracy of translating Greek words into English words, but on the agreement of the final product with their own beliefs about what the Bible must say. In practice, people who do not read Greek compare a new translation with an existing one of which they approve. Any difference is judged negatively, and is considered to be changing or distorting the text of the Bible. But differences are bound to arise in new translations because Greek words often can mean several different things in English and, besides that, the good news is that with every passing generation we are learning to read Koine Greek better as we learn more about it.

So the first question you should ask anyone who claims to have the credentials to speak about the translation of the New Testament is: Do you know how to read Koine Greek? If not, then you have no basis to render an opinion, other than to rely on other people who do read Koine Greek. If we Greek readers disagree among ourselves, then you must examine our arguments and evidence and decide who has the better case.

When it comes to using literary context to assess the accuracy of a translation, anyone who has spent a lot of time reading the New Testament has made a beginning on mastering this credential. It involves recognizing the different types of writing contained in scripture. Paul's letters are a very different sort of literature than a narrative such as the Gospel according to Mark, which again is quite distinct from a visionary account like the Book of Revelation. These discrete forms of writing shape the meaning of the passages they contain. The distinctive vocabularies, metaphors, and emphases of the individual authors also supply the context for understanding individual passages they wrote.

But knowing the New Testament inside and out is only the beginning. The books of the New Testament belong to a larger literary context that includes early Jewish and Christian traditions of writing. The Jewish scriptures (the Christian Old Testament), for example, form an essential context for understanding the expression of the New Testament. Other Jewish and Christian writings produced at the same time as the New Testament, such as the Dead Sea Scrolls or the Christian apostolic fathers, help us to grasp the literary conventions followed in the New Testament, as well as the characteristics that set the New Testament apart. The New Testament was not written in isolation, but emerged from a larger literary world by which, and against which, it was shaped. So familiarity with literary context in both the narrow and broad sense is an important skill to apply to assessing Bible translations.

Knowing the dictionary definition of isolated Greek words, or having a sense of literary conventions are good starting points, but they are not sufficient to make someone able to make or assess Bible translations. Words change their meaning over time, and one has to be familiar with how particular words and phrases were understood in particular times and places by reading writings other than the biblical ones. Moreover, when we write or talk, the full meaning is not in the dictionary meaning of the words alone, but in the references and allusions of our imagery, metaphors, and figures of speech. Some terms have very specialized meaning for particular groups of people. Some statements assume familiarity on the part of their hearers about the topic being spoken of. For example, a great deal of what Jesus had to say refers to and builds upon the ideas and images of 1st century Judaism. Without education in how 1st century Judaism operated and what it valued, it is easy to misunderstand what Jesus is talking about, or to be downright baffled by it.

This kind of background knowledge is available to historians from the literature and archaeology of the period. The exact nuance of a phrase or argument in the New Testament may depend on this background knowledge. So it is important to have some credentials in this area. If you haven't had the opportunity to receive this sort of education, it is never too late. You can easily fill your home library with books on the subject, of which dozens are published every year. In this area, too, we are learning more all the time. But if someone ignores the historical context of the Bible, and has no background in the subject, they are in a poor position to assess a translation of the Bible. All they can do is argue the dictionary meaning of a term, or the normative understanding of a concept found in their church, against a translation that takes cognizance of the language in its own time and place, as it was known to the actual authors of the Bible.

Thousands of biblical researchers in America have these three credentials, not to mention the many more in other English-speaking countries, and I am one of them. That is why I feel somewhat justified in writing this book. But just as importantly, I have an attitude that puts me at a distinct advantage to write a book such as this. I am a committed historian dedicated to discovering what Christians said and did two thousand years ago. I have no stake in proving that *those* Christians are most like a particular modern denomination of Christianity, or that they adhered to particular doctrines that match those of modern Christians. If it turns out that they did, fine; if not, then I certainly am not going to fault them for that. If you are looking for my bias, I guess you could say that I have a bias in favor of historical truth, the accurate reconstruction and comprehension of the past. If the Bible as it was written two thousand years ago presents obstacles and challenges to modern Christians, if it does not so simply conform to what modern Christians want or expect it to say, I consider that a problem for modern Christians, not for the Bible.

That said, I'm not asking you to just take my word for things. I would be a pretty poor educator if I expected you to adhere to the cult of the expert. In fact, I encourage distrust. I don't want you to trust me; I want you to be *persuaded* by the information I provide. Check my claims; scrutinize my arguments. I haven't studied all of this material for so many years for you to trust me without proof. Proof is the coin of the academic trade. If I don't have evidence -- linguistic, literary, and historical facts -- to back up what I say, I would be uttering nothing but idle opinion. I have set out for you the necessary tools of the work we have before us. Walk with me awhile in the pages that follow as we put these tools to use, so you can see how they help us to determine accuracy and bias in Bible translation. When we are finished, I hope you will be motivated to continue your exploration and to develop your ability to use these tools to pursue further questions of your own.

ONE

THE ORIGINS OF MODERN ENGLISH BIBLES

This chapter is about how it is that we, living at the dawn of the 21st century, have a book in our possession that was written two thousand years ago. Most of the books on our shelf are not that old. The Bible, of course, owes its uniquely long life to its importance within the Christian religious tradition. But that does not answer the whole question, because the Bible goes back so far in time that it predates the invention of printing, and even the formation of the English language itself. So, obviously, this book has gone through some changes over the years. And since its exact wording and meaning is so crucial to Christians, those changes need to be understood and scrutinized very closely in order to be sure that what we have today is as close to the original book as possible.

A great deal rests on the meaning of that last "as possible," because the Bible has to be useful for modern people, and that fact necessitates some change. A crumbling manuscript written in Greek would not have much use in a typical modern Christian's home. The steps of adaptation from that crumbling manuscript to a modern, compact, convenient, and readable Bible are what interest us here.

I will not be addressing the ultimate origin question about the Bible, namely, was it inspired by God? Nor will I look into questions of biblical authorship, date, and so forth. Our starting point is the completed Greek compositions of the biblical authors, and we are interested here in how those already written texts are transformed into English Bibles. Translators are not inspired, and the fact that translations are revised over the years shows a healthy appreciation of human fallibility. Not only are translators not perfect, but the manuscripts from which they make their translations are imperfect copies of lost originals. No two manuscripts of the Bible agree completely. With imperfect base texts, translators cannot possibly produce perfect translations. The best they can hope to achieve is the most accurate rendering of the most likely original text based on the actual manuscripts we have at present. So whether or not the original compositions of the biblical authors were inspired by God, modern English translations would be twice removed from any such inspiration: first by fallible human copyists, and second by fallible human translators.

That brings me to my first point about how we come to have a Bible. The actual original manuscripts written by Mark, Paul, and the other writers of the New Testament -- what technically are called the "autographs" -- no longer exist. We have the Bible only in the form of copies of copies of copies of the originals, at best. There is nothing mysterious or diabolical about the disappearance of the original autographs. Keep leafing through a book over and over again for a few hundred years and see what kind of shape it's in. Carry it around with you, stuff it into tight hiding places several times, drop it in the rain and mud a few times, and loan it to people time and again. Books wear out. They get damaged; they fall apart; they fade. This is what happened to the original writings of the biblical authors. I don't mean to sound disrespectful; I am sure the early Christians did their best to take care of these writings. But times were tough, and these manuscripts apparently circulated widely. Eventually, they simply crumbled away.

Fortunately, before that happened, copies were made. And then these copies were copied, and so on, until a fairly large number of copies were in circulation for each book of the New Testament. But copying a manuscript is tricky business, and the longer the text, the trickier it is. Copyists make mistakes. When I make this point in the classes I teach, I make an analogy to copying a friend's class notes. If I were to collect the interdependent notebooks of my students, I would get a lot of amusement out of the transformations and slips of the copyists. Now, certainly, most people who copied books of the Bible were a little more concerned and dedicated to get it exactly right than students who want to copy just accurately enough to pass a test. But the actual manuscripts of the Bible we have show that concern and dedication are not enough. No two manuscripts read exactly alike because through copy after copy errors crept in.

Most biblical manuscripts were made by a scribe working with a source text which he (usually it was a he) looked at and copied onto the blank pages which were going to become the finished copy. The manuscript he was working from would have been made by hand, with letters written in ink on papyrus (a plant-fiber paper) or parchment (an animal-skin paper). He would work by candlelight or lamplight or sunlight, sitting for hours at a writing bench.

Under these conditions, the eye can play tricks on you. Letters may be imperfectly written and mistaken for other letters. Imperfections in the paper may look like letters or alter the appearance of written letters. Words, phrases, even whole sentences may be skipped because, in copying, the scribe must look back and forth from his source to the copy he is making, and in the process he loses his place. It is very easy for the eye to jump from one occurrence of a word to another occurrence of the same word on the page. In the sentence I have just written, it would be very easy for a scribe to jump from the first "occurrence" to the second "occurrence" and to produce a copy that reads: "It is very easy for the eye to jump from one occurrence of the same word on the page." If you stop to think of how many times "and," "of," and "to" appear on a typical page, you can start to imagine the potential for error in making copies. This kind of thing happens all of the time in the manuscripts we have of the Bible. Not only do scribes omit material, they also duplicate lines by jumping *back* to the previous occurrence of a word.

But copying manuscripts is even more complicated than that. Ancient Greek manuscripts did not use marks of punctuation, and these marks only developed very gradually and sporadically over time. So the oldest biblical manuscripts have no periods, commas, quotation marks, or anything of the kind. Even worse, ancient Greek manuscripts were written without spaces between words, so that a scribe would be looking at *atextthatreadslikethis*. By this point, you may be wondering why on earth manuscripts were written this way. The standard answer is that the culture was still largely oral, and that texts served as aids to memory more than as sources of novel information. But admittedly, if someone had thought of the improvements of spacing words and using punctuation the scribes would have jumped at the innovation, and they did when these inventions were made. Meanwhile, many scribes worked by sight at blocks of letters rather than sentences and units of meaning, and many mistakes were made. You can do an experiment at home into this sort of work simply by copying an acrostic from a newspaper or magazine. Imagine doing page after page of this kind of copying for hours on end.

For those scribes who worked with units of meaning, looking at the source manuscript and reciting aloud an entire clause, then repeating it to themselves as they copied the words, other sorts of problems arose. Again, we have the usual slips as a person recites something back to him- or herself: words drop out or get transposed, ideas get rephrased. Then there is the additional problem that the New Testament contains a great deal of related or parallel content. In the Gospels, for instance, the same stories are told in different ways by the four evangelists. If the scribe has a favorite version among the four, or is used to hearing a story in only one of the four retellings, he may accidentally remember and write that version rather than the one he is supposed to be copying.

Some scribal operations used a method of mass-producing manuscripts that involved taking dictation. In this process, a whole set of scribes would sit at their benches with only blank pages in front of them. A reader would stand in the front of the room and read the Bible aloud, and the scribes would write down what they heard. In this way, many copies could be made at once. The motivation to produce more Bibles faster can be understood, but the consequences for accuracy can be readily imagined. In this instance, reconstructing one of my class lectures from my student's notebooks would be the appropriate analogy (although students rarely copy lectures word for word anymore, as used to be the case). I suppose a language dictation class like the one I had in high school would be a closer analogy. But the point is the same: all kinds of errors of the ear are made under these conditions.

By now you may be getting pretty pessimistic about the Bible, but take heart. Modern biblical scholars have developed all sorts of strategies for compensating for all of these errors, and the Bible today is in better shape than it has ever been. This will become clear as I continue the story of how we come to have a Bible.

At some point, Christians began to collect the individual books of the New Testament and form them into sets. Up until then, the Bible of the Christians was the same as the Bible of the Jews, or what Christians now call the Old Testament. In addition to that Bible, there were the books that were taken very seriously as sources of distinctly Christian teaching, or what one early writer called "the memoirs of the apostles." These additional books were read from when Christians gathered on Sundays, and were used in private study. It became clear by the use they were being put to that these books were every bit as important to Christians as the books of the Bible, and so they should become part of it. Not all of the local Christian communities agreed which books were worthy of such a status and which were not, but over the centuries a consensus developed among the Christian leadership, and by the end of the 4th century, the list of books to be included in the New Testament, what we call the "canon," was generally agreed upon.

Involved in the collection process was a concern over having manuscripts that agreed with each other and were relatively error free. Since the autographs were already long gone, there was no way to know for sure how the manuscripts should read, but examples that differed dramatically from the many other copies to which they could be compared were destroyed. In each city, the local bishop had the authority to approve the biblical text and to confiscate defective copies. As Christianity grew and prospered, the individual manuscripts were used as sources from which to make copies of the entire Bible. Eventually, complete Bibles replaced the library of separate books that had been used, and people began to speak of the Bible as a single book, rather than as a collection of individual books, which it originally was.

In the first few centuries of Christian history, missionaries traveled widely to spread the "good news," and translated as they went. Thus, Jesus' own disciples, who probably spoke a local Galilean variety of Aramaic, a Semitic language, found that they had to translate their teachings into Greek to reach many of the people they wished to convert. Christian tradition tells us that Mark, the gospel writer, got his start as Peter's interpreter in front of Greek-speaking audiences. Paul knew Greek himself, and wrote his letters directly in that language since he was writing to people who spoke Greek. At that time, Greek was to the ancient world what English is to the modern world -- a kind of international language that people learn if they want to have business, social, or intellectual dealings beyond their own country.

But eventually Christian missionaries reached places where even Greek wasn't spoken. By this time, the books of the New Testament had been written, and so the missionaries began to translate these books into local languages such as Latin, Syrian, Armenian, Coptic (Egyptian), Gothic (a language related to German and Scandinavian languages), and so on. For a while, then, everyone had Bibles in their own language.

Languages change over time; some die out, others evolve into forms that differ substantially from their older forms. Latin, for example, evolved into French, Spanish, Italian, and Portuguese. English and German have a common linguistic ancestor from which they evolved, although English vocabulary has been heavily influenced by French. As these changes occurred, Christian leaders started to worry about translation. They knew that all translation involves some degree of interpretation, and they were afraid that biblical truth would be distorted by translation. Besides, in the Middle Ages, Latin served Europe as Greek had served the ancient Roman Empire, as an international language that transcended local politics and culture. The Christian leaders wanted to foster unity, not diversity, in the Christian community. If Christians were reading different translations of the Bible, they inevitably would start to diverge from one another in their understanding of biblical truth.

So the Christian leaders of Western Europe (the Catholic bishops, lead by the Pope in Rome) had their own good reasons for not keeping up with language change by making translations of the Bible. In hindsight, we can say that they drew the wrong conclusions from their concerns. The outbreak of the Protestant Reformation shows that many Christians felt alienated from the well-springs of their faith, at least in part because of their inability to have access to and read the Bible. Today, translation into local languages is standard practice for all denominations of Christianity, including the Catholic church. But I am getting ahead of myself.

Because many Christians wanted to read the Bible for themselves, the motivation existed to make translations. While the Christian leadership forbade the making of translations, people did so secretly and at great personal risk. Only in the 16th Century did it become possible for translations to be made openly, as local rulers allied themselves with the Protestant Reformation and refused to go along with the Catholic ban on translation, thus protecting those inside their borders who wished to undertake this work. This turn of events came at precisely the right time to have maximum impact, because the translators were able to make use of a revolutionary new medium of communication: printing. Now a Bible manuscript could be type-set and mass produced. Printed Bibles could be made much more quickly and inexpensively than ever before. They also could be made much smaller and easier to handle than a handwritten manuscript. And, of course, there was an eager market for the book. As a result, the Bible became the first best-seller of the print era, and has remained the world's best selling book ever since.

All of these developments occurred in the specific case of the English translation of the Bible, too. At first, the kings of England enforced the church ban on translation with force. Translations were confiscated and burned, sometimes with their authors. But eventually the English swung over politically and ideologically to the pro-translation camp. The established Church of England sought to maintain control over of the process, however, and so only one, officially sanctioned translation was produced: the Authorized Version, popularly known by the name of its royal sponsor as the King James Bible, completed in 1611.

The King James Bible really marks the dawn of modern Bible translation, even more than the parallel effort of Martin Luther in German nearly a century earlier does. I say this because the King James Bible is a translation made by committee, a procedure which has come to be the norm in modern translations. It is reasoned that the combined knowledge of many scholars is better than the lone labors of a single scholar, no matter how gifted. In theory, this is a strategy to overcome bias. One person's personal bias may be compensated for by the biases of others, until the consensus opinion is as close to objectivity as can be achieved. This is the theory, although it doesn't always turn out this way, as we shall see.

How did the King James committee do its work? Its first task was rounding up some Bible manuscripts to compare with one another to make sure the most accurate biblical text was used as a base to work from in making a translation. Most of the existing Bible manuscripts in England at the time were, of course, in Latin. But there were printed editions of the Greek text, based on the few, recent manuscripts -- many generations removed from original autographs of the biblical authors -- that could be found in western Europe at the time. At times, then, the committee suspected that the Greek manuscripts were in error, and chose to follow the Latin version instead.

Once the committee had agreed on the base text, translation could begin. The well-understood meaning of the Latin Vulgate (from the early 5th century) filled in for any uncertainty about the meaning of the original Greek. But the committee worked in earnest to produce the most clear, accurate, and aesthetically pleasing translation possible. It is universally acknowledged that in the latter goal they succeeded. The King James Bible is a beautiful piece of English literature. In terms of the other two goals, however, this translation falls short, although for its time it was pretty good.

The members of the committee worked on various sections of the Bible, then assembled to examine and discuss what they had accomplished. Verse by verse, a consensus was reached. Theological and other intellectual differences could be found among the members of the committee, and debates about translation often hinged on the implications for Christian doctrine and practice as much as they did on the linguistic meaning of a Greek word. Obviously, the overwhelming majority of the members of the committee came from a common background in the Christian mainstream, and shared commitments to certain basic Christian truths quite apart from the Bible. They certainly had biases, and when those biases were held in common they went unrecognized and unaddressed in the work of translation.

This built-in theological bias in the work of Bible translation has continued to the present day. Bible translation is usually undertaken by people with theological training who also happen to be reasonably competent in biblical languages. These may be members of missionary societies, or individuals involved in denominational leadership, or the more intellectually inclined among ministers. The vast majority of Bible translations are produced by and for specific denominations of Christianity, or cooperatively among members of related denominations.

The main advantage of contemporary Bible translations over the venerable King James Bible is not that they are made by people with less bias towards the material, but that they are based upon a much larger, and therefore better, set of Greek manuscripts. In the centuries since the King James committee did its work, biblical scholars have gone throughout the world, finding every surviving manuscript of the Greek New Testament they could. We now have not only many more manuscripts, but also much older ones, closer to the autographs of the biblical authors.

The work of comparing all of the manuscripts, and drawing conclusions about the most likely original wording of the books of the New Testament, reached a point of maturity in the work of B. F. Westcott and F. J. A. Hort in the late 19th century. Some modern translations are based upon the conclusions of Westcott and Hort. But the work on the text of the New Testament continued in the 20th century. New manuscript discoveries were made, and new ideas about how to compare and weigh the evidence emerged. As a result, researchers came to slightly different conclusions from those reached by Westcott and Hort about the "best" text of the New Testament.

In the early part of the 20th century, Eberhard and Erwin Nestle produced such a new edition of the New Testament text. Their work now appears in the "Nestle-Aland" edition (re-edited under the leadership of Kurt Aland). The United Bible Society also produced a new edition of the text. Many modern translations are based on either the Nestle-Aland or UBS text editions. By the end of the 20th century, the Nestle-Aland and the UBS editions of the Greek text of the Bible were practically identical, in large part because the editorial team of the two "independent" editions was by that time identical. Questions might be raised about this monopoly on deciding the "best" text of the New Testament, but that would take us on a detour from our main subject.

In any case, these editions are vastly superior to anything that existed before them. The advantage of having these modern editions of the Greek text of the New Testament is simple to understand: a more accurate Greek text makes possible a more accurate translation. But that advantage can be squandered by the bias of translators.

With thousands of biblical scholars in America alone, you may think that Bible translation is mostly a scholarly enterprise. It isn't. Although biblical scholars have been the key players in identifying the more accurate Greek text of the New Testament, most have never been involved in a Bible translation project. Instead their research involves investigating specific biblical books and passages in the original Greek, and publishing their findings in specialized academic journals for their academic peers to consider. At some point, they may write a textbook for use in college Bible courses. Only a handful ever get involved in Bible translation projects.

Although there have been quite a few translations made by individuals, only a few have succeeded in gaining a wide readership. Most of the "big" translations are the work of committees, combining the talents of several translators. These committees are sponsored by religious groups and operate under principles they all agree to in advance. As a committee, they discuss and debate the results of their work, and find the best reading they can all agree on.

The conditions that produce Bible translations naturally shape the outcome of the work. Since translations are made under the authority of denominations, a translation team must create something that will be acceptable to its sponsors. Translations are made not in the environment of academic freedom, but under the limitations of creedal commitment. The members of the team, drawn from a common religious community, share assumptions about the meaning of the Bible, rather than representing different viewpoints that must stand up to the scrutiny of other perspectives. These are far from ideal conditions for delivering accurate, unbiased English Bibles.

I want to make it clear that I am not assuming any sort of intellectual dishonesty on the part of Bible translators. I think it is the rare individual who goes into a Bible translation project thinking, "I am going to make the Bible fit my beliefs." I believe that by far the majority of people involved in this work are honest, earnest people who want to produce the most accurate, understandable Bible they can. Bias is not the same as maliciousness or dishonesty. Biases are unconscious assumptions, or unrecognized blind spots. The failings of most modern English Bibles are not deliberate; they are lapses, oversights, and inconsistencies. The faults of translators are of training and approach, not character.

The responsibility of making new translations rests upon people who are largely ill-suited to the task, through no fault of their own. They do not have the full complement of training. That is, they usually have the language skills but little or no exposure to information about the cultural context that helps make sense of the language. Their focus is more on making the language fit a modern context than an ancient one. They also are not conditioned to objectivity, that is, they are people most deeply involved in public roles of theological commitment that they must uphold. For an academic to come up with a new reading of a biblical verse may be celebrated; for a theologian to do so may result in expulsion from his or her church. Get a group of theologians together who share a common creed, and they will only reinforce each other's assumptions, with no voice in the room to point out the blind spots. So, in my opinion, most Bible translations are born in adverse conditions. It is not really too surprising, therefore, to find inaccuracies and biases in them. Yet I must admit to occasional astonishment at the audacity of some translators. There has been more than one occasion, while working on this book, that I have jumped up out of my seat shouting, "I can't believe they translated it that way!"

TWO

THE WORK OF TRANSLATION

You can think about Bible translation as a process of steps or phases, taking us not only from Greek to English, but also from a "rough-draft" English translation to smoother and clearer English prose. There are any number of steps to ever greater smoothness and clarity, but at some point along the way the original meaning can be eclipsed by polish and paraphrase. The question with Bible translation, as with most things, is knowing when to stop. I will walk you through the possible phases of translation, describing, giving examples, and commenting on the pros and cons of stopping or moving forward to the next possible phase.

Lexical ("Interlinear") Translation
Translation begins with the identification of each Greek word. This is done using a dictionary or lexicon. Such reference works are compiled from the vast body of Greek literature we have at our disposal. Since new discoveries of Greek literature are made quite frequently, dictionaries and lexicons must be constantly updated with new information. For any given Greek word, there may be anywhere from two to a dozen English equivalents. The correct English equivalent for a Greek word as it is used in the New Testament will be determined by the time of composition (since some meanings are attested in earlier periods, and others in later times), the context of use, and other factors. Using the dictionary or lexicon, the translator will determine what part of speech the word is (a noun, verb,

adjective, adverb, preposition, and so on), and the range of possible meanings it has in its time and context of use in the New Testament. The translator will also determine the word's grammatical form, that is, the modification of the word's root by markers that signal its relation to other words in its sentence. The translator will recognize grammatical form either from his or her training in Greek, or with the help of a Greek grammar.

The best Greek lexicon is that of Liddell & Scott (updated by several subsequent editors) published by Oxford University Press. In its resources, it covers the whole history of ancient Greek, from classical through the Christian period. A more specialized lexicon is the one originally edited by Walter Bauer (which has also been revised by many later editors), published by the University of Chicago Press and focused more on the later Greek of the Christian period.

There are, of course, many lexicons devoted to the Bible alone; but in the work of Bible translation, these should be used only secondarily, if at all. Biblical lexicons have many weaknesses. They tend to be based on existing English translations, rather than offering resources for fresh translation. They are deeply flawed by containing information only from the Bible itself, instead of including information from Greek literature in general. They are inherently biased towards harmonization of meaning for a particular word among its many uses in the Bible. But the same word can have quite different meanings according to its context of use, particularly when used by different biblical authors. Most biblical lexicons are handicapped by a mistaken etymological approach to word meanings. This is the idea that words only mean what their constituent parts mean. The actual history of use is much more reliable in determining a word's meaning.

For a given passage of the New Testament, then, you can write out a line of Greek, and write beneath each Greek word its probable meaning, with any modification based upon its marked role in the sentence. The result is what is often called an "interlinear translation." But, of course, it's not a translation at all, as a quick glance will show you immediately. It's only a stepping stone on the way to a translation. The lexical phase of translation provides the building blocks from which a coherent English sentence can be developed. Interlinears are published not because they can serve as translations in their own right, but because they allow a reader to see what Greek word stands behind an English word that has been incorporated into a translation. Published interlinears are study aids, not Bible translations.

Here's an example:

> This for is will of the God, the holiness of you, to abstain you from the fornication, to know each of you the of himself vessel to possess in holiness and honor, not in feeling of desire according to which also the nations the ones not knowing the God, the not to trespass and to defraud in the matter the brother of him. (1 Thessalonians 4:3-6)

To make this a usable translation, the words must be rearranged according to normal English syntax. Some words should be dropped because they are not necessary in English (such as the article "the" before "fornication"), and other words need to be added to complete the sense (for example a verb such as "do" in the clause "according to which the nations also *do*"). Even when rearranged and touched up in these ways, the meaning of the passage will remain ambiguous, primarily because of uncertainty about what "the of himself vessel" is.

Literal ("Formal Equivalence") Translation

Once all of the individual words have been more-or-less identified, they can be assembled into sentences. The grammatical markers that modify word roots point the way in this work. As the assembly-work goes on, the translator will modify individual word meanings according to clues from the context that is emerging. One of the most important steps from the interlinear to the literal phase is changing word order from what is acceptable in Greek to what works in English. Greek grammar is much more flexible about word order than English is, and it is not possible for English sentences to follow Greek word order. If you try to stick too closely to the original Greek in word order, you will produce sentences like nothing heard in any normal English composition. The King James Version occasionally lapses into this kind of hyper-literalism.

But in attempting to make a literal translation, you want to adhere to the rhetorical style of the original, even if you cannot follow exactly the Greek word order. This is what is called "formal equivalence" translating. "Formal equivalence" means that one translates not only what a text says, but as much as possible in the way the text says it, reproducing to a certain degree the stylistic elements of the original in its structure and word play. A formal equivalence translation "is designed so as to reveal as much of the original form as possible" (Ray, page 47).

There is much good to be said of literal, formal equivalence translation. Even though it is not an interlinear, this kind of translation still brings the reader very close to the original Greek. Literal translations tend to be very conservative about how many different English words they use for a given Greek one, and do not bring in synonyms merely for the sake of variety. They permit the reader to notice differences in style between the books of the New Testament. They do not offer much opportunity for interpretive rephrasing.

On the other hand, literal, formal equivalence translation has some shortcomings as well. Its conservative handling of vocabulary usually involves an overreliance on technical theological terminology. Words such as "justification," "grace," "Gentile," and so on, fail to communicate meaning to the average reader. They either have no common, non-technical meaning in English the way the Greek words that stand behind them did, or they suggest a wrong meaning because of changes in ordinary English usage. As a result, such words lose their freshness and immediacy, their resonances with daily life and reality that they would have had with early readers of the Bible.

A second, related weakness frequently found in formal equivalence translation is a much too narrow definition of what constitutes formal equivalence. Older and less sophisticated applications of formal equivalence often lapse into the etymological fallacy. That is, translators make the mistake of thinking a word has a core meaning based upon the lexical meaning of its constituent parts that is *always* the same and *always* intended when the word is used, regardless of context. Too much emphasis on formal uniformity makes it impossible to accurately convey an equivalent meaning in translation.

A third weakness often found in formal equivalence translations is an inability to deal with implicit information embedded in the Greek. Translations frequently fail to convey such implicit information to the reader because the translator believes that formal equivalence demands the minimum possible wording rather than the fullest communication of meaning. The words carry connotations that would have been recognizable to their original audience. But the tremendous cultural changes of the last two thousand years put up barriers between these connotations and a modern audience. A translation really cannot be said to be complete until the modern English reader has as much access to meaning as the original Greek readers did.

But the text of the New Testament itself cannot be the place for commentary. There are limits on what constitutes implicit information. Nida and Taber have set out this point very well:

> [O]ne may make explicit in the text only what is *linguistically* implicit in the immediate context of the problematic passage. This imposes a dual constraint: one may not simply add interesting cultural information which is not actually present in the meanings of the terms used in the passage, and one may not add information derived from other parts of the Bible, much less from extra-biblical sources, such as tradition. When one attempts to make too much explicit, one falls into eisegesis [reading into the text] rather than exegesis [reading out of the text] (Nida and Taber, page 111).

So it is legitimate to draw out the full meaning of words, and to make more plain the expression of sentences and the structure of a passage by spelling out what the passage suggests subtly. A writer like Paul, who leaves many verbal gaps that he assumes the reader is able to fill by the logic and parallelism of what he says, really cannot be understood by the typical reader without some "filling in" -- that is, making explicit what is implicit in his writing. In each case, however, there must be a defensible basis in the words that are there for any claim about what is implied. We will see several cases where there is wide disagreement about implicit information in the New Testament.

Many modern English translations belong to the literal, formal equivalence category. The King James Version is at the most conservative end of the category, at times verging on being an interlinear in its loyalty to Greek word order at the expense of acceptable English forms of speech. The New American Standard Bible and the New World Translation are also very literal, although they are more accommodated to proper English style than the King James. The New Revised Standard Version, the New American Bible, and the New International Version are three popular Bibles that, while generally literal, give some attention to making implicit information explicit. The degree to which they do this varies considerably from passage to passage. The NRSV and NIV sometimes make uncharacteristic leaps into the next phase or category of translation. But for the most part, all of these translations were the product of translators who felt content to stop with the literal, and not to continue into a further, "dynamic" transformation of the English text.

We return to our example, 1 Thessalonians 4:3-6, to see what literal, "formal equivalence" translation looks like.

KJV: For this is the will of God, *even* your sanctification, that ye should abstain from fornication: That every one of you should know how to possess his vessel in sanctification and honor; Not in the lust of concupiscence, even as the Gentiles which know not God: That no *man* go beyond and defraud his brother in *any* matter . . .

NW: For this is what God wills, the sanctifying of you, that you abstain from fornication; that each one of you should know how to get possession of his own vessel in sanctification and honor, not in covetous sexual appetite such as also those nations have which do not know God; that no one go to the point of harming and encroach upon the rights of his brother in this matter . . .

NASB: For this is the will of God, your sanctification; *that is*, that you abstain from sexual immorality; that each of you know how to possess his own vessel in sanctification and honor, not in lustful passion, like the Gentiles who do not know God; *and* that no man transgress and defraud his brother in the matter . . .

The KJV, NW, and NASB offer very literal translations, definitely formal equivalence in following the flow of Paul's rhetoric. As a result, the KJV has some phrasing that is not recognizable as proper English (for example: "even as the Gentiles which know not God"), while the NW sounds stilted and wooden. The NASB, on the other hand, manages to flow smoothly as modern English by adding a few transition words that do not have any effect on the meaning, other than to make it clearer. The KJV and NASB retain the archaic English word "Gentiles," while the NW translates more accurately as "nations." The KJV and NW retain the archaic English word "fornication" (a transformed loan-word from the Greek *porneia*), while the NASB uses the modern expression "sexual immorality," which is generic enough to cover most possible meanings of the original Greek term. All three translations retain the theological technical term "sanctification," which has little or no meaning for the average reader.

None of these translations interpret Paul's statement about knowing how to "possess one's own vessel" within the translation itself. The NASB quite properly suggests some possible understandings of the expression in a footnote ("I.e., body; or possibly, wife"). The meaning of this expression is not clear to the modern reader as it stands, but these translations are careful not to promote a possible interpretation to the status of scripture. Interpretation built upon the literal rendering of Paul's words is left to the reader.

That's not to say that the KJV and NW do no interpreting of their own. The KJV adds the word "any" to the clause "defraud his brother in *any* matter." That's a nice sentiment, but it is not what the Greek says. The KJV translators have added a teaching to the passage that is not there in the text, even though they and we would be happy if it was. The KJV and NW have interpreted the Greek phrase *en pathei epithumias* (literally: "in the feeling of desire") to mean "in the lust of concupiscence" and "in covetous sexual appetite," respectively. Both of these readings heighten the strength of Paul's rhetoric, making it sharper and more negative. Both translations in this case owe more to the Latin Vulgate (the source of the word "concupiscence") than they do to the original Greek. Paul can warn against something without sounding quite so shrill as these translations make him. The NASB is slightly more in line with the tone of the original Greek: "in lustful passion."

"Dynamic Equivalence" Translation

"Dynamic equivalence" refers to a method of working with blocks of meaning larger than the word or phrase in order to produce English passages whose simplicity and straightforwardness make for better reader comprehension than passages which adhere to Greek rhetorical forms. In dynamic equivalence one translates what a text says, but not in the way it says it, replacing the latter with a style considered most appropriate for a modern reader. Partisans of dynamic equivalence insist that this is the only really correct way to translate, and that anything else falls short of bridging the gap between the original text and the readers who do not speak the original language.

The advantages of moving translation to the "dynamic equivalence" phase are obvious: such a translation reads well, is simplified for reader comprehension, and does not confront the reader with the challenging obscurities of the original. Technical terminology is avoided, and nuances implicit in the original Greek are made explicit. But there are also serious drawbacks to this sort of translating. Although proponents of dynamic equivalence translation always characterize it as a more modern, sophisticated method, it is actually based on an outmoded view of language as mere packaging around ideas. This basic flaw in dynamic equivalence theory is well stated by A. H. Nichols:

> The truth is that language is not a mere receptacle. Nor does the Bible translator work with some disembodied "message" or "meaning". He is struggling to establish correspondences between expressions of the different languages involved. He can only operate with these expressions and not with wordless ideas that he might imagine lie behind them. Translators must not undervalue the complex relationship between form and meaning (Nichols, page 83-84).

Linguistic theory in the last thirty years has shifted decidedly towards viewing language as the stuff of which ideas are made, as the provider of "metaphors we live by." Meaning is rooted in language, not merely carried by it.

A second weakness of dynamic equivalence translation is that it adds an extra layer between the literal meaning of the Greek and the reader. This layer has the effect of hiding from the Bible reader the interpretive work of the translator. Robert Bratcher, a leading proponent of dynamic equivalence translating, himself says,

> While there is widespread agreement, if not unanimity, on the meaning of most of the Hebrew (and Aramaic) Old Testament and of the Greek New Testament, there are many places where scholars are sharply divided, and translations reflect those differences. This lack of consensus poses no great difficulty for students of the original texts, but many faithful Bible readers who have little if any technical knowledge of such matters may find it difficult to believe that a word or a phrase can be understood in so many different ways. (Bratcher 1990/91, page 293)

The disagreement among scholars to which Bratcher refers can occur in two different phases of research. There can be disagreement over the lexical meaning of a word or phrase, and there can be disagreement over the meaning of sentences and even whole passages even after the lexical meaning of the individual words and phrases is agreed upon. Most arguments in biblical studies are over the latter. In his dynamic equivalence translation work, Bratcher chooses *one* among the disputed meanings to include in his English Bible. The reader usually is not told of alternative theories of the meaning, nor is he or she supplied with the literal wording of the passage upon which these rival interpretations are based. So, dynamic equivalence translations exercise greater control over the reader, putting narrower limits over what the reader is allowed to know about the original text of the Bible.

A third weakness of dynamic equivalence translation is its stated goal of making the Bible comfortable and familiar to its readers. Certainly, we want people to feel able to understand what the Bible says. But do we really achieve that by "dumbing-down" its content? The Bible is not well served by being made comfortable, familiar, and conformed to modern sensibilities. Its greatest religious value lies in its challenges to the all-too-confidant assurance of modern life.

In the words of Bratcher, "[M]ore is involved in a literal translation than words and grammar, and that is the strangeness of the cultural setting of the original, so that a series of words strung together that faithfully represent the meaning of the individual words of the original may be quite meaningless to readers who belong to a completely different culture" (Bratcher 1990/1, page 291). Bratcher's observation is quite correct. The question is: What should we do about it? His solution is to strip away this cultural difference, and make the Bible fit into the cultural perspective of the reader. In my view, such a transformation of the meaning of the text runs the risk of disguising or distorting the sense of the original.

The fact is that the earthly career of Jesus took place in a world very different from our own. To communicate his purpose and vision to his disciples, Jesus employed the cultural reality around him as a starting point -- its values and symbols, its social arrangements and religious vocabulary. The meaning of his teaching, and of the conveyance of that teaching in the writings of the New Testament, was rooted in this ancient, alien cultural context. We -- that is scholars, translators, and religious leaders -- understand the meaning of this material only by doing historical, contextual research that allows us to define and catch the nuance of these cultural references. On the basis of this research we produce commentaries on the Bible.

The ambition of dynamic equivalence translation is to condense all of this explanatory commentary into a paraphrase of the biblical passage itself, so that the reader will not need to turn to published commentaries, or study Bibles, or extensive footnotes to grasp the meaning. That's an honorable goal, but one that is impossible to achieve. In the process, distortion occurs. The paraphrase is too loose to communicate the exact way in which the passage conveyed its meaning, and too constrained by the limits of translation to give a full explanation of meaning. It falls somewhere in between, in that unsatisfactory region of not-quite-this and not-quite-that. Subtleties and nuances of the original are lost, and the temptation to add new nuances to the meaning is too readily accommodated.

The principal example of a dynamic equivalence translation is the Today's English Version, commonly known as the "Good News Bible," whose New Testament was translated by Robert Bratcher. But the New Revised Standard Version and the New International Version often incorporate "dynamic" readings in their generally literal text.

We return to 1 Thessalonians 4:3-6 in some dynamic equivalence versions:

NRSV: For this is the will of God, your sanctification: that you abstain from fornication; that each one of you know how to control your own body in holiness and honor, not with lustful passion, like the Gentiles who do not know God; that no one wrong or exploit a brother or sister in this matter . . .

NIV: It is God's will that you should be sanctified: that you should avoid sexual immorality; that each of you should learn to control his own body in a way that is holy and honorable, not in passionate lust like the heathen, who do not know God; and that in this matter no one should wrong his brother or take advantage of him . . .

NAB: This is the will of God, your holiness: that you refrain from immorality, that each of you know how to acquire a wife for himself in holiness and honor, not in lustful passion as do the Gentiles who do not know God; not to take advantage of or exploit a brother in this matter . . .

TEV: God wants you to be holy and completely free from sexual immorality. Each of you men should know how to live with his wife in a holy and honorable way, not with a lustful desire, like the heathen who do not know God. In this matter, then, no man should do wrong to his fellow Christian or take advantage of him.

You can see that the NRSV, NIV, and NAB are very close to being literal translations; they read very similarly to the NASB. But a couple of differences push these translations in this passage into the dynamic equivalence category. The TEV, on the other hand, is the classic example of a dynamic equivalence translation. The translator has reduced the entire passage to three basic "kernals" of meaning, which are then rendered into the simplest, most straightforward English possible.

When it comes to the expression "possess one's own vessel," the NRSV, NIV, and TEV translators did not retain the literal wording in the text while offering possible interpretations in a footnote, as the NASB translators did. Rather, they chose one possible interpretation for inclusion in the text, and used footnotes to warn the reader of uncertainty (NRSV: "Or *how to take a wife for himself*"; NIV: "Or *learn to live with his own wife*; or *learn to acquire a wife*"; TEV: "live with his wife; *or* control his body"). To me, this is an acceptable way to handle a difficult passage. Having the footnotes makes all the difference, although I think it would be better to include the literal phrasing in the footnote as well, so that the reader knows what the interpretations are based upon. The NAB in this case fails to offer a footnote, giving the reader a false sense of certainty about the interpretive choice made by its translators.

Both the NRSV and NIV choose the most broadly applicable possible meaning ("control one's own body"). This has neither more nor less probability than the other possible interpretations, so the choice was most certainly made for its value for religious instruction. It's a bit of a stretch for the Greek verb *ktasthai* ("to acquire," "to possess") to mean "control," and that's a weak point in this interpretation. The NAB and TEV follow the equally possible understanding of "vessel" as "wife." The NAB, therefore, speaks about knowing how to "acquire a wife." But it seems to be beyond the stretch of the Greek verb *ktasthai* to mean "live with" as the TEV has it, and the translator apparently made that fundamental shift of meaning in order for the passage to match modern sensibilities, which might be uncomfortable with language about "acquiring" a wife. This is typical of dynamic equivalence translation. It's true that the reader of such a translation might feel more comfortable with the content; but he or she is not being exposed to what the Bible actually says.

The NRSV can be considered a dynamic equivalence translation in this passage also because it renders the conventionally androcentric Greek "to not wrong or exploit his brother" into a form that conveys the accurate implicit meaning to a modern audience: "no one wrong or exploit a brother or sister." Ancient Greek, like English before the last couple of decades, used masculine forms for the generic, inclusive sense. When Paul writes "his brother" he means "his or her brother or sister." He doesn't mean that only men should not defraud, but it's alright for women to do so; or that one should not defraud only brothers, but it's alright to defraud sisters. Paul's Greek has no subject at all where many English translations add "no man" (KJV, NASB, TEV, AB). The NRSV's use of gender-inclusive language in line with modern English standards is an example of dynamic equivalence at its best.

The NRSV also exhibits dynamic equivalence characteristics in this passage when it translates *hagiasmos* as "sanctification" in verse 3, but as "holiness" in verse 4. This shows the dynamic tendency to "mix it up," to add variety into the translation in order to make it more lively and less repetitive. The problem with this principle is that it obscures the parallelism of words that helps to make passages hold together and make sense. It makes it impossible for the reader to trace the subtle connections between ideas in the biblical text. There is no gain in understanding achieved by such variety in translation. It is done solely for the sake of stylistics. This is an example of dynamic equivalence at its worst.

The NAB interprets *porneia* ("fornication," "sexual immorality") as generic "immorality." I don't know whether this should be considered dynamic equivalence or simply poor translation. *Porneia* always has a sexual connotation in Greek, even if its exact nuance of meaning can shift from one passage to the next.

The NIV and TEV venture into paraphrase when they replace "the nations" (or "the Gentiles") with "the heathen." This is a highly interpretive rephrasing of Paul's words that cannot be defended. It obscures the Jewish background of Paul's rhetoric, and so the continuity between Christianity and Judaism. How Paul uses the expression "nations" must be carefully considered, not oversimplified into a Christian statement of "us" vs. "them." The TEV makes a similar paraphrastic oversimplification when it changes "brother" to "fellow Christian." This has the effect of narrowing the range of Paul's concern. Is Paul really saying that one should take care not to defraud only fellow Christians, and that it's alright to defraud other people, the "heathen"? I don't think so; and I would like to see a demonstration that Paul used the expression "brother" only of Christians, and not of one's fellow human being in general.

Most of these translations usually fall into the formal equivalence category. The fact that they must be considered dynamic equivalence translations here shows how difficult passages push translators to their limits. Dynamic equivalence and paraphrase are resorted to when the formally equivalent wording does not convey an obvious meaning to the modern reader. The desire to make the Bible more clear to the reader cannot be faulted in principle. Rather it should be praised. At the same time, however, we have to scrutinize the lengths to which translators go to make the Bible make sense. We have to check to see that they are not introducing clarity at the expense of accuracy. Whenever a translation that usually follows one approach to translating jumps into another approach, we must be particularly concerned about accuracy and bias.

Paraphrase
The word "paraphrase" is used quite commonly in English for restating something in other words. In Bible translation, a paraphrase has the same primary goal as a dynamic equivalence translation -- that is, to make the meaning as plain and understandable as possible for the reader. The idea of making a Bible paraphrase is based upon the notion that the Bible's own phrasing is too difficult for the average reader. In a paraphrase, the translator is able to remove difficult rhetoric, harmonize passages with one another, and draw out implications for the reader. It is a perfect opportunity to make the Bible consistent with the translator's own theology.

For these reasons, a paraphrase should never be mistaken for a Bible. It should not be packaged as a Bible, sold as a Bible, or used in place of a Bible. It should pass under the name of its author, as a commentary or interpretation of the Bible. When, instead, it is handled as if it is a Bible translation, and the author's name is left off of the title page as if he or she had no role in determining the contents of the book, a terrible deception is happening.

Properly speaking, paraphrases do not belong to the consideration of this book. But two paraphrases enjoy such widespread use as Bibles, and so often are quoted and cited as if they are legitimate translations, that I felt it was my duty to scrutinize them alongside actual translations. Only in this way will the general public be educated about their true character. The two paraphrases I am speaking about are the Living Bible, by Kenneth Taylor, and the Amplified Bible, by Frances Siewert.

The move from dynamic equivalence to paraphrase entails an additional layer of interpretation. It is a step that is part of understanding the Bible, but a step that leads us beyond translation. Throughout this book, I will make the distinction between translation and interpretation. It is true that translation always involves a degree of interpretation, even in deciding which lexical meaning of a word to choose among the many possibilities. But there is a basic difference between linguistic and contextual interpretation that reveals the meaning of Greek sentences, and theological interpretation that constructs systems of belief from those sentences. It is my contention that such theological interpretation can only be valid if it is based upon a carefully considered and sound translation of the biblical text, and that translation must precede interpretation in that sense. But it is a hard distinction to maintain when many Bible translators have felt free to add interpretation to translation in their work.

Here, one more time, is our example, 1 Thessalonians 4:3-6, in paraphrase:

AB: For this is the will of God, that you should be consecrated (separated and set apart for pure and holy living): that you should abstain *and* shrink from all sexual vice, That each one of you should know how to possess (control, manage) his own body in consecration (purity, separated from things profane) and honor. Not [to be used] in the passion of lust like the heathen, who are ignorant of the true God *and* have no knowledge of His will, That no man transgress and overreach his brother *and* defraud him in this matter *or* defraud his brother in business.

LB: For God wants you to be holy and pure, and to keep clear of all sexual sin so that each of you will marry in holiness and honor -- not in lustful passion as the heathen do, in their ignorance of God and his ways. And this is also God's will: that you never cheat in this matter by taking another man's wife . . .

The character of the Amplified Bible as a commentary on the Bible should be obvious from this example. But in the correspondence I receive it is clear that many people are using it as a Bible, treating all its "amplifications" as authoritative. These amplifications are not limited to paraphrases in parentheses, but are embedded in the text itself, connected by italicized *and* or *or*. In this passage the LB looks very much like a dynamic equivalence translation, reducing the contents of the passage to its "kernels" and conveying them in clear and straightforward language. In other passages, it more freely expands and transforms the biblical text, as we will see.

The AB interprets "vessel" as "body" and adds an extensive footnote defending that choice. The LB chooses the "wife" interpretation of "vessel," but doesn't inform readers that an interpretive choice has been made. The LB goes on to make explicit what "this matter" is in which one should not defraud his brother ("by taking another man's wife"). With either the "body" or the "wife" interpretation of "vessel," the LB's interpretation of "this matter" is likely to be correct.

Both the AB and the LB use "heathen" in place of "nations" without letting the reader in on the change. I have already spoken above about how illegitimate this interpretation is. The AB adds an additional clause ("*and* have no knowledge of His will") without justification, and totally misses the point of "defraud one's brother in the matter" (the matter being sexual boundaries) by suggesting that it means "defraud his brother in business" (!). The slightest attention to literary context should have prevented the latter mistake.

Sorting out the differences

The common contrast between "formal equivalence" and "dynamic equivalence" is, in my opinion, something of a false dichotomy. In both models of translation, you render ordinary words in the same, literal way. There is no difference in how a "formal" translator and a "dynamic" translator would render the Greek words for "dog," "boat," or "house" into English. The same goes for common verbs such as "come," "go," or "speak." The two approaches diverge only when it comes to problematic vocabulary, culturally constituted objects or actions, metaphors, technical terms, and so on.

When it comes to such culturally constituted vocabulary, a formal equivalence translator tends to work lexically, identifying a consistent term in English that corresponds as completely as possible with the range of meaning of the Greek word, accepting the fact that in some passages the chosen translation may not convey all of the nuance of the Greek phrasing, or that a contemporary reader may not be able to grasp without commentary the significance of the words or images involved in the passage in their original environment.

In the same situation, a dynamic equivalence translator works more flexibly and contextually, varying the English terms matched to the same Greek original, and more freely searching out analogies in modern culture that would communicate to the contemporary reader the meaning and significance of the original, at the expense of some of the rootedness of the meaning in its original cultural setting.

But whichever approach one prefers, the key word in both is "equivalence." Both are committed to this. "Formal" means simply sticking closely to the original syntax; "dynamic" allows freer play with syntax for the sake of semantics. But the test of a translation of either kind is *equivalence* -- that is, does the translation actually convey a meaning equivalent to the one readers in the original linguistic, literary, and cultural setting received?

The best approach to Bible translation, therefore, is to not be a partisan of either model exclusively, but to combine the best features of each while avoiding their chief pitfalls. Translators of both schools tend naturally to follow a formal, *denotative* equivalence when dealing with ordinary vocabulary, and a more nuanced, *connotative* equivalence for difficult, technical, or ambiguous terms or phrases. In the latter case, a good translation should avoid both resorting too easily to technical vocabulary that has no meaning to the "un-churched" and using too freely modern analogy that has only a tenuous connection to the meaning of the original. The translation should give careful attention to the cultural environment of the text's origin, and footnotes should be used to explain this contextual meaning where translation alone cannot convey a sufficient understanding. This combined, eclectic approach has been adopted in principle by the NRSV, with its famous dictum of "as literal as possible, as free as necessary," and by several other modern translations although, as we will see, not consistently.

My vote in favor of the eclectic approach is dictated by how the Bible is being read today: individually, outside of a classroom or educational environment. More literal, formal equivalence translations have the advantage of not hiding things from the reader by overtranslating or making the meaning seem too familiar and day-to-day. In fact, more literal translations bring to the reader's attention the need to look into explanatory material, and can start the reader on the quest for larger understanding of the full context of the Bible. On the other hand, there is no good reason to be needlessly pedantic and obscure. The English used should be contemporary, and should be as fully informative and as clear in meaning as the original Greek allows.

THREE

MAJOR ENGLISH TRANSLATIONS

Between the 1952 publication of the Revised Standard Version and the 1990 issuing of the New Revised Standard Version, fifty-five English translations of the New Testament appeared (Metzger 1993, page 397). Most of these were the work of individuals with their own peculiar axe to grind, and they quickly faded into obscurity in the bargain bin of bookstores. But several of these translations were major publishing events, because they were issued under the authority of large interdenominational groups, because they were key moments in a single denomination's handling of the Bible, or because the result of an individual translator's work gained wide popularity.

In this book, I have selected eight of these major translations to include along with the venerable King James Version for an exploration of accuracy and bias.

The King James Version
The Authorized Version is widely known as "The King James Bible," or "The King James Version" (KJV) because King James I of Great Britain sponsored it. It was completed in 1611, the work of a translation team that numbered somewhere between forty-five and fifty-five individuals (accounts vary). They worked from the foundation of earlier English

translations, most significantly William Tyndale's Bible published a century earlier. Many church leaders strongly criticized the KJV when it was first published, beginning a long tradition of rejecting anything new in favor of older translations that were themselves criticized when they first came out.

The KJV was based upon the best texts of the New Testament available at the time, principally those published by Desidarius Erasmus between 1516 and 1535 and Theodore Beza between 1565 and 1604.[1] But by the standards of modern biblical scholarship, the quality of those texts was dismal. Erasmus based his text editions on manuscripts of the 13th, 14th, and 15th centuries. He worked with only three manuscripts of the Gospels, five of Paul's letters, and four of the rest of the New Testament. The improvements in text editions in the time between Erasmus and the production of the KJV were minor at best. "The King James scholars could have known fewer than twenty-five late manuscripts of the New Testament, and these were carelessly used. Today there are 5,358 known New Testament manuscripts and fragments" (Lewis, page 42). The superior text base used today allows us to identify over a dozen verses included in the KJV that are not authentic parts of the New Testament.[2] Dozens of other words or phrases are included in the KJV that have little or no basis in Greek manuscripts[3]; likewise many words or phrases are missing from the KJV that are found in reliable Greek manuscripts. Many of these differences have their basis in the Latin Vulgate, which the King James translators turned to too often as their guide. Often, the meaning is changed dramatically (see Lewis, pages 42-44). The KJV also introduced an error into the title of the Letter to the Hebrews, ascribing its authorship to "St. Paul," even though the identity of the author has always been, and remains, unknown. Some other versions have repeated this mistake.

The KJV is a "formal equivalence" translation. It tends to be quite literal, following the Greek idiom even when it makes little sense to the average reader. That doesn't means the KJV avoids all paraphrase; it frequently introduces English idioms of its own time in place of the literal meaning of the Greek. It is arranged by verses; that is, every verse is a distinct paragraph.

The KJV's formal equivalence translation is careful and accurate within the knowledge of Greek in the time it was produced. Our knowledge of Greek has improved greatly in the last four hundred years, and we are now able to recognize many mistranslations in the KJV (for a representative sample, see Lewis, pages 46-47). Some of these mistranslations, however, appear to be distortions due to bias. For example "slave" (*doulos*) is replaced with "servant." "Love" (*agapē*) is sometimes translated instead as "charity." The names of female leaders of the early Christians are changed into male names (Junia in Romans 16 and Euodia in Philippians 4). There is notable inconsistency in how particular Greek words are rendered into English (Lewis, page 49); among these are *psuchē*, translated as both "soul" and "life"; *dikaios*, translated as both "righteous" and "just"; *hagiasmos*, translated as both "holiness" and "sanctification"; *exousia*, translated as both "authority" and "power"; and *logizomai*, translated variously as "count," "reckon," and "impute" (even side by side in Romans 4!). Lewis also points to cases where a single English word is used for two different Greek words, obscuring important distinctions (page 50).

The greatest drawback of the KJV is that the English it employs is not modern English. Besides the notorious "thee" and "thou," dozens of words found in the KJV have dropped out of the language completely. More importantly, many words now mean something different than they did in 1611. "Meat" was used of any kind of food. "Corn" was any grain, particularly wheat, not American maize (which, of course, was unknown in the Old World in New Testament times). "His" was used where we would use "its." "Prevent" meant "come before," not "hinder." "Let" meant "prevent"; now it means "allow." "Suffer" meant "allow"; now is used for experiencing pain. "Conversation" meant "interaction"; now it is limited to "talking." "Evidently" meant "clearly"; now it means "apparently." To be "careful" meant to worry, rather than being cautious. To be "pitiful" meant to be compassionate, rather than wretched or miserable. "Worship" referred to a physical bowing or prostration; now it is used of a mental state of reverence. "Quick" meant "alive," rather than "fast." And so on.

Even though all of these archaic expressions are retained in today's KJV, the original King James Bible of 1611 was different in several ways from what is now so widely reprinted as the KJV (Lewis, pages 37-40). It had marginal notes containing variant readings of the text, and it had chapter headings. Both are now omitted. The Apocryphal books of the Old Testament (those which are part of the Catholic and Orthodox canon, but not of the Protestant canon) were in the 1611 edition, but were removed in 1629. Literally hundreds of improvements of the translation were made in subsequent reprintings, beginning already in 1613. Printing mistakes have been gradually corrected over the last four centuries. In the 1760s, language, spelling, and punctuation were "modernized" and the use of italics to mark words added for sense was made more systematic. It is the revision of the mid-1700s that forms the base of the modern KJV. But even that was touched up in the 1930s and 1960s by changes in spelling, punctuation, and the running headers at the top of pages.

In 1979 something called "The New King James Bible" appeared. This was simply an effort to save the KJV from abandonment throughout Christian denominations by removing the more archaic examples of Shakespearean English. Whoever did this "clean-up" work on the KJV (the individuals responsible have remained anonymous) brought little new scholarship to their work, and rather completely ignored all of the advances in textual and linguistic knowledge achieved in the 450 years between the KJV and the NKJB. Most astonishingly, the NKJB uses the same text base as the KJV, which is different in nearly 6,000 places from modern critical texts of the New Testament, and in some passages has no basis in Greek manuscripts at all.

Since there has been no improvement in the text base, the only changes found between the KJV and NKJB are the use of more modern English words and phrases and some corrections of poor translations. Many examples of archaic forms survived the revision, however. The KJV's use of italics to mark added words is dropped. In the end, the NKJB team produced a merely cosmetic touch-up of the KJV that does not amount to a new translation. So we will not include the NKJB in the comparisons of this book. Instead, we will compare the KJV, as the "old standard," to eight translations produced in the second half of the 20th century.

The (New) Revised Standard Version

The Revised Standard Version (RSV) New Testament was published in 1946, under the sponsorship of the National Council of Churches, through its educational arm, the International Council of Religious Education. It was the fruit of a translation team consisting of thirty-two scholars, under the leadership of Luther Weigle, dean of Yale Divinity School, nearly all of whom were connected to Protestant denominations. The translators explicitly committed themselves to not bring theological influences to their translation work. In his article explaining the "Method and Procedure of the Revision," William Irwin wrote that, "there is no place for theology in Bible translation, whether conservative or radical or whatever else. A 'theological translation' is not a translation at all, but merely a dogmatic perversion of the Bible" (Irwin, page 14).

The RSV and NRSV translations have been published as "authorized" revisions of earlier translations, leading back through the American Standard Version to the KJV. This claim begs the question: authorized by whom? The answer is the National Council of Churches of Christ in the U.S.A. So the reader's attitude towards this authorization will depend on what he or she thinks of this religious body. To me, the claim looks a bit too much like an advertising ploy, implying that other translations are somehow "unauthorized." This implication would be particularly directed against the NASB and NW, both of which present themselves as, like the RSV, revisions of the American Standard Version.

The RSV and NRSV are formal equivalence translations, although the NRSV is considerably looser than its predecessor, moving in the direction of dynamic equivalence. The RSV and NRSV were based upon the best and most up-to-date critical editions of the thousands of biblical manuscripts now available, the Nestle-Aland and United Bible Societies editions. These versions have also benefitted from advances in our understanding of Greek grammar and syntax. The text is arranged in sense paragraphs, rather than having every verse a separate paragraph.

From the inception of the project, the RSV translation committee has had as its goal making its Bible *the* Bible of the English-speaking world, replacing the venerable KJV. Bruce Metzger of Princeton Theological Seminary, chair of the RSV committee since 1977, sums up the story of the making of the RSV as "an account of the triumph of ecumenical concern over more limited sectarian interests. At last (and for the first time since the Reformation) one edition of the Bible had received the blessing of leaders of Protestant, Roman Catholic, and Eastern Orthodox churches alike" (Metzger 1993, page 401). Metzger repeats this testimonial to the RSV's unique universality over and over again as its chief virtue. The drive to attain that goal has resulted in a definite tendency to "revise-to-please" on the part of the editors over the years. Revision has most often been back towards more traditional understandings of passages, at the expense of accuracy. There also has been regression towards a more traditional text-base (this regression was based upon a similar conservative reaction in the UBS Greek New Testament in its third edition).[4] Revision can be a good thing, as improved readings are incorporated into a translation. But the history of the revision of the RSV reflects an over-eagerness on the part of the editors to please readers by catering to their preconditioned biases. This compromising attitude has grown as the number of scholars actually responsible for the translation has shrunk to a handful.

Metzger oversaw the developments leading from the RSV to the NRSV. These included very commendable efforts to use more gender inclusive language in English where it could be considered to be implied in the Greek, the continued modification of English expression to bring it out of the KJV past and into the present, and of course further changes necessitated by advances in biblical scholarship. Ten scholars worked on the New Testament of the NRSV. The translation committee was selected primarily on the basis of representing the vested denominational interests; that is, Metzger saw to it that Protestant, Catholic, and Eastern Orthodox participation was involved, so that the finished product would be acceptable to all parties. The principle of translation followed defied the tidy categories of "formal" and "dynamic" equivalence, putting in their stead the motto "as literal as possible, as free as necessary." The NRSV was published in 1990.

The New International Version
The New International Version (NIV) was initiated by translators representing the Christian Reformed Church and the National Association of Evangelicals. Eventually, over one hundred translators representing over a dozen evangelical denominations became part of the team. The translation work was sponsored by the International Bible Society, headquartered in New York, and the New Testament was completed in 1973. A decade later, it was reissued with nine-hundred-thirty changes. In 1985 and 1986 further changes were made, twenty-five in all. Most of the changes are in English style, and do not substantially alter the meaning of the earlier edition.

The NIV is a formal equivalence translation. It is less formal than the NRSV, and closer to the NAB. But there are many dynamic equivalence bolts from the blue. In fact, Robert Bratcher's TEV seems to have been primary reading material for the translation committee. The best and most recent critical editions of Greek manuscripts were used, and the handling of the text-base is generally careful. The theological stance of the translators, however, makes them more conservative in their text decisions than those of the NRSV or NAB. Bruce Metzger points out examples where the NIV ignores the underlying Greek text and where it makes additions not supported by the Greek "for what appears to be doctrinal reasons" (Metzger 1992, page 9; he cites the addition of "your" in Matthew 13:32 and "now" in 1 Peter 4:6). The text is arranged in sense paragraphs.

Carolyn Johnson Youngblood gives a sympathetic account of the origins of the NIV in her article, "The *New International Version* Translation Project: Its Conception and Implementation." She describes the need recognized in certain segments of the Christian public to have a Bible in modern English. In her words, "the new Bible must of necessity be done by scholars from a broad spectrum of evangelical communions who held to a high view of scripture" (Youngblood, page 240). These specific criteria (evangelical, high view of scripture) were shaped by reaction to the RSV, which was widely criticized by more conservative Christians for its departures from the KJV. This outcry against the RSV was understandable coming from a general public who had no means to assess the new translation in comparison to the original Greek of the New Testament manuscripts. All they could see was that the RSV was different from the KJV. But was that difference "better," or "worse"?

Even the NIV's defenders freely admit that it is "a theological translation, given birth by evangelical dissatisfaction with the theology of the RSV" (Jackson, page 208). Prospective members of the NIV translation committee were recruited only from "evangelical seminaries and Christian colleges" (Youngblood, page 245), and had to subscribe to particular creeds of faith (the Westminster Confession of Faith, the Belgic Confessions, and the Statement of Faith of the National Association of Evangelicals). Creedal commitment, of course, has nothing to do with linguistic skill or the other necessary criteria of accurate translations. So bias was woven into the NIV from the very beginning, despite whatever integrity the translators brought to their work. I have found nothing in print to suggest that the NIV committee imposed any test of linguistic or historical knowledge on a par with its theological test.

Edwin H. Palmer, "a theologian and former pastor of a Christian Reformed church" (Youngblood, page 245) was named director of the project. At the time he was a professor of systematic theology at Westminster Theological Seminary. In his own description of the fifteen-person governing committee of the project, it was "made up of theologians from different American colleges, universities, and theological seminaries" (quoted in Worth, page 149). Even though the translation team of over one hundred persons included many who specialize in biblical research, it was the fifteen theologians of the governing committee who had final say over every verse.

The New American Bible

The New American Bible is the Catholic contribution to modern Bible translations. Work on the New Testament began in 1956, and was completed in 1970. The translation team consisted of fifty-nine Catholic and five Protestant scholars, under the sponsorship of the Confraternity of Christian Doctrine.

The NAB's text-base is derived from both the Nestle-Aland and the UBS Greek texts (which in the most recent editions are basically identical). Initially, the NAB stood very near the transition point between formal equivalence and dynamic equivalence translation. A revised edition was published in 1986, with significant changes from the original in favor of a more consistent formal equivalence style. The Preface to the new edition states:

> The primary aim of the revision is to produce a version as accurate and faithful to the meaning of the Greek original as is possible for a translation. The editors have consequently moved in the direction of a formal-equivalence approach to translation, matching the vocabulary, structure, and even word order of the original as closely as possible in the receptor language.

Another notable change in the 1986 edition is its effort to use gender inclusive language whenever practical. This move towards formal equivalence is a definite advance over the earlier edition's apparent indecisiveness about how free to be in its renderings. But there is still considerable inconsistency to be found. The text is arranged in sense paragraphs.

Although a few Protestant biblical scholars participated in the translation, it is largely the work of Catholic scholars and received the sanction of the Catholic church. One might assume a distinctly Catholic bias in the finished product. But ideologically the Catholic church is under less pressure to find all of its doctrines in the Bible than is the case with Protestant denominations, and this fact, combined with the vast resources of Catholic biblical scholarship, seems to have worked to the NAB's advantage.

The New American Standard Bible
The New American Standard Bible was produced under the auspices of the Lockman Foundation, reaching publication in 1963. The translation committee has been kept anonymous, although, according to the foundation itself, it consisted of qualified individuals from many Protestant, predominantly conservative, denominations (Presbyterian, Methodist, Southern Baptist, Church of Christ, Nazarene, American Baptist, Fundamentalist, Conservative Baptist, Free Methodist, Congregational, Disciples of Christ, Evangelical Free, Independent Baptist, Independent Mennonite, Assembly of God, North American Baptist, and "other religious groups").

The translation team expressly committted itself to "be true to the original Hebrew and Greek." The translators claim to have followed the 23rd edition of the Nestle-Aland Greek text, and they often do. But in several cases they have reverted to the deeply flawed KJV text. This hardly seems to fulfill the commitment to be true to the original text. The translation is of the formal equivalence variety, including, like the KJV, the use of italics to mark added words (although this is not completely consistent). Although the NASB New Testament was published ostensibly as a rival revision of the American Standard Version to that of the RSV, it often reverts to KJV stylistics, including making every verse a separate paragraph.[5]

The Amplified Bible
The Amplified Bible (AB) is a curiosity, also produced by the Lockman Foundation, that enjoys widespread use. The book is the work solely of Frances E. Siewert, completed in 1958. Ostensibly, it sets out to provide the many possible nuances, or to expand upon the inherent sense, of the original Greek phrases. But Siewert does not confine herself to this sort of "amplification." Instead, she freely expands the biblical text with doctrinal content totally alien to the Bible, imported from later Christian theology. So the AB is inherently and explicitly interpretive, not a translation at all.

Siewert claims to follow the Westcott and Hort Greek text, which is a fine one, but in fact sneaks in readings not found in Westcott and Hort, always inferior readings whose substitution for the Westcott and Hort text occurs in every case for tendentious theological reasons. The main translation follows the formal equivalence approach, but the extensive glosses added amount to a workbook for a dynamic equivalence alternative. The text is arranged by verses, as in the KJV and NASB.

In addition to the strong theological slant throughout the AB, it suffers from the complexity of the glosses (synonyms and other explanatory insertions) it uses. Siewert seems to have lost control of the layers involved in the translation, between main text, italicized text, parentheses, and brackets. Removing the commentary enclosed in brackets often results in totally incoherent sentences. The heaping of synonyms is usually highly redundant and pointless, and very often extremely biased towards particular theological interpretations.

The Living Bible
The Living Bible (LB), completed in 1967, is not a Bible translation at all, and it would not even be considered in this book were it not for its great popularity and widespread use among people who have no idea that they are not dealing with a legitimate Bible translation. The author, Kenneth N. Taylor, did not even work from the original languages of the Bible. The LB is not based upon any Greek text, but rather upon the American Standard Version English translation of 1901, checked against other translations, such as the KJV and NASB. It includes passages known to be not original parts of the books of the Bible.[6] These additions have a theological slant that Taylor favors, and so he includes them despite the best textual evidence. He also freely omits from the Bible material he does not like,[7] and adds interpolations of his own, theological statements that have no basis in the biblical text.[8] The text is arranged in sense paragraphs.

Taylor claims that his goal in the LB is "to say as exactly as possible what the writers of the Scriptures meant, and to say it simply, expanding where necessary for a clear understanding by the modern reader" (Preface). The questions to be put to such a claim include "On what basis do you determine what the writers meant?" and "Is saying what they meant exactly compatible with saying it simply?" The only legitimate means to determine what the writers meant is to understand the language they used in its linguistic, literary, and cultural contexts. To communicate the meaning of the Bible exactly, one cannot oversimplify the complexities and nuances of its expression. But Taylor has not investigated the linguistic background of the text; he freely harmonizes between the books of the Bible, thus ignoring literary context; and he constantly introduces anachronisms into his reworkings of biblical material, thus distorting the conditions in which the Bible was produced. His simplifications of the Bible's meaning are usually tendentious, bringing the Bible into line with his own personal theology.

Orlinsky and Bratcher are of the opinion that "Taylor is guilty of distorting the biblical text, omitting and adding material, all dictated by his lodestar, a rigid evangelical position" (Orlinsky and Bratcher, page 243),[9] and "*The Living Bible* is an unfaithful, tendentious misrepresentation of the biblical text" (Orlinsky and Bratcher, page 244). Bruce Metzger says that "the text is greatly expanded by imaginative details for which there is no warrant in the original," and that "Taylor takes unwarranted liberties with the text" (Metzger 1992, page 9). One might argue that as a paraphrase the LB is entitled to less stringent standards than regular translations. But a paraphrase, by any definition, must contain the same meaning as the original, even if in different words. The LB's accuracy is hit-and-miss. Taylor at times grasps the meaning of the original text (through the medium of other translations he has consulted). But far too often he indulges in creative rewritings of the Bible that might be defended as interpretation, but cannot be called translation by any stretch of that term.

Today's English Version
The Today's English Version Bible (TEV), widely known as the "Good News Bible" is the product of the American Bible Society. In the 1960s, members of this society hit upon the idea to produce an English translation according to the same principles used when making translations of the Bible into indigenous languages around the world for the purposes of proselytization. The TEV would be a test of the principal of "dynamic equivalence" -- composing a translation based upon the presumed meaning in context of whole passages, rather than adhering more cautiously to the exact mode of expression for that presumed meaning employed by the original authors. The obstacles of the ancient, alien culture of the Bible's origin would be as much as possible stripped away to make the translation inviting and familiar.

The principal translator for the TEV New Testament was Robert Bratcher. He worked under the authority of the Translations Department of the ABS, headed by Eugene Nida, the great proponent of "dynamic equivalence." Bratcher had the assistance of a "consultative committee" consisting of two former missionaries, a representative of the British counterpart to the ABS, a representative of the National Council of Churches, and one bona fide Bible scholar, Howard Clark Kee, then a professor at Drew Theological Seminary. So the team involved was primarily theological in character and approach. They were undertaking, in effect, missionary work to the English speaking world.

The TEV New Testament was completed in 1966. Revisions were made rapidly in the following years, and the translation had reached its fourth edition by 1976. The TEV was a runaway best-seller. In the case of both the TEV and the LB, the Bible-reading public revealed an exception to the rule that they generally reject new Bible translations at first. The public appears willing to embrace an easily comprehensible translation despite its departure from the traditional translation, and regardless of its accuracy. Because the public is not informed of issues of accuracy and bias in Bible translation, it has no way to judge new translations other than on their familiarity or readability. Sales of the TEV were greatly aided by the fact that the Catholic Church approved its use by its members in 1969. New editions were issued with improvements -- nearly eight-hundred already by 1981. In 1992 a new edition appeared that incorporated gender-inclusive language.

The TEV follows the United Bible Society's Greek text, with the exception of fourteen passages where it prefers other readings.[10] The text is arranged in sense paragraphs, and is supplied with subject headings every few paragraphs. These "aids" actually serve to control what the reader focuses on in the passage and guides them to interpret the text in the same way the editor does.

The words of Bruce Metzger are apt: the TEV "has made clear some passages that are unclear in the original" (Metzger 1992, page 9); in other words, the translator has decided for himself the meanings of ambiguous parts of the text, and conveyed only his preferred meanings to the readers of the TEV Bible. This is interpretation, not translation.

The New World Translation
Like the NAB, the New World Translation is a product of a single Christian denomination, in this case, the Jehovah's Witnesses, through their publishing arm, the Watchtower Bible and Tract Society of New York. Because of its association with the Jehovah's Witnesses, the NW is often and readily pointed to as an example of a translation which must have a theological bias, unlike the supposedly objective, neutral, and scholarly Bibles more widely used today. The attention to bias is heightened by the fact that the theology of the Jehovah's Witnesses does not correspond to that of the mainstream denominations. This difference creates a hostile atmosphere in which representatives of that mainstream theology charge

that any variation in the NW from more familiar translations must serve the ulterior motives of distorting the "truth." But the facts are that all of the translations considered in this book are products of people with theological commitments, that all contain biased translations of one sort or another, and that the NW deserves to be assessed for accuracy by the same standards applied to the others.

The NW's text-base is the Westcott and Hort edition, which is the foundation of modern critical editions, and closely related to the more recent Nestle-Aland and UBS texts. It stays true to this text-base, and does not draw in readings from the inferior traditional text, as happens with the NASB, AB, and LB. The NW is a formal equivalence translation, with occasional ventures into dynamic equivalence where the meaning was felt to be obscured by potential misunderstandings of Greek idiom. This approach puts the NW very close to the NRSV's principles of "as literal as possible, as free as necessary." But the NW is free of the shadow of King James, and so reads quite differently than the KJV-dependent NRSV. One systematic peculiarity of the NW is the substitution of "Jehovah" for "Lord" in well over two-hundred verses.[11]

The NW New Testament was first published in 1950, and was most recently revised in 1984. The members of the translation team remain anonymous, just as they do for the NKJB and the Lockman Foundation's NASB.

NOTES

1. The text editions of Stephanus, published between 1546 and 1551, and the Complutensian Polyglot, published in 1522, also apparently were consulted.

2. Matthew 17:21; 18:11; 23:14; Mark 7:16; 9:44; 9:46; 11:26; 15:28; Luke 17:36; 23:17; John 5:4; Acts 8:37; 15:34; 24:7; 28:29; Romans 16:24.

3. The KJV Book of Revelation alone contains thirteen verses for which no manuscript support whatsoever exists (1:9; 1:11; 2:3; 2:20; 2:24; 3:2; 5:10; 5:14; 15:3; 16:5; 17:8; 17:16; 18:2); they all derive from errors in the publications of Erasmus and Beza. Passages of similar origin in the rest of the KJV include Acts 9:5-6; Romans 7:6; and 1 Peter 3:20.

4. Mark 16:9-20 and John 7:53-8:11 were reinserted into the main text with no new textual justification, and despite the fact that, if anything, the scholarly consensus had solidified in agreeing that these passages were inauthentic. Luke 22:19b-20 and 24:47a were also restored to the main text, while Luke 22:43-44 and a clause from Luke 12:39 were removed to footnotes.

5. The original edition of the NASB had the innovation of marking with asterisks places where Greek present tense verbs used as a "historical present" are made into English past tense verbs to conform to proper English grammar (see, for example John 1:43). Since Greek verbal tenses do not agree exactly in their sense and usage with English tenses, and a rote obedience to the Greek forms would produce sentences that sound ridiculous in English, all translations make this sort of verbal tense adjustment. On this subject, see chapter ten. The practice of marking such verbal adjustments was dropped in subsequent NASB editions.

6. For example, Matthew 17:21; 18:11; Mark 15:28; John 5:3b-4; Acts 8:37; 14:6b-8a; Romans 16:24.

7. For example, Matthew 5:18; Mark 13:30; John 12:14.

8. For example, in 2 Timothy 2:8; Hebrews 9:18.

9. The words "rigid evangelical position" are Taylor's own self-characterization, from the Preface of the LB.

10. Mark 6:20, 22; Luke 21:19; Acts 7:46; 10:19; 12:25; Romans 8:28; 1 Corinthians 13:3; 2 Corinthians 8:7; Hebrews 4:2; 2 Peter 3:10; Jude 5; Revelation 14:3; 21:3. Later changes in the UBS Greek text came into line with the TEV in three cases (Mark 6:20; Acts 10:19; Jude 5; see *Bible Translator* 18 [1967], pages 167-174).

11. On this peculiarity, see the Appendix.

FOUR

BOWING TO BIAS

We begin our exploration of accuracy and bias by looking at the most basic component of translation: the accurate definition of single words, or what we might call lexical accuracy. A source of trouble in English translations of the New Testament occurs when translators become fixated on a very narrow, specialized significance of a word that actually has a much broader meaning in its original context of use in the Bible. In such cases, the accuracy of the translation is hampered by a bias towards a restricted, theological importance invested in a term. I will illustrate this problem with the example of the Greek verb *proskuneō*.

Ancient Mediterranean societies tended to be very hierarchical. It was a world where everyone knew their place in relation to countless superiors and inferiors. Those who neglected or forgot this stratification of rank would be readily reminded by those around. In the highest place stood God or the gods. Below that in the Roman Empire ranked the emperor, followed by senators, governors, and a very complex system of local officials, priests, and landowners. The very bottom was occupied by slaves who might be owned by the lowliest of peasant.

Social convention dictated gestures of deference and respect from inferior to superior at every point along this hierarchy. In the presence of someone of high rank, low bows or prostrations were expected. The Greek verb that expresses making such a prostration was *proskuneō*. In the modern world, the best example of a prostration can be seen in the prayers of Muslims. Dropping to your knees, you bend forward and lower your head to the ground.

In the time of Jesus, prostrations were quite common throughout the eastern Roman Empire, both in official circles and in the less formal daily dealings of people of widely different rank. The Greek verb *proskuneō* gradually expanded its meaning to include a wide variety of formal gestures of respect. It even came to be used colloquially with the meaning "kiss" or a welcoming embrace.

The verb *proskuneō* is used fifty-eight times in the New Testament. When the King James translation was made, the word picked to best convey the meaning of the Greek word was "worship." At that time, the English word "worship" had a range of meaning close to what I have suggested for the Greek word *proskuneō*. It could be used for the attitude of reverence given to God, but also for the act of prostration. The word was also used as a form of address to people of high status, in the form "your worship." So the King James translation committee made a pretty good choice.

But modern English is not King James English, and the range of meaning for the word "worship" has narrowed considerably. Today, we use it only for religious veneration of God, so it no longer covers all of the uses of the Greek verb *proskuneō*, or of the English word in the days of King James. For this reason, it is necessary that modern translations find appropriate terms to accurately convey precisely what is implied by the use of *proskuneō* in the various passages where it appears. If they fail to do this, and cling to the old English word "worship" without acknowledging its shift of meaning since the days of King James, they mislead their readers into thinking that every greeting, kiss, or prostration in the Bible is an act of worship directed to a god.[1]

Let's look at some concrete examples. I will quote all nine translations we are comparing, giving the full text first from the NAB, and then just the pertinent phrase from the others.

Matthew 18:26
NAB: At that, the servant fell down, did him homage, and said, 'Be patient with me and I will pay you back in full.'
NW: ... began to do obeisance to him ...
NASB: ... prostrated himself before him ...
NIV: ... fell on his knees before him ...

NRSV:	... fell on his knees before him ...
TEV:	... fell on his knees before the king ...
AB:	... fell on his knees, begging him ...
LB:	... fell down before the king, his face in the dust ...
KJV:	... and worshipped him ...

Here Jesus is telling a story in which a slave, in trouble with his owner, the king, begs for leniency with a gesture of subservience. Clearly Jesus himself could imagine situations in which a person would do such a thing, with no intention of suggesting that one was "worshiping" the person to whom one bowed. In his story-telling, Jesus accurately reflects the social conventions of the world around him. All of the translations accurately convey the meaning of *proskuneō* here. The KJV's "worship" had the same meaning in the time the translation was made.

Revelation 3:9

NAB:	Behold, I will make those of the assembly of Satan who claim to be Jews and are not, but are lying, behold I will make them come and fall prostrate at your feet, and they will realize that I love you.
NW:	... do obeisance before your feet ...
NASB:	... come and bow down at your feet ...
NIV:	... come and fall down at your feet ...
NRSV:	... come and bow down before your feet ...
TEV:	... come and bow down at your feet ...
AB:	... come and bow down before your feet ...
LB:	... fall at your feet ...
KJV:	... come and worship before thy feet ...

Here Jesus tells the "angel of the congregation in Philadelphia," probably meant to represent the community itself, that he will make the "false Jews" of the "assembly of Satan" come and prostrate themselves at their feet. The gesture is one of subservience towards superiors, not an act of worship of the Christians, or their angel, as a god.

Mark 15:18-19

NAB:	They began to salute him with, 'Hail, King of the Jews!' and kept striking his head with a reed and spitting upon him. They knelt before him in homage.

NW:	. . . bending their knees, they would do obeisance to him.
NASB:	. . . and kneeling and bowing before him.
NIV:	Falling on their knees, they paid homage to him.
NRSV:	. . . and knelt down in homage to him.
TEV:	. . . fell on their knees, and bowed down to him.
AB:	. . . and kept bowing their knees in homage to Him.
LB:	. . . and went down on their knees to 'worship' him.
KJV:	. . . and bowing *their* knees worshipped him.

This scene is well known to most readers of the Bible. It has been depicted quite accurately in numerous films of the life of Jesus. The Roman soldiers who have Jesus in custody are mocking what they understand to be his claim to be king of the Jews. In their mockery, they kneel down and prostrate themselves to the "king." There is absolutely no reference here to religious veneration or worship of Jesus as a god. It is (mock) homage to a king.

Notice that in the above examples the King James translators employed "worship" even though they fully recognized that the religious sense of that term did not apply. You can see in each of these cases that the modern translations understand the meaning of the verb *proskuneō*, and leave behind the King James Version's "worship" as inaccurate in a modern English context.

But in other passages, translations revert to the KJV's "worship" inappropriately. They do so primarily because the gesture of prostration is directed to Jesus, and in that circumstance they translate differently, under the pressure of theological bias. Here is an example.

Matthew 2:1-2, 8, 11

NAB:	When Jesus was born in Bethlehem of Judea, in the days of King Herod, behold, magi from the east arrived in Jerusalem, saying, 'Where is the newborn king of the Jews? We saw his star at its rising and have come to do him homage.'... He sent them to Bethlehem and said, 'Go and search diligently for the child. When you have found him, bring me word, that I too may go and do him homage.'... and on entering the house they saw the child with Mary his mother. They prostrated themselves and did him homage.
NW:	. . . falling down, they did obeisance to it.
NASB:	. . . fell down and worshiped Him.

NIV:	. . . bowed down and worshiped him.
NRSV:	. . . knelt down and paid him homage.
TEV:	. . . they knelt down and worshiped him.
AB:	. . . fell down and worshiped Him.
LB:	. . . they threw themselves down before him, worshiping.
KJV:	. . . fell down, and worshipped him.

The magi drop to their knees and prostrate themselves to the baby Jesus. They do so because he is the "king" their astrological observations had led them to. The majority of translations (NASB, NIV, TEV, AB, LB) lapse into language of "worship" that simply does not apply to this context. Rendering homage to a king is not the same as worshiping a god.

The magi were priests of the Zoroastrian faith, which like Judaism is monotheistic. In this story, their astrological talents have revealed to them the birth of a new king. Herod and his advisors correctly discern that this new king -- not one of Herod's sons -- must be the messiah. So Herod feigns willingness to go himself to render homage to the new king. In the Jewish tradition, the messiah is merely a chosen human being; there is no suggestion that he is a divine being. The whole episode works with royal images and privileges, and language of "worship" has no place here.

We can take the other passages in the Gospel according to Matthew where *proskuneō* is used, and see how "worship" works its way into modern translations. If the word is used to refer to the actions of a leper (Matthew 8:2), a local Jewish authority (Matthew 9:18), or women (Matthew 15:25 and 20:20) most translations stick with the literal meaning of kneeling, or bowing (only the AB and LB, along with the KJV, regularly employ "worship" in these passages). But when the disciples of Jesus are the actors, suddenly we see "worship" everywhere.

Matthew 14:33

NAB:	Those who were in the boat did him homage, saying, 'Truly, you are the Son of God.'
NW:	. . . did obeisance to him . . .
NASB:	. . . worshiped him . . .
NIV:	. . . worshiped him . . .
NRSV:	. . . worshiped him . . .
TEV:	. . . worshiped Jesus . . .
AB:	. . . knelt and worshiped Him . . .
LB:	. . . sat there, awestruck . . .

KJV: . . . worshiped him . . .

Jesus has just performed the superhuman feat of walking on water. In awe at Jesus' power, and in some fear of it, the disciples prostrate themselves in the boat. Within the cultural context of the events, the gesture makes perfect sense. In the ancient world, one bows to power. Most translations choose to import the modern meaning of "worship" into the passage, apparently because of the recognition by the disciples that they are in the presence of "a son of God." Yes, that's what the Greek says: "a son of God." This title was used of someone especially chosen and protected by God, and bestowed with power by him -- especially a king. The idea was used of Solomon (2 Samuel 7:14) in the Old Testament, as well as of Alexander and Augustus in the larger Greco-Roman world. By misreading the words used of Jesus by the disciples, by wrongly reading them in light of the Christian doctrine about Jesus' divinity as "the Son of God," most translations add to the text the false idea that the disciples are depicted worshiping Jesus, when in fact, in this particular episode, they merely are reacting to his evident powers with awe.

Matthew 28:9
NAB: And behold, Jesus met them on their way and greeted them. They approached, embraced his feet, and did him homage.
NW: . . . did obeisance to him.
NASB: . . . worshiped Him.
NIV: . . . worshiped him.
NRSV: . . . worshiped him.
TEV: . . . worshiped him.
AB: . . . worshiped Him.
LB: . . . worshipping him.
KJV: . . . worshipped him.

The situation in this example is very similar to the previous one. Struck with amazement and fear at seeing Jesus alive when they thought him dead, the disciples cower at his feet. Touching the head to someone's feet while clutching them with the hand is a gesture of total subservience. The emotions involved in this scene are made plain by the words Jesus uses in the next verse in response to the gestures of his disciples: "Do not be afraid." The disciples are not "worshiping" Jesus, but throwing themselves to the ground in the presence of someone of apparently superhuman power.

The prostrations made to Jesus fit within the cultural attitudes I discussed at the beginning of this chapter. They are gestures of respect made to a superior, in either the spiritual, social, or political sense. In every case, we are dealing with a physical gesture that was used more broadly than just the context of "worship." You can see, however, that the nine translations we are comparing show varying degrees of inconsistency in how they translate *proskuneō*. Rendering a single Greek word into more than one English alternative is not *necessarily* inaccurate in and of itself. Since Greek words such as *proskuneō* have a range of possible meanings, it is not practical to insist that a Greek word always be translated the same way. There are more valid and less valid contexts to consider in making a choice. But in our exploration of this issue, we can see how theological bias has been the determining context for the choices made by all of the translations except the NAB and NW. There are passages where many translators have *interpreted* the gesture referred to by the Greek term *proskuneō* as implying "worship." They then have *substituted* that interpretation in place of a translation.

I am not going to enter into a debate over interpretation. It is always possible that the interpretation of the significance of the gesture *may be* correct. But the simple translation "prostrate," or "do homage," or "do obeisance" is *certainly* correct. So the question is raised, why depart from a certain, accurate translation to a questionable, possibly inaccurate one?

The answer is that, when this occurs, the translators seem to feel the need to add to the New Testament support for the idea that Jesus was recognized to be God. But the presence of such an idea cannot be supported by selectively translating a word one way when it refers to Jesus and another way when it refers to someone else. Since such "acts of worship" are made to others beside Jesus in the New Testament, and Jesus even tells a story in which such a gesture is made to an ordinary person, we can rule out the idea that "prostration" means "worship" in the modern sense of that English word. When we observe how these same translators choose "worship" when the gesture is made to Jesus by certain persons, and choose other English words to translate the very same Greek term when the gesture is directed to someone other than Jesus, or is directed to Jesus by someone whom they regard as not qualifying as a true believer, their inconsistency reveals their bias.

They might argue that the context of belief surrounding Jesus implies that the gesture is more than "obeisance" or "homage." It's not a very good argument, because in most of the passages the people who make the gesture know next to nothing about Jesus, other than that it is obvious or rumored that he has power to help them. One final example proves that, even among the disciples, the word *proskuneō* means a physical gesture, and not a faith-based "worship."

Matthew 28:16-17

NAB:	The eleven disciples went to Galilee, to the mountain to which Jesus had ordered them. When they saw him, they worshiped, but they doubted.
NW:	. . . they did obeisance, but some doubted.
NASB:	. . . they worshiped *Him*; but some were doubtful.
NIV:	. . . they worshiped him; but some doubted.
NRSV:	. . . they worshiped him; but some doubted.
TEV:	. . . they worshiped him, even though some of them doubted.
AB:	. . . they fell down and worshiped Him; but some doubted.
LB:	. . . worshiped him -- but some of them weren't sure it really was Jesus!
KJV:	. . . they worshipped him: but some doubted.

Here all translations except the NW have recourse to "worship" -- a rendering which makes no sense in this context. How can someone worship and doubt at the same time? Notice how all eleven disciples prostrate themselves, but not all believe what they are experiencing (actually, the NAB is the only version to correctly translate the Greek "but they doubted"; there is nothing in the Greek from which you could get "some"). The word can't possibly mean "worship" as we use that word today, as a mental state of reverence, since "they doubted." It only refers to the outward physical act of bowing down, which may or may not reflect how the one making the gesture really feels about the person to whom they make it. This contradiction seems to have been missed by all the translators except those who prepared the NW.

In our exploration of the Greek word *proskuneō* in the New Testament, therefore, the NAB and NW receive the highest marks for accuracy, while the others show a tendency to lapse into interpretive judgments guided by their theological biases.

It is perfectly legitimate for readers of the Bible to have different opinions about what is implied in a gesture of reverence such as prostration. Some will give it great theological importance; others will find it too broadly used to necessarily have theological import. But this debate of interpretation is the right of the readers, and should not be decided for them by translators whose biases lead them to restrict what they will allow the readers to be able to consider.

The reader can make a case that the prostrations given to Jesus are meant to signify a unique, even divine status. This interpretation can be built upon the text, but is not inherently and necessarily given in the text, which may also be interpreted in other ways. The Reformation fought for the access of all believers to the Bible and the right of the individual to directly encounter and interpret the text. Modern translators undermine that cause when they publish interpretations rather than translations, still trying to direct readers to the understanding acceptable to the beliefs and biases of the translators themselves.

Few Christians still incorporate prostrations into their worship of God, and the prostrations once due to kings and other high officials have been refined into graceful bows and curtsies. The world of the Bible was quite different, and if we forget that fact we are apt to misunderstand what is on the page in front of us.

NOTES

1. Donald W. Burdick lists "altered meanings in the English language" as one of three reasons new translations are necessary ("Bible Translation: Why, What, and How?," *Seminary Review* 21 [1975], pages 3-7).

FIVE

GRASPING AT ACCURACY

In his letter to the Philippians, Paul encourages his readers to imitate Jesus. To give them some idea of the attitude they should be imitating, he quotes a poem or hymn that gives a very condensed, stylized account of just what Jesus did (Philippians 2:5-11). The proper interpretation of this passage has been debated since the letter was written, and is still hotly debated today. As throughout this book, I will not attempt here to settle the interpretive debate. Instead, I will be looking at translation of the passage to determine whether it has been handled accurately and without bias. We need to make sure that translators have not rigged the debate by making a translation that fits the interpretation they want for the passage.

It is true that the exact nuance of the Greek will only become clear with a decision about interpretation. Translation and interpretation are not *absolutely* separable. But there are limits to how far the Greek can be stretched; and an interpretation is less likely the more it stretches the Greek to make it fit.

As in the previous chapter, we are dealing with lexical matters, that is, the definition of individual words. It is the opening lines of the poem that make for difficulty in translation, and provide an opportunity to either resist or yield to the temptation of biased translation. Here are the results:

KJV: Christ Jesus: Who, being in the form of God, thought it not robbery to be equal with God: But made himself of no reputation, and took upon him the form of a servant, and was made in the likeness of men.

NASB: Christ Jesus, who, although He existed in the form of God, did not regard equality with God a thing to be grasped, but emptied Himself, taking the form of a bond-servant, *and* being made in the likeness of men.

NW: Christ Jesus, who, although he was existing in God's form, gave no consideration to a seizure, namely, that he should be equal to God. No, but he emptied himself and took a slave's form and came to be in the likeness of men.

NIV: Christ Jesus: Who, being in very nature [Or *in the form of*] God, did not consider equality with God something to be grasped, but made himself nothing, taking the very nature [Or *the form*] of a servant, being made in human likeness.

NRSV: Christ Jesus, who, though he was in the form of God, did not regard equality with God as something to be exploited, but emptied himself, taking the form of a slave, being born in human likeness.

NAB: Christ Jesus, Who, though he was in the form of God, did not regard equality with God something to be grasped. Rather, he emptied himself, taking the form of a slave, coming in human likeness.

TEV: Christ Jesus . . . He always had the nature of God, but he did not think that by force he should try to become [*or* remain] equal with God. Instead of this, of his own free will he gave up all he had, and took the nature of a servant. He became like man and appeared in human likeness.

AB: Christ Jesus: Who, although being essentially one with God *and* in the form of God, did not think this equality with God was a thing to be eagerly grasped *or* retained, But stripped Himself, so as to assume the guise of a servant, in that He became like men *and* was born a human being.

LB: Jesus Christ, who, though he was God, did not demand and cling to his rights as God, but laid aside his mighty power and glory, taking the disguise of a slave and becoming like men [Literally, "was made in the likeness of men."].

The first lexical issue concerns the Greek word *morphē*. The translators of the NIV, TEV, AB, and LB have taken it upon themselves to change Paul's language about Jesus being *en morphē theou* (literally: "in the form of God") to "being in very nature God" (NIV), "always had the nature of God" (TEV), "being essentially one with God" (AB), and "he was God" (LB).

What exactly Paul means by "in the form of God" is part of the interpretive debate about this passage. At least one possibility is that it is meant to echo the characterization of human beings as being made "in the image of God" in Genesis 1 (in other words, Christ possessed that perfect form/image of God that humans originally had, but had lost through doing the opposite of what Christ is reported here to have done). The translators of these four versions have gone out of their way to prevent such a possible understanding of the passage, apparently concerned that Paul's choice of words failed to make clear that Christ was more than a human being at the beginning of the story.

Now, the Greek word *morphē* ("form") is fairly generic, and can mean a number of things. But it does not mean "nature" or "essence," nor does it signify that anything "was" or was "one with" something else. These four translations (NIV, TEV, AB, LB) do not translate the Greek, but substitute interpretations of their own that are not based in Paul's language at all. Therefore they are inaccurate; and their bias is evident in what they try to import into the passage. The TEV and NIV have tried to introduce a "two-nature" Christology (first worked out by Christians at the Council of Chalcedon over three hundred years after the New Testament was written). The LB and AB have attempted to eradicate the distinctions between Jesus and God the Father that Paul makes in this very passage. We do not gain much confidence in their interpretation of the passage when we see how they tamper with the text to support it.

The second lexical issue with this passage, and the one to which we will give the most attention, is the meaning of the Greek noun *harpagmos*. You can see above that it is translated similarly by four translations as "something to be grasped" (NAB, NIV), "a thing to be grasped" (NASB), and "a thing to be eagerly grasped" (AB). The English word "grasp" can mean either grabbing at something one does not have in order to get it, or clinging to something one already has in order to hold on to it. So by using "grasp," these four translations leave it ambiguous whether Paul means that Christ already had equality with God and refrained from clinging to it, or did not yet have it and refrained from snatching at it.

It may be the most diplomatic choice to go with the translation that is open to the most possible interpretations; but that should not be the primary concern of translators. The question we must consider is whether or not this ambiguity is found in the original Greek word *harpagmos*, or whether accuracy in this case demands that diplomatic ambiguity must yield to a more definitive meaning.

Other translators apparently felt the word *harpagmos* falls pretty clearly on one side or the other of the two possible meanings mentioned above. On one side are the KJV and NW, which translate *harpagmos* as "robbery" and "seizure," respectively. These two words suggest snatching at something one does not possess.[1] On the other side are the NRSV and LB, which offer "something to be exploited" and "cling," respectively. These two phrases suggest holding on to something one already possesses. The TEV and AB, however, offer options on both sides. The TEV has both "by force he should try to become" and, in a note, "*or* remain." The AB tries "a thing to be eagerly grasped *or* retained." So which is it?

The Liddell & Scott Greek dictionary, which is based upon the whole of Greek literature, defines *harpagmos* as "robbery," "rape," and "prize to be grasped." But the third definition is itself based on Philippians 2:6; no other case is given by Liddel & Scott where *harpagmos* means this. In fact, the word is quite rare. So we have to do a little linguistic investigation to get a better sense of what it might mean.

Rolf Furuli states correctly that, "When a noun with the ending *-mos* was made from a verb, it became a verbal noun entailing the activity of the verb" (Furuli, page 263). *Harpagmos* is such a noun, based upon the verb *harpazō* (there are many variations in the exact spelling and pronunciation of the Greek verb over time). The Liddell & Scott dictionary provides the following meanings for this verb: (1) snatch away, carry off; (2) seize hastily, snatch up; (3) seize, overpower, overmaster; (4) seize, adopt; (5) grasp with the senses; (6) captivate, ravish; (7) draw up.

Sprinkled through the lexicon entry are uses meaning: to be a robber, thievish, to be torn from someone's possession, greedily, snap up, and plunder. The noun *harpagē* is used for: (1) seizure, robbery, rape; (2) thing seized, booty, prey; (3) greediness; as well as for a hook, grappling-iron, or rake. Similarly, the noun *harpagma* means booty, prey, or windfall. Other words formed of this root include the following: "robber" (*harpaktēr*; *harpaktēs*), "greedily" (*harpakti*), "rapacious, thievish" (*harpaktikos*), "robbing, rapacious" (*harpax*), "gotten by rapine, stolen" (*harpaktos*), "carried away (*harpastos*), "ravished, stolen" (*harpagimos*), "hurriedly, violently" (*harpagdēn*), "bird of prey" (*harpasos*), "hook" (*harpagos*).

You can see that every one of these related words has to do with the seizure of something not yet one's own. There is not a single word derived from *harpazō* that is used to suggest holding on to something already possessed. In light of this, the KJV's "robbery" and the NW's "seizure" look to be most accurate, with the other translations either inaccurate or unnecessarily ambiguous.

Of course, we will want to consult not only a good dictionary, but also how the word is used in the writings of the New Testament itself. Unfortunately, *harpagmos* occurs only in Philippians 2:6. But several of the closely related words we noted above are used in the New Testament. We should see how our translations handle them.

First, the root verb *harpazō* can be found in thirteen verses of the New Testament: Matthew 11:12; 13:19; John 6:15; 10:12; 10:28-29; Acts 8:39; 23:10; 2 Corinthians 12:2; 12:4; 1 Thessalonians 4:17; Jude 23; Revelation 12:5. Paul himself uses the verb *harpazō* three times to refer to a person being carried off to heaven (2 Corinthians 12:2; 12:4; 1 Thessalonians 4:17). Unfortunately, modern translations are so under the spell of the KJV that most duplicate the latter's rather bland "caught up" in these verses. The TEV, however, has "snatched up" and "gathered up." In any case, it is clear that Paul is using the verb with the meaning given first by Liddel and Scott: "snatch away, carry off." The other writers of the New Testament use it in precisely the same way. I provide the relevant citations in two tables.

	Mt. 11:12	Mt. 13:19	Jn 6:15	Jn. 10:12	Jn. 10:28-29
KJV	take by force	catcheth away	take by force	catcheth	pluck
NASB	take by force	snatches away	take by force	snatches	snatch
NIV	lay hold of	snatches away	make by force	attacks	snatch
NRSV	take by force	snatches away	take by force	snatches	snatch
NAB	taking by force	steals away	carry off	catches	take
AB	seize by force	snatches away	seize	chases; snatches	snatch
TEV	seize	snatches away	seize	snatches	snatch
LB	(omitted)	snatches away	take by force	leaps on	snatch; kidnap
NW	seizing	snatches away	seize	snatches	snatch

TABLE 5.2

	Acts 8:39	Acts 23:10	Jude 23	Revelation 12:5
KJV	caught away	take by force	pulling	caught up
NASB	snatched away	take away by force	snatching	caught up
NIV	took away	take away by force	snatch	snatched up
NRSV	snatched away	take by force	snatching	snatched away
NAB	snatched away	rescue	snatching	caught up
AB	caught away	take forcibly	snatching	caught up
TEV	took away	get away	snatching	snatched away
LB	caught away	take away by force	snatching	caught up
NW	led away	snatch	snatching	caught away

As you can see, in the New Testament the verb *harpazō*, which is the root underlying the noun *harpagmos* used in Philippians 2:6, always means to snatch something away, to seize and take it. All nine of our translations consistently recognize that meaning. They never translate it to mean holding on to something one already has. Why then do many of them shift the meaning in Philippians 2:6?

The adjective *harpax* appears in four passages of the New Testament: Matthew 7:15; Luke 18:11; 1 Corinthians 5:10-11; 1 Corinthians 6:10. In the latter three of those passages, it is used as a substantive, that is, it functions as a descriptive noun for a group of people. Paul is the author of two of these passages. So we get more information about the connotations of the word for him.

TABLE 5.3

	Matthew 7:15	Luke 18:11	1 Cor. 5:10-11	1 Cor. 6:10
KJV	ravening	extortioners	extortioners	extortioners
NASB	ravenous	swindlers	swindlers	swindlers
NIV	ferocious	robbers	swindlers	swindlers
NRSV	ravenous	thieves	robbers	robbers
NAB	ravenous	greedy	robbers	robbers
AB	devouring	extortioners; robbers	cheats; thieves	extortioners; robbers
TEV	wild	greedy	thieves	thieves
LB	will tear apart	cheat	thieves; swindler	robbers
NW	ravenous	extortioners	extortioners	extortioners

You can see that the word has connotations of seizing something violently or unjustly. This meaning is recognized by all nine of our translations, yet not followed by many of them when it comes to Philippians 2:6.

The noun *harpagē* appears three times in the New Testament, though not used by Paul: Matthew 23:25; Luke 11:39; Hebrews 10:34.

TABLE 5.4

	Matthew 23:25	Luke 11:39	Hebrews 10:34
KJV	extortion	ravening	spoiling
NASB	robbery	robbery	seizure
NIV	greed	greed	confiscation
NRSV	greed	greed	plundering
NAB	plunder	plunder	confiscation
AB:	extortion; prey; spoil; plunder	greed; robbery; extortion	plundering; confiscation
TEV	gotten by violence	violence	seized
LB	extortion	greed	taken
NW	plunder	plunder	plundering

Once again, the meaning follows the same basic idea of seizure, and all of our translators show that they know that. All of the words we have looked at, all related to the verb *harpazō*, have this sense of seizing something from someone else, even when it is the Holy Spirit or some other divine force seizing someone in inspiration. Incidentally, the Greek mythological beings known as *harpies* get their name from the same root we have been considering. They are bird-like predatory creatures that harass and seize people who have offended the gods. The English word "harpoon" also comes from this Greek root, as a name for a spear with hooks on it for grabbing onto the flesh of the animal it pierces. The idea of justly retaining something of one's own would seem to be just about the opposite in meaning from words derived from *harpazō*.[2] While it is true that context and use can modify the lexical meaning, it would be going to far to suggest that context and use could reverse the lexical meaning. There is no credible argument to support such a reversal of meaning for *harpagmos* away from its obvious sense as a seizure, robbery, or snatching of something.

In light of this lexical investigation, we can conclude that the NRSV translators have misunderstood *harpagmos* by taking it as referring to grasping at something one already has, that is, an "exploitation."[3] The same mistake is found in the alternatives given by the AB ("retained"), TEV ("remain"), and LB ("cling"). Nothing in the use of this word or its related terms, either within the New Testament or in Greek literature in general, supports these translations. Since the old RSV had the more neutral "grasped," we see that the NRSV has moved in the direction of more limited interpretation and, in this instance, an erroneous meaning.

Needless to say, the LB translation bears little if any resemblance to the meaning of the original Greek, which says nothing about Christ's "rights as God," nor about "his mighty power and glory." Correcting the LB's mistranslation of *harpagmos* ("demand and cling") would do little to improve this piece of creative rewriting.

The TEV translation, on the other hand, simply leaves readers scratching their heads. On the one hand it says that Christ "had the nature of God." On the other hand, "he did not think that by force he should try to become equal with God." To have the same nature, yet not be equal, is theologically complex enough to demand some sort of explanation in a footnote. As it stands, the translation is simply confusing, which would be perfectly acceptable if the original was equally difficult. Paul's original, however, is not at all difficult or confusing. He says that Christ had the "form" of God, not the "nature" of God. Equality is not at all implied in the word "form." For example, a child can have the "form" of its parent -- a particularly appropriate point in the context of Philippians 2:5-11, as suggested by C. A. Wanamaker.[4]

The NAB, NIV, NASB translations, and the primary reading of the AB, can be considered "acceptable" because the phrases they use all involve the English word "grasp," which can mean what the Greek word *harpagmos* means. But the Greek *harpagmos* does not have the same ambiguity that English "grasp" has, and so "grasp" is not the best possible word to use in a translation of this verse.

The NW translators, on the other hand, have understood *harpagmos* accurately as grasping at something one does not have, that is, a "seizure." Christ did not even think of grabbing at equality with God, but instead humbled himself to self-sacrifice. The literary context supports the NW translation (and refutes the KJV's "thought it not robbery to be equal"), because this portion of the "Philippians Hymn" is setting up a contrast between what Christ might have done (grab at equality) and what he did do (humble himself). But, having agreed that the NW gets the sense of the verse right, I have to say that "gave no consideration to seizure, namely, that he should be equal," while a hyper-literal rendering of the Greek, is too convoluted and awkward. It could be conveyed much more simply, as something like, "gave no thought to a seizure of equality," or "did not consider seizing equality," or "did not consider grabbing at being equal."

If the Greek in Philippians 2:6 means that Christ "did not consider seizing equality," to what exactly is Paul referring? A possible answer to this question is to be found in Paul's understanding of Christ as the New Adam. Christ's behavior is depicted as the opposite of the actions of Adam, who "snatched at" equality with God by eating of the Tree of Knowledge in the garden of Eden. According to Paul, Christ is the "New Adam" who restarts the human race, and does it all right this time, avoiding the errors of Adam and his descendants. Whether or not it is correct to interpret Philippians 2:6 in line with what Paul says elsewhere about Christ as the New Adam is open to debate. The main point here is that the most likely meaning of the word *harpagmos* guides how we are able to interpret the passage. We cannot legitimately interpret the passage in a way that ignores the meaning of the words within it.

No one should take offense at the fact that, in this particular passage, Paul chooses to focus on Christ as a human being, and on how his path to glory was through humble service and sacrifice. This certainly is not all Paul has to say about Christ. What this passage says is clear enough. But how it is to be fit to a larger set of beliefs about Christ is something up to the individual community of belief. It is a matter of moving from translation to interpretation, and from interpretation to a systematic account of biblical theology as a whole.

Since the passages of the Bible can be fit together to form many different interpretations and theologies, we must be aware of how easy it is to reverse the process, and read those interpretations and theologies back into the individual passages. It is perfectly legitimate for those various interpretations to be made and maintained on the basis of a biblical text that does not preclude them. What is not legitimate is changing the Bible so that it agrees with only one interpretation, that is, changing it from the basis of interpretation into a product of interpretation. Historians call that a falsification of evidence, a lie about the past. Christians don't look too favorably on it either. They don't want a "corrected" Bible that conforms with what the minister, priest, theologian, or scholar believes to be true. They want such experts and authorities to base what they teach on what the Bible really, originally says. The only way to know what that is, is to translate accurately and without bias.

NOTES

1. But it must be noted that the KJV reverses the meaning of the Greek by reading Greek syntax as if it were English. So the KJV reads: "thought it not robbery to be equal with God." All modern translations recognize that this is a misunderstanding of the Greek, as you can see by comparing them.

2. It should be noted that a lexical investigation such as this is not the same as a strictly etymological analysis of a word. The meanings recorded in the Liddel & Scott dictionary, for example, are meanings *in use* that can be demonstrated in the context of specific literary passages, and not derived from etymology. The consistency of meaning among the various derivations of the verbal root *harpazō* does not depend on etymology, but is evidence of widespread cultural agreement on the constellation of meaning for a set of related words.

3. This choice was made apparently on the basis of the argument of R. W. Hoover, "The Harpagmos Enigma: A Philological Solution," *Harvard Theological Review* 64 (1971) 95-119. But Hoover's entire argument was demolished in just four pages by J. C. O'Neill, "Hoover on *Harpagmos* Reviewed, with a Modest Proposal Concerning Philippians 2:6," *Harvard Theological Review* 81 (1988) 445-449.

4. C. A. Wanamaker, "Philippians 2.6-11: Son of God or Adamic Christology?" *New Testament Studies* 33 (1987) 179-193.

SIX

WHEN IS A MAN NOT A MAN?

The New Testament was written in a language that, like many languages throughout the world, was formed in a male-dominated society. Greek and English are similar in this respect. Both have grammatical rules that are male-biased.

In the last several decades, increased attention has been given to this problem of our language, and how it shapes the meaning of what we communicate. To refer to the world's population as "mankind" or even simply as "Man," and to standardly use "he" as the appropriate pronoun when referring to any title or position in our society when the specific occupant is not identified, suggests that males are the most important, even the only important, inhabitants of the globe.

Reform of English into more gender-neutral or gender-balanced grammar has been taking place gradually. Aside from the fact that this reform corresponds with the values our society espouses, such changes reflect the reality of our actual lives. The male bias in English is a residue of past conditions, and does not accurately reflect the fact that our present society is full of female doctors, lawyers, business owners, and political leaders. As we compose writings in today's English, it is a good thing to have it match our present conditions and values.

But what does this issue have to do with Bible translation? It is one thing to change how we write new things in English, but quite another to go back and change things already written. Doubts about the appropriateness of changing works of the past are particularly strong when it comes to a "classic": a great work of literature, or something as sacrosanct as the Bible. If the Bible says "he," who are we to change that to "she" or "he or she"? That's a legitimate and important concern to raise.

As I said, Greek, like English, is a male-biased language. The authors of the New Testament books were taught to use that language in its standard, male-biased form. The society they lived in was itself very male-biased. Power over every public institution was almost exclusively in male hands. Most, if not all, of the New Testament authors were themselves males (it is possible that the unknown author of the Letter to the Hebrews could have been a woman). In their public speaking as well as their writing, they would have assumed a mostly male audience, because males could more freely attend public events and had more opportunities to learn to read. But even a woman author thinking of a female audience would be likely to use Greek in its standard form, laced with male-biased grammar, simply because that was "proper" Greek.

In dealing with the issue of gender language in the New Testament, then, I resort to the basic principles that I apply throughout this book. Accuracy means being true to the original Greek language of the text, to the literary context of the passage in question, and to the known facts of the larger society and culture in which the New Testament was written. When we adhere to these principles we discover some interesting things.

On the one hand, the KJV and other translations that adhere rather conservatively to the standards set by the KJV are actually *more* male-biased than the original Greek of the New Testament. This is true because certain gender-neutral terms used in Greek are translated with gender-specific (that is, masculine) words in these translations.

On the other hand, those translation teams that have made a conscious attempt to produce more gender-balanced translations have achieved very mixed results, due in part to uncertain notions of how to proceed towards their goal. So they at times change the story, removing from the text expressions that reflect accurately the conditions in which Jesus and his disciples created Christianity.

Man and woman
Greek has distinct, specific words for "man" and "woman." The word for

"man" is *anēr*, and can also mean "husband." The word for "woman" is *gunē*, and can also mean "wife." The distinctive meaning and use of these two words is obvious and straightforward, and offers little difficulty to the Bible translator. But in a couple of instances, those translations that have been produced with gender neutrality in mind remove or obscure references to "man" or "men" that the translators considered unnecessary for the basic meaning of the passages where they occur.

For example, In the book of Acts, many people are depicted making public speeches. In that time and culture, the public spaces where someone might make a speech were likely to be full of men, but considered to be not the best place for a woman. There were, of course, exceptions. Some women had enough wealth and power to defy most social conventions. But the general assumption would be that public speeches were made to a male audience, and the standard way for delivering such speeches had that assumption built right into it. So when Peter or Paul or someone else launches into a speech in Acts, he (and it always is a he in Acts) begins by calling out to "Men!"

Several translations, in a commendable effort to make the Bible as gender neutral as possible, remove this form of address, and make the openings of speeches in Acts more generically directed. Phrases such as "Men! Galilaeans!" (Acts 1:11) or "Men! Judaeans!" (Acts 2:14) or "Men! Israelites!" (Acts 2:22; 3:12; 5:35; 13:16; 21:28) or "Men! Athenians!" (Acts 17:22) or "Men! Ephesians!" (Acts 19:35) are neatly trimmed to omit "men." The NRSV, NAB, and TEV are fairly consistent in doing this.[1] The NIV, AB, and LB join in the practice at Acts 2:14. Why they do so just this one time is a mystery to me.

Sometimes this effort to broaden the references of biblical language comes up against the tendency of the New Testament authors themselves to think primarily of men when making a statement that could apply to women just as well. In Acts 2:5, Luke speaks of "Jews, devout men." The NRSV, NAB, NIV, and LB rephrase this to eliminate the gender reference. James frequently says "man" in expressions he uses to talk about human behavior in general (for example, James 1:8; 1:12; 1:20; 1:23; 3:2). The NRSV consistently makes these passages gender-neutral, and the TEV and LB do so less consistently.

In such cases, the reader loses a little of the historical authenticity of the biblical language. If I were making a translation, I would be disinclined to follow this practice. But nothing of the core meaning of these passages is lost by such a change, and I think it is within the tolerable range of translator option. If someone can think of a serious objection, I would be interested to hear it.

Human being

Greek also possesses a word, *anthrōpos*, that means a human being, whether male or female. There is nothing in the word *anthrōpos* itself that specifies whether it is meant to refer to either a man or woman. Such a narrowing of its meaning can only come from the immediate context of the passage. If the context does not provide a more specific determination of meaning, the reader must assume that the word is meant generically, as "human being."

In narrative passages of the New Testament, it is legitimate to translate *anthrōpos* as "man" if the immediate context tells us that the "person" or "individual" (possible options to use for *anthrōpos* that might be less awkward than "human being") was, indeed, a man. There is no grounds for criticizing a translation that adopts such a contextual translation.

On the other hand, there are several translations that persist in translating *anthrōpos* as "man" in passages where it is obvious the more generic "human being" is meant. I say it is obvious because in these passages instructions are being given which we have no reason to think are limited only to men. Ask yourself if the following thoughts are true:

Matthew 4:4	"Man shall not live by bread alone" . . . but woman can get by fine on a bread-only diet.
Matthew 6:1	"Take care to not do your righteous acts in front of men" . . . but feel free to show off in front of women.
Matthew 6:14	"For if you forgive men their trespasses, your heavenly father also will forgive you" . . . but if you want to continue to hold women's trespasses against them, that's quite alright.
Matthew 10:33	"Everyone who denies me in front of men, I will also deny in front of my father who is in the heavens" . . . but I don't care one way or another whether you deny me in front of women.
Matthew 12:31	"All sins and blasphemies will be forgiven to men" . . . but women won't get off so easy.

Mark 2:27	"The sabbath was made for man" . . . so woman must work seven days per week.
Luke 2:14	"Glory in the highest to God, and on earth peace among men" . . . but women are out of luck.
John 1:4	"The life was the light of men" . . . while women, sadly, remained in darkness.
Romans 2:9	"(There will be) affliction and distress upon every soul of man who performs evil" . . . but women will get away with murder.
Romans 2:16	"In the day when God judges the secrets of men" . . . but won't be able to figure out what women have been up to.
Romans 3:28	"A man is justified by faith without works of (the) Law" . . . but a woman has to work for it.
Romans 5:12	"Death spread to all men" . . . while women, as we all know, live forever.
Romans 12:18	"Be at peace with all men" . . . but give women as hard a time as possible.
Colossians 1:28	"Teaching every man in all wisdom, so that we may present every man perfect in Christ" . . . while leaving women to their own devices.
1 Timothy 4:10	"The living God, who is the savior of all men" . . . but, unfortunately, not of all women.
Titus 2:11	"For the gift of God has appeared (as) salvation for all men" . . and, with a little luck, the women might get some help, too.

I hope that my little, slightly irreverent concoctions make it perfectly clear that to use "man" and "men" to translate *anthrōpos* in these verses is inaccurate, and very easily can lead to incorrect conclusions about the meaning of what is being said. Of course, as translators we should not rule out beforehand that the Bible *could* make distinctions between men and women in the instructions that it gives. If the literary context of any of the above examples suggested such distinctions, we would have a reason to translate *anthrōpos* as "man." But such is not the case. *Anthrōpos* does not mean "man" unless the context dictates it. The contexts of the above passages clearly do not so dictate.

Yet the KJV and NASB have "man" or "men" in all sixteen of these verses, the NW does in all but one of them (once using "mankind"), the NIV does in thirteen of them (using "everyone" or "human being" occasionally), and the AB in twelve of them (adopting "everyone" or "mankind" in some cases). The NRSV, NAB, TEV, and LB, on the other hand, are more attentive to accurately conveying to the Bible reader that these passages refer to all human beings. Even the TEV and LB, however, often resort to the term "mankind," and in a couple of cases actually use "man" in a saying so widely known as to have become a popular refrain ("Man shall not live by bread alone" and "The sabbath was made for man").

It can and has been argued that at the time the King James translation was made "man" and "men" were used as the proper generic reference to human beings, and that this remained true up until very recently. That argument is debatable; even Shakespearean English had the words "human," "person," "someone," and so forth. The fact is that the KJV translators were all men, and the vast majority of translators of the other versions have been as well. They have taken the Bible to be speaking first and foremost to them. It never occurred to them to be careful about being inclusive. Remember, that is the essence of bias: unconscious assumptions and blind spots, not malicious distortion.

In any case, the modern reader no longer understands "man" in the generic sense, and translations need to keep up with that change of English usage. A translation, after all, is meant to convey the accurate meaning of the original to the modern reader. If it is frozen in time and preserved as an artifact of an earlier form of English, it ceases to be a translation at all, and will need to be itself translated.

No one

The same experiment in meaning that we did with passages that refer to "human beings" and yet are often translated as referring to "men" can be used to bring clarity to the Bible's use of the expression "no one" (*oudeis*). The Greek word *oudeis* is so generic, and so ungendered, that

WHEN IS A MAN NOT A MAN?

it is used in the New Testament with the meaning "nothing" as often as it is used to mean "no one." To add to it the specificity of "man" by translating it "no man" creates the potential for serious misunderstanding.

Matthew 6:14	"No man can serve two masters" . . . but women frequently must.
Matthew 11:27	"No man knows the Son" . . . but women are quite familiar with him.
Mark 13:32	"But of that day and hour no man knows" . . . only the women know.
John 1:18	"No man has seen God at any time" . . . but women have been known to catch a glimpse of him.
John 3:2	"No man can do these miracles that you do" . . . usually only women work miracles such as these.
John 3:13	"No man has ascended up to heaven" . . . that is a privilege that has been reserved for women.
John 8:15	"I judge no man" . . . I only judge women.
2 Cor. 5:16	"From now on we know no man according to the flesh" . . . but naturally we'll keep on knowing women according to the flesh.
2 Cor. 7:2	"We have wronged no man, we have corrupted no man, we have defrauded no man" . . . but please don't ask us about our treatment of women.
Galatians 3:11	"No man is justified by the law" . . . but it works fine for women.

In most of the examples given, it is only the KJV which uses the misleading expression "no man." The more modern translations generally keep to the more literal, and more accurate "no one" (although the LB frequently changes the wording so radically as to completely eliminate the sentence in which "no one" should appear). But there are lapses. The NW has the most problems in this respect, using "no man" in four out of the ten verses sampled (John 1:18; John 3:13; John 8:15; 2 Corinthians 5;16). The NASB slips into "no man" twice in the same sample (John 1:18 amd 2 Corinthians 5:16), and the AB once (John 1:18). This sort of inconsistency needs to be corrected in future editions of these translations.

The one and this one
Greek abounds in *gerunds*, verb phrases used as nouns, often as the subject of a sentence. In Greek the definite article "the" (*ho*) is added to a verb to create the subject "the one who does x." Up until recently, the preferred English wording for such a verbal subject was "he who does x." This male bias in English intrudes into many New Testament passages where the more neutral Greek expression is translated. Greek also frequently uses the demonstrative pronoun, "this" (*houtos*), where in English we would use a personal pronoun ("he," "she," or "it"). These are examples of how Greek is *less* male-biased than English, because sometimes when we are speaking of a generic person it is inaccurate to specify the person as either male or female.[2]

How do our translations handle these gender neutral Greek expressions? Let's look at the most straightforward examples.

> But the one who endures (*ho hupomeinas*) to the end, this
> one (*houtos*) will be saved (Matthew 24:13; Mark 13:13).

The KJV, NASB, NIV, NW, and AB, substitute "he" for one or other of the two ungendered Greek expressions. The NRSV, NAB, TEV, and LB more accurately avoid making the subject a "he."

> The one who is the least (*ho mikroteros huparchōn*) among
> you all, this one (*houtos*) is great (Luke 9:48).

The KJV, NASB, NIV, NW, AB, and TEV substitute "he" for one or both of the ungendered Greek expressions. The NRSV, NAB, and LB avoid "he."

> This one was in the beginning with God (John 1:2).

The NASB, NIV, NRSV, NAB, and AB replace "this one" with "he," confusing the pre-incarnate Word, which as a divine being transcends human gender, with the incarnate Jesus, who certainly was a man. Only the KJV, NW, and TEV use ungendered language that accurately reflects the original Greek.[3]

> If someone does not have a spirit of Christ, this one (*houtos*) is not of him (that is, of Christ) (Romans 8:9).

The KJV, NASB, NIV, AB, and LB substitute "he" for the Greek "this one." The NRSV, NAB, NW, and TEV keep the language correctly generic.

> If someone is a hearer of the word and not a doer (of it), this one (*houtos*) is like a man who . . . (James 1:23).

The comparison is to a man, but the comparison applies to anyone (male or female) who hears the message of Christianity without putting it into practice. Nevertheless, the KJV, NASB, NAB, AB, and LB limit James' point to men, by substituting "he" for "this one." The NIV, NRSV, NW, and TEV maintain the proper neutral reference here.

> Who is the liar unless it be the one who denies (*ho arnoumenos*) that Jesus is the Messiah? This one (*houtos*) is the anti-Christ, the one who denies the Father and the Son (1 John 2:22).

In establishing the clear boundary between Christians, who are by definition pro-Christ, and the opponents of Christians, whom he considers anti-Christ, John makes use of "this one" to match his generic expression "the one who denies." Such a person, of course, could be either a man or a woman. Despite that, the KJV, NIV, AB, TEV, and LB specify "he" or "the man who." The NRSV, NAB, NASB, and NW remain true to the neutral quality of the original Greek.

> The one who remains (*ho menōn*) in the teaching, this one (*houtos*) has both the Father and the Son (2 John 9).

The KJV, NASB, AB, and NW limit this promise to "he," while the NIV,

NRSV, NAB, TEV, and LB more accurately convey the gender-neutral sense of the Greek.

Sex-change operations
One sort of gender bias that cannot be blamed on the English language is the actual altering of characters in the Bible from women into men. This occurs in at least two places in some New Testaments: Romans 16:7 and Philippians 4:2. Since the alteration is more common in Romans 16:7 (only the KJV makes the change in Philippians 4:2[4]), we will use it as our example.

In Romans 16, Paul sends greetings to all those in the Roman Christian community known to him personally. In verse 7, he greets Andronicus and Junia. All early Christian commentators thought that these two people were a couple, and for good reason: "Junia" is a woman's name. It appears that way, correctly, in the KJV, NRSV, and NAB. But the translators of the NIV, NASB, NW, TEV, AB, and LB (and the NRSV translators in a footnote) all have changed the name to an apparently masculine form, "Junias." The problem is that there is no name "Junias" in the Greco-Roman world in which Paul was writing. The woman's name "Junia," on the other hand, is well-known and common in that culture. So "Junias" is a made-up name, at best a conjecture. Why have so many translations substituted a probably fictitious man's name for the woman's name in Romans 16:7?

Walter Bauer, in his *Greek-English Lexicon of the New Testament and Other Early Christian Literature*, (right after he admits that the name "Junias" is unknown outside of Romans 16:7) says, "The possibility, from a purely lexical point of view, that this is a woman's name . . . is probably ruled out by the context" (page 380). He means that the context refers to Andronicus and Junia as "apostles," and it seems unreasonable to him, and apparently to dozens of other modern translators, that a woman could be called an "apostle." But that is purely an assumption on their part, one that they hold before translating, rather than based upon what the text actually says. That's not a very good way to do translation.

Paul generally uses the term "apostle" broadly of people who have been formally "sent out" (the meaning of *apostolos*) on a mission by God or a Christian community, and who occupy a very high status in the leadership of the Christian movement. Paul rarely, if ever, uses the term in a way that restricts it to "The Twelve," the inner circle of Jesus' original disciples. After all, he considers himself an "apostle," and he was not among "The Twelve," and in Romans 16:7 he considers Andronicus, as well as Junia, to be "apostles" as well.

Paul says that Andronicus and Junia are "prominent (*episēmoi*) among the apostles." The Greek adjective *episēmos* is translated variously as "prominent" (NRSV, NAB), "outstanding" (NIV, NASB), "of note" (KJV, NW), "well known" (TEV), and "held in high esteem" (AB). The ambiguity of the English phrasing "among the apostles" seems to cause some readers to think it can mean something like "well known *to* the apostles," or, as the LB has it, "respected *by* the apostles." But the Greek phrasing that stands behind the English does not mean that. Rather it says that these two are prominent "in (the group of) the apostles." Most translators understand that meaning, and those who find it inconceivable that a woman would be "in (the group of) the apostles" simply write her out of the group by changing her to a man.[5] Such a move is not translation at all. It is changing the Bible to make it agree with one's own prejudices.

Conclusion

No translation we are comparing receives a perfect score on the accurate translation of Greek gender-neutral language. The lure of common English male-centered forms of speech frequently leads translators astray. The NAB and NRSV are the most careful in avoiding unnecessarily gendered expressions, and these same two translations have allowed Junia to be the woman she is. The TEV also does fairly well on the gender issue, but slips into male-biased expressions more frequently than either the NAB or the NRSV, and has changed Junia into a man for what seems to be bias against the idea of a woman being considered an apostle.

The NW and LB are inconsistent on the gender issue, and for very different reasons. The NW often follows the Greek quite closely, and so maintains the neutrality of phrases such as "no one" and "this one." On the other hand, it freely uses "man" in place of "human being" and frequently uses "he" when a more generic "one who" is intended. The LB is so free with paraphrase that its avoidance or use of male-biased expressions seems to be purely a matter of chance, a question of what the translator found to be the most "dynamic" way of saying something, regardless of the gender issue. Both translations change Junia into a man.

The NIV, NASB, and AB tend to follow the archaic male bias of the KJV tradition, and in doing so are both less accurate in their

74   TRUTH IN TRANSLATION

translation and less up-to-date in their English style than the other translations. All three alter Junia's sex in line with their biases against a woman being counted among the apostles of early Christianity.

All of the translations considered in this volume could be improved in future editions if their translators attended more carefully and consistently to the ways in which the male bias of traditional English introduces a narrowing element not present in the original Greek of the New Testament, and to the ways in which modern assumptions about gender roles in the Christian community might interfere with accurate representations of women's roles in the Bible.

NOTES

1. The NRSV and NAB do not do so in Acts 1:11, because the context mentions only "the apostles" as present, and Luke, the author of Acts, uses this term for the twelve disciples specially chosen by Jesus as his inner circle (Paul uses the term more loosely, in a way that applies to some early Christian women as well as men). Simple oversight seems to be behind the NRSV failure to make the change in Acts 2:14 and the TEV failure to do so in Acts 21:28.

2. Technically, the Greek *ho* is the masculine form of the article, so there is some male bias already in the original Greek when it uses the masculine article for the generic meaning "the one who." The article *ho* can be used with the meaning "he," but it does not *necessarily* have that meaning. So English is *more* biased when it uses "he."

3. The LB omits John 1:2 entirely.

4. The LB translator unwittingly copies the KJV's male name Euodias, even though he goes on to refer to the person as a woman.

5. The AB and NW strengthen the change by referring to both Andronicus and Junias as "men," while the KJV, NASB, and AB use the expression "kinsmen."

SEVEN

PROBING THE IMPLICIT MEANING

One of the greatest challenges in any translation is finding the right words in English to carry all of the meaning of words in the original language. Since languages did not arise together, and no one made sure that a single word in one language would have one and only one corresponding word in another language, translators often find themselves using several words together to communicate the full meaning of only one word in the original language of a text. This is as true in Bible translation as it is in any other kind of translation.

This problem is what we call the issue of implication, that is, what is implied in the original Greek, and how much are we responsible to make what is implied visible and clear to Bible readers. According to A. H. Nichols, "It has long been recognized in the history of translation that a source text ... has implicit meaning that may need to be made explicit if its translation is to be understandable in the receptor language" (Nichols 1988, page 78). The Amplified Bible can be seen as a translation that has taken this duty most seriously, although it takes the opportunity of "amplification" to not only make what is implicit explicit, but also import theological interpretation into the text. Obviously, we cannot burden the text of the Bible with all of the commentary and interpretation we may want a reader to have. Rather, translators should follow the principle referred to by Nichols; they should make what is implicit in the original Greek explicit only if the passage would otherwise be incomprehensible to the general reader.

This idea is expanded upon by Bratcher, in his article introducing "The Nature and Purpose of the New Testament in Today's English Version." He says that there are some passages we must leave alone, because we are not sure what is implied in the shared context of the writer and his original audience (he uses the example of 1 Corinthians 7:36-38). But he contrasts to that situation another kind of implication that is embedded in the words themselves. Bratcher insists that, "where there is information implicit in the text itself the translator may make it explicit in order to allow his readers to understand the meaning of the text. Contrary to what some might think this does not add anything to the text: it simply gives the reader of the translation explicit information which was implicitly made available to the original readers."

His language rings a bell with me, because I have often heard members of the general public accuse certain Bible translations of "adding words." This accusation is based upon a naive understanding (or rather misunderstanding) of how translation is done. The irony of such accusations is that they are made by people who only notice "added words" by comparing a new translation to an already existing one they like. What they don't realize is that the older translation has hundreds of "added words," too. Only a couple of translations actually take the trouble to mark their "added words" so that readers will know what is going on in the translation process. Most translations don't bother to do this because the necessity of making implicit elements of the original Greek explicit is so widely accepted.

When the Revised Standard Version came out in 1946, Luther Weigle demonstrated the issue of "added words" by counting the number of English words used to translate the Greek of several chapters of the New Testament in the King James Version, American Standard Version, and Revised Standard Version.[1] For example, Matthew, chapter five, has 1,081 words in the King James version, 1,056 words in the American Standard Version, and 1,002 words in the Revised Standard Version. Does that mean that the KJV added seventy-nine words to Matthew, chapter five? Well, yes and no. What it really means is that stylistic issues and efforts at clarity produce differences in how a biblical passage reads in English. Sometimes several English words are thought to be needed to bring out the full meaning of a single Greek word. At other times, complex Greek phrases come out as simple English terms.

Added words are often essential in translation and do not necessarily involve any change in meaning -- but rather the clarification of meaning. The majority of the added words in the major translation are inserted to clarify the subject (Greek uses the pronoun "he" a lot; what it refers to is usually identifiable by noun and pronoun case endings which are found in Greek but are not used in English; therefore an English translation must make explicit the implied reference of the pronoun), or to smooth out the flow of ideas. Paul, for example, often adopts the high style of a polished man of letters. Since saying complex things with the fewest possible words was considered the epitome of high style in Greek, Paul's expression is often terse. But translators have a commitment to meaning over style, and necessarily sacrifice some of Paul's sophistication in turning a phrase for the sake of clarity. Such additions are innocuous and, as should be obvious, often necessary.

But it must be admitted that in some cases the translators have snuck an *interpretation* of a verse into the translation itself. They might defend this practice by insisting that they are only clarifying the meaning of the Greek. But there is a key difference between clarification and interpretation. Clarification draws out the potential meaning of a word or phrase; interpretation closes and limits the meaning in a specific way. Interpretation goes beyond what the Greek itself gives and adds words that give the Greek a meaning imposed from outside the biblical text.

To explore the issue of implied meaning and "added words," I have chosen Colossians 1:15-20. This passage comes up in some discussions of this issue I have heard, and it should. It is a tricky passage where every translation does and must "add words. The KJV and NASB use italics to mark words added for understanding, to make what is implicit in the original Greek explicit in English. The NW uses brackets to indicate the same thing. But readers of the other major translations probably think that every word they read in their Bibles actually corresponds to words explicit in the Greek text. They are wrong to think that.

In order to show you what is hidden beneath the fine polish of modern Bible translations, in this chapter I will print the text of the translation of this passage using the system of italics used by the KJV and NASB to indicate English words that have no matching word in the original Greek text. All of these are "added words," which their respective translators believe to be implied in the original Greek. So confidant are they that they are right, they haven't bothered to let their readers know about it. The question for us to consider will be whether these words change the meaning of the Greek, whether they "add" more than merely what is implied.

First, the translations that employ ways of marking "added words":

KJV: Who is the image of the invisible God, the firstborn of every creature: for by him were all things created, that are in heaven, and that are in earth, visible and invisible, whether *they be* thrones, or dominions, or principalities, or powers: all things were created by him, and for him: and he is before all things, and by him all things consist. And he is the head of the body, the church: who is the beginning, the firstborn from the dead; that in all *things* he might have the preeminence. For it pleased *the Father* that in him should all fullness dwell; and, having made peace through the blood of his cross, by him to reconcile all things unto himself; by him, *I say*, whether *they be* things in earth, or things in heaven. (Total: 135 words)

The KJV accurately marks all additions to the text, even though the additions serve merely to fill out the flow of the passage in English.

NASB: And He is the image of the invisible God, the first-born of all creation. For by Him all things were created, *both* in the heavens and on earth, visible and invisible, whether thrones or dominions or rulers or authorities -- all things have been created by Him and for Him. And he is before all things, and in Him all things hold together. He is also the head of the body, the church; and He is the beginning, the first-born from the dead; so that He *Himself* might come to have first place in everything. For it was the *Father's* good pleasure for all the fulness to dwell in Him, and through Him to reconcile all things to Himself, having made peace through the blood of His cross; through Him, *I say*, whether things on earth or things in heaven. (Total: 139 words)

The NASB fails to italicize the word "Himself" in the expression "He Himself"; otherwise it marks all additions with italics. The meaning of the passage is not significantly altered.

NW: He is the image of the invisible God, the firstborn of all creation; because by means of him all [*other*] things were created in the heavens and upon the earth, the things visible and the things invisible, *no matter* whether they are thrones or lordships or governments or authorities. All [*other*] things have been created through him and for him. Also, he is before all [*other*] things and by means of him all [*other*] things were made to exist, and he is the head of the body, the congregation. He is the beginning, the firstborn from the dead, that he might become *the one who is* first in all *things*; because [*God*] saw good for all fullness to dwell in him, and through him to reconcile *again* to himself all [*other*] things by making peace through the blood [*he shed*] on the torture stake, *no matter* whether they are the things upon the earth or the things in the heavens. (Total: 160 words)

Only the italicized words in brackets are marked as additions in the NW; those that appear outside of brackets above are not marked in any way in the text. But none of those unmarked additions alters the meaning of the passage.

Now let's look at translations that do not mark "added words" in any way. In the following translations, all of the italics are mine; none of these translations makes any effort to mark added words. From this comparison, you will immediately see that no translation renders this passage without "adding words." What will be most interesting is what words are added and why.

NAB: He is the image of the invisible God, the firstborn of all creation. For in him were created all things in heaven and on earth, the visible and the invisible, whether thrones or dominions or principalities or powers; all things were created through him and for him. He is before all things, and in him all things hold together. He is the head of the body, the church. He is the beginning, the firstborn from the dead, that in all *things* he *himself* might be preeminent. For in him all the fulness was pleased to dwell, and through him to reconcile all things for him, making peace by the blood of his cross

80 TRUTH IN TRANSLATION

[through him]², whether those on earth or those in heaven. (Total: 123 words)

Although the NAB adds words that it does not mark for its readers, the additions only sharpen and clarify the meaning of the original Greek; they do not shift or alter the meaning.

NIV: He is the image of the invisible God, the firstborn *over* all creation. For by him all things were created: things in heaven and on earth, visible and invisible, whether thrones or powers or rulers or authorities; all things were created by him and for him. He is before all things, and in him all things hold together. And he is the head of the body, the church; he is the beginning *and* the firstborn from among the dead, so that in everything he might have the supremacy. For *God* was pleased to have all *his* fullness dwell in him, and through him to reconcile to himself all things, whether things on earth or things in heaven, by making peace through his blood, shed on the cross. (Total: 127 words)

NRSV: He is the image of the invisible God, the firstborn of all creation; for in him all things in heaven and on earth were created, things visible and invisible, whether thrones or dominions or rulers or powers -- all things have been created through him and for him. He *himself* is before all things, and in him all things hold together. He is the head of the body, the church; he is the beginning, the firstborn from the dead, so that he might come to have first place in everything. For in him the fullness *of God* was pleased to dwell, and through him *God was pleased* to reconcile to himself all things, whether on earth or in heaven, by making peace through the blood of his cross. (Total: 127 words)

AB: [Now] He is the *exact* likeness of the unseen God [the visible representation of the invisible]; *He is* the Firstborn of all creation. For it was in Him that all things were created, in heaven and on earth, things seen and things unseen, whether thrones, dominions, rulers, or authorities; all things were created *and exist* through Him [by His service, intervention] and *in and* for Him. And He Himself existed before all things, and in Him all things consist (cohere, are held together). He is also the Head of [*His*] body, the church; *seeing* He is the Beginning, the Firstborn from among the dead, so that He *alone* in everything *and in every respect* might occupy the chief place [stand first and be preeminent]. For it has pleased [*the Father*] that all the *divine* fullness (the sum total of the divine perfection, powers, and attributes) should dwell in Him *permanently*. And God purposed that through (by the service, the intervention of) Him [*the Son*] all things should be *completely* reconciled *back* to Himself, whether on earth or in heaven, as through Him, [*the Father*] made peace by means of the blood of His cross. (Total: 194 words)

The additions to the text made by the NIV, NRSV, and AB are much more significant, in quantity and in alteration of meaning, than those of the translations we have already considered.

In the NIV, the translators have first of all replaced the "of" of the phrase "firstborn of creation" with "over." This qualifies as addition because "over" in no way can be derived from the Greek genitive article meaning "of." The NIV translators make this addition on the basis of doctrine rather than language. Whereas "of" appears to make Jesus part of creation, "over" sets him apart from it.

Secondly, the NIV adds "his" to the word "fullness," in this way interpreting the ambiguous reference in line with a specific belief about Christ's role in the process being described. The NRSV, likewise, adds the phrase "of God" to "fullness," for the same purpose. Both translations are inserting words to lead to the same doctrinal conclusion that the AB spells out in one of its interpretive brackets, that "the sum total of the divine perfection, powers, and attributes" are to be found in Christ. Whether this is true or not, and whether this is one of the ideas to be found in Paul's letters or not, it certainly is not present in the original Greek wording of this passage.[3] Notice that the AB does not limit its interpretation to brackets, but also repeatedly adds words designed to maximize the doctrinal content of the passage, adding "divine" to "fullness" and building up Christ's uniqueness with such qualifiers as "exact," "alone," "in every respect," and "permanently." I marvel at the translator's assumption that Paul needed so much help to make clear what he thought of Christ.

TEV: *Christ* is the *visible* likeness of the invisible *God*. He is the first-born *Son, superior to* all created things. For through him *God* created everything in heaven and on earth, the seen and the unseen things, including *spiritual* powers, lords, rulers, and authorities. *God* created the whole universe through him and for him. *Christ existed* before all things, and in union with him all things have their proper place. He is the head of his body, the church; he is the source *of the body's life*. He is the first-born *Son, who was raised* from death, in order that he alone might have the first place in all things. For it was by *God's* own decision that the *Son* has in himself the full *nature of God*. Through the *Son, then,* God decided to bring the whole universe back to himself. *God* made peace through *his Son's* sacrificial death on the cross *and so brought back to himself* all things, both on earth and in heaven. (Total 166 words)

The TEV goes even further than the previously considered translations in substituting theologically-motivated interpretation for a valid translation. One of the most unfortunate things it does is artificially separate phrases in such a way as to create a whole new meaning not found in the Greek. "He is the first-born of creation" becomes in the TEV "He is the first-born Son, superior to all created things." Like the NIV, the TEV introduces the wholly unscriptural language of "superior" (compare the NIV's "over"), which is in no way implied in the Greek genitive "of." To further safeguard the phrase from a meaning that he does not want it to have, the TEV translator creates the phrase "the first-born Son," also not implied in the Greek, which has "first-born of creation" instead. In this way, the TEV divorces Christ from creation, making the sentence mean the exact opposite of what Paul wanted to say here. In fact, Bratcher and Nida have admitted that, "translated literally (as RSV), it implies that Christ is included in the created universe" (Bratcher and Nida 1977, page 22). Their claim that such a literal translation is "inconsistent with the context of the whole passage" is an extreme example of circular reasoning, and rests upon their predetermined position on the nature of Christ, rather than on the literary context as it stands in the original Greek.

The same alteration of the text occurs a few verses later, where the TEV has "He is the first-born Son, who was raised from the dead" in place of the original's "He is the first-born from the dead." Here again, the

TEV makes the passage into something dealing with Christ's sonship, his relation to God, rather than its actual focus on his relation to creation. Since Bratcher, the TEV translator, is a completely competent Greek scholar, we cannot attribute these changes to error. Since the words that are added are not anything implied in the Greek, we cannot say his translation is made necessary by the duty to make the implied sense clear. We can only conclude that Bratcher deliberately altered the meaning of the passage to "protect" it from interpretations which did nt match his own theological commitments and interests.

LB: *Christ* is the *exact* likeness of the unseen God. He existed before *God made* anything *at all*, and, *in fact, Christ himself is the Creator* who made everything in heaven and earth, the things we can see and the things we can't; *the spirit world with its* kings and kingdoms, *its* rulers and authorities; all were made by *Christ* for his own use *and glory*. He was before all else *began* and it is his *power* that holds everything together. He is the Head of the body *made up of his people -- that is, his* church -- *which he began*; and he is the Leader of all those who arise from the dead, so that he is first in everything; for *God* wanted all *of himself* to be in *his* Son. It was through *what his Son did* that *God* cleared a path for everything to come to him -- all things in heaven and on earth -- for *Christ's death on* the cross has made peace *with God for all* by his blood. (Total: 171 words)

As a paraphrase, the LB has license to freely rephrase and reorder content. But a paraphrase must still communicate the content of the work being translated, and not rewrite the substance of the book. In my analysis, I have given the LB the benefit of the doubt, and accepted every phrase that has some equivalent in the Greek, regardless of how the LB renders it. But what stands out is how much content the LB has added to this passage, much more even than has the AB, which is, after all, "amplified." The LB translator is guilty of all the doctrinal importation discussed above with reference to the NIV, NRSV, and TEV, and even surpasses them in this respect.

So it is the NIV, NRSV, TEV, and LB -- the four Bibles that make no attempt to mark added words -- that actually add the most significant, tendentious material. Yet in many public forums on Bible translation, the practice of these four translations is rarely if ever pointed to or criticized, while the NW is attacked for adding the innocuous "other" in a way that clearly indicates its character as an addition of the translators. Why is that so? The reason is that many readers apparently want the passage to mean what the NIV and TEV try to make it mean. That is, they don't want to accept the obvious and clear sense of "first-born of creation" as identifying Jesus as "of creation." "Other" is obnoxious to them because it draws attention to the fact the Jesus is "of creation" and so when Jesus acts with respect to "all things" he is actually acting with respect to "all other things." But the NW is correct.

Perhaps it is the word "thing" that readers are uncomfortable associating with Christ. But the Greek *pan*, various forms of which are used in this passage, means simply "all," and the phrase could just as well be translated "all [others]." "Thing" is added in English because we don't usually use "all" without a following noun of some sort. But one shouldn't stress "thing" as essential to what Paul refers to as "all." Rather, Paul uses "all," after identifying Christ as the first-born of creation, to refer to "the rest." "All" includes every being and force and substance in the universe, with the exception, of course, of God and, semantically speaking, Jesus, since it is his role in relation to the "all" that is being discussed.

"All" is commonly used in Greek as a hyperbole, that is, an exaggeration. The "other" is assumed. In one case, Paul takes the trouble to make this perfectly clear. In 1 Corinthians 15, Paul catches himself saying that God will make all things subject to Christ. He stops and clarifies that "of course" when he says "all things" he doesn't mean that God himself will be subject to Christ, but all *other* things will be, with Christ himself subject to God. There can be no legitimate objection to "other" in Colossians 1 because here, too, Paul clearly does not mean to include God or Christ in his phrase "all things," when God is the implied subject, and Christ the explicit agent, of the act of creation of these "all things." But since Paul uses "all things" appositively (that is, interchangeably) with "creation," we must still reckon with Christ's place as the first-born of creation, and so the first-born of "all things."

Similar uses of "all" in expression of hyperbole are not hard to find. In Luke 21:29, Jesus speaks of "the fig-tree (*sukē*) and all the trees (*panta ta dendra*)." The fig-tree is obviously a tree, and the ancients knew it as a tree. This phrase actually means "the fig-tree and all *other* trees," just as the NW, NAB, and TEV have it (the LB similarly: "the fig tree, or any other tree"). By woodenly translating the phrase as "the fig-tree and all the trees," the NIV and NRSV translators violate their own commitment to use modern English style (the KJV, NASB, and AB, which are not committed to modern English style, also use this strange phrasing). As for the NAB, TEV, and LB, they show an understanding of this idiom here in Luke 21:29, but fail to apply that understanding to Colossians 1:15-20. Such inconsistency often signals the intrusion of bias into the more theologically significant biblical text.

Another example can be seen in Luke 11:42, where Jesus speaks of Pharisees tithing "mint and rue and every herb (*pan lachanon*)." Since mint and rue are both herbs, and were thought to be so by the cultures from which the Bible comes, the phrase "every herb" must mean "every other herb" (NW) or "all the other herbs" (TEV) or "all other kinds of ... herb" (NIV). The KJV, NASB, NRSV, NAB, and AB translate in such a way as to imply that mint and rue are not herbs. That is inaccurate translation. But the TEV and NIV show here that they understand the idiom by which "other" is implied by "all." Why then do they not similarly bring out that implication in Colossians 1:15-20? Once again, theological bias would seem to be the culprit.

So what exactly are objectors to "other" arguing for as the meaning of the phrase "all things"? That Christ created himself (v.16)? That Christ is before God and that God was made to exist by means of Christ (v.17)? That Christ, too, needs to be reconciled to God (v.20)? When we spell out what is denied by the use of "other" we can see clearly how absurd the objection is. "Other" is implied in "all," and the NW simply makes what is implicit explicit. You can argue whether it is necessary or not to do this. But I think the objections that have been raised to it show that it is, in fact, necessary, because those who object want to negate the meaning of the phrase "firstborn of creation." If adding "other" prevents this misreading of the biblical text, then it is useful to have it there.

The need to make implicit information explicit in translating a passage is widely accepted, especially among "dynamic equivalence" translators. Nida and Taber, in their book, *The Theory and Practice of Translation*, insist that making what is implicit explicit is necessary if the text is likely to be misunderstood by readers (Nida and Taber, page 110). Even the KJV, the mother of all formal equivalence translations, has words added in order to make the implicit explicit (for example, in 1 John 3:17, where the KJV has "bowels *of compassion*" to help its readers understand the meaning the early readers of the Greek would have been able to grasp easily in the sole word "bowels").[4]

But once the issue of "adding words" is raised, and all of the versions are put side by side and compared to the Greek, we discover a shocking willingness of translators to freely add words and ideas not supported or in any way implied in the Greek, without any method to indicate these additions to their readers. In the name of "clarifying" a passage, these translators often import their own interpretations. The amount of work they put in to altering the text so that it conforms to their theology gives striking testimony to the power of bias. When the Bible says something that does not match their religious understanding, there seems to be little resistance to the temptation to make it say something else, something more in line with what they expect and are comfortable with.

It is ironic that the translation of Colossians 1:15-20 that has received the most criticism is the one where the "added words" are fully justified by what is implied in the Greek. And if we, under other conditions, might have said that making the implied "other" explicit is not altogether necessary, we now recognize by the gross distortion of the passage in other translations that what the NW translators have done is certainly necessary after all. If the NIV, NRSV, TEV, and LB translators are willing to "add words" in order to shift the meaning of the passage away from Christ's connection with creation and "all things," then it is clearly justifiable for the NW to cement that connection, explicitly expressed in the passage, by bringing to the foreground of translation those implied nuances which go along with the meaning of the passage as a whole. Since several major translation teams themselves have misunderstood Colossians 1:15-20, it seems this is a clear case where Nida and Taber's principle applies, and we are called upon to make the implicit explicit.

All translations "add words" in an effort to make coherent English sentences out of Greek ones. Even interlinears, which are something less than translation, often have two or more English words for a single Greek one, while very frequently having nothing, or a dash, for a Greek word that does not have a necessary English equivalent. Translators decide how aggressively to make implicit parts of the meaning of the Greek explicit in English. The decision whether or not to make something implicit explicit is up to the translators, and cannot be said to be either "right" or "wrong" in itself. Accuracy only comes into it when assessing whether something made explicit in the translation really is implied in the Greek. If it is, then it is accurate to make it explicit. In Colossians 1:15-20, it is accurate to add "other" because "other" is implied in the Greek.

But if words are added that cannot be shown to be implied in the original Greek, then the translation that adds them is inaccurate in that particular passage. In Colossians 1:15-20 it is inaccurate to add the word "over" in place of "of" in the phrase "first-born of creation." This is a distortion of the possible meaning of the Greek. It is also inaccurate to add the words "of God" or "divine" to "fullness," or to substitute "all of himself" for it. These are all very tendentious and unproven interpretations of Paul's wording. Implicit meaning should only be made explicit when what is implicit is unambiguous. If what is implied is open to debate, it is not the translators' job to decide the debate for the reader (and without informing the reader). It is their job to render the Greek into English in a way that conveys all that the Greek suggests, without adding to or subtracting from its meaning. Already in the KJV the Greek was rendered well "all fullness"; the NW follows suit, while the NASB gives the equally accurate "all the fullness." The NAB also accurately conveys the literal meaning, while rearranging the sentence's structure to make a smoother English sentence. The other versions force a particular interpretation on "fullness," and in doing so they violate the principles by which they ought -- and claim -- to be working.

So the mere fact that words are "added" in the process of translation is unremarkable. Everything depends on what the added words are -- whether they are part of the implied meaning of the Greek or not. Unfortunately, most modern English translations do not identify what they have added to the text. I'm not talking about the ordinary use of more than one English word to accurately convey the meaning of the underlying Greek. I am talking about substantial, significant additions that change the meaning. Most translators seem to feel justified in not revealing those kind of additions. Bias is the culprit here. It creates in translators the false assurance that they are reading the passage the only way it can be, and it leads them to forego providing the reader with information about the literal form of the underlying expression of the Bible.

NOTES

1. "The English of the Revised Standard Version," in *An Introduction to the Revised Standard Version of the New Testament* (International Council of Religious Education, 1946); reproduced in Worth, page 117.

2. The NAB brackets this phrase not because the translators have added it, but because Paul's repetition of this phrase is a redundancy typical of Greek style but a little awkward in English, as shown by the way the KJV and NASB deal with it. The NW actually goes a step further than the NAB and omits the redundancy altogether.

3. To what, exactly, "fullness" is meant to refer here is ambiguous. Those translators who add words to identify the fullness as God's (whatever that may mean) are influenced by Colossians 2:9, where Paul again uses the noun "fullness" in a phrase (not the same as that found in Colossians 1:19) that can be translated "the fullness of deity" or "the fullness of divinity" (again, leaving aside how that is to be interpreted). But the context of the two statements is quite different, and the assumption that whenever Paul talks about "fullness" he means something divine is baseless (in fact, most of the times he uses "fullness" it is not in reference to God), and illegitimately restricts Paul's possible meaning. The "fullness" that dwells in Christ in Colossians 1:19 *may* refer to the fullness of God, so that Christ stands in for God in the reconciliation process Paul is talking about (in this way reflecting back to verse 15's statement that Christ is the "image' of God). Or it *may* refer to the fullness of creation, so that Christ stands in for creation in the reconciliation process (in this way pointing forward to verse 20's references to Christ's blood and the cross). Or it may have been Paul's precise intention to suggest both kinds of fullness, and to indicate that Christ forms a bridge between God and creation in the mediation of reconciliation. By over-determining what "fullness" refers to, some translations drain the passage of its richness and subtlety.

4. I owe this example to Ray, page 54.

EIGHT

WORDS TOGETHER AND APART

So far, we have been dealing with lexical problems, where the meaning of a single word is at issue. I want to turn now to questions of grammar, the rules governing the relation between words.

In Titus 2:13, Paul refers to the situation of "awaiting the happy hope and (the) manifestation of the glory of the great God and our savior Christ Jesus," (where the crucial Greek phrase is *tou megalou theou kai sōtēros hēmōn Xristou Iēsou*). Paul's phrasing is somewhat ambiguous, and on first glance there seems to be two possible ways to understand the phrase. It could be read as "the glory of our great God and Savior, Christ Jesus," as if the whole phrase was about Jesus only and he is called both "God" and "Savior." Or it could be read as "the glory of the great God, and of our savior, Christ Jesus," as if both God and Jesus, as distinct figures, are mentioned.

Here is how our translations render this verse:

KJV:	the glorious appearing of the great God and our Saviour Jesus Christ
NAB:	the appearance of the glory of the great God and of our savior Jesus Christ

NW:	the . . . glorious manifestation of the great God and of [the] Savior of us, Christ Jesus
NRSV:	the manifestation of the glory of our great God and Savior (Or of the great God and our Savior), Jesus Christ
TEV:	when the glory of our great God and Savior Jesus Christ (or the great God and our Savior Jesus Christ) will appear
NASB:	the appearing of the glory of our great God and Savior, Christ Jesus
NIV:	the glorious appearing of our great God and Savior, Jesus Christ
AB:	the glorious appearing of our great God and Savior Christ Jesus
LB:	the glory of our great God and Savior Jesus Christ

The translations fall into easily discernible groups, even though all can be characterized as "literal."

The KJV, NAB, and NW understand Paul to refer to both God the Father and Jesus Christ here. All three retain both "the" (with "God") and "our" (with "savior" -- the NW has the more woodenly literal "of us"). The NAB and NW use a second "of," which is an implicit part of the genitive ("of") form of the nouns in this phrase, and is as legitimately added to "of our savior" by these two translations as it is to "of . . . God" by all translations.[1]

The NASB, NIV, AB, and LB translators all prefer to see Paul referring to Jesus as "God" here, and accordingly shift the possessive pronoun "our" to a position before "God" to draw the two phrases completely together. The NRSV and TEV occupy the middle ground between these two readings, placing in their main texts a translation that equates "God" and "Savior," but offering the version that distinguishes between "God" and "Savior" as an alternative reading in a footnote. The NRSV and TEV translators are to be commended for fully informing their readers about the alternatives.

When we find ourselves facing an ambiguous passage, frustrated in our attempt to make a decision one way or another about how to translate, it is always a good idea to look for similar passages in order to make a comparison of expression, and so help to clarify the possible meaning of the words we are translating. The closest parallel to Titus 2:13 is just a chapter away, in Titus 1:4. Compare:

Titus 2:13   *tou megalou theou kai sōtēros hēmōn Xristou Iēsou*
              of the great God and (of the?) savior of us Christ Jesus

Titus 1:4   *apo theou patros kai Xristou Iēsou tou sōtēros hēmōn*
              from God Father and (from) Christ Jesus the savior of us

The variations between the two verses are entirely incidental. The phrases "Christ Jesus" and "savior of us" switch positions in the two passages. This rearrangement results in "Christ Jesus, the one who is our savior" (1:4), compared to "our savior Christ Jesus" (2:13). Repeating the idea he introduced in 1:4, Paul can afford to me more succinct in 2:13. The word modifying "God" is changed from "father" to "great." But that does not change the identity of the God spoken of. In fact, it can be said without qualification that if Paul had simply repeated "father" in Titus 2:13, there would never have been any controversy over the meaning of the passage.   Another comparable verse is 2 Thessalonians 1:12. Compare:

Titus 2:13   *tou megalou theou kai sōtēros hēmōn Xristou Iēsou*
              of the great God and (of the?) savior of us Christ Jesus

2 Thess. 1:12 *tou theou hēmōn kai kuriou Iēsou Christou*
              of the God of us and (of the?) Lord Jesus Christ

The form of this passage is the same as Titus 2:13. Yet all but one of the translations (the NAB is the exception) add "the" before "Lord," showing that they understand "God" and "Lord" to be distinct here (the TEV and LB even add a second "of"). The NIV and TEV offer alternatives closer to Titus 2:13 in footnotes. That leaves the NRSV, NASB, NAB, AB, and LB translators with some explaining to do. Why are they inconsistent in how they translate the two passages? If the distinctness of Jesus in the second phrase of 2 Thessalonians 1:12 is certain to them, why is it not also certain in Titus 2:13 (or vice versa in the case of the NAB)?

The same issue arises in regard to 2 Peter 1:1. The author refers to "the righteousness of our God and (of the?) savior Jesus Christ." The NW adds "the" in brackets before "Savior Jesus Christ," making explicit a reading that distinguishes between the latter and "our God."[2] The NRSV offers this reading in a footnote, but places in its main text "the righteousness of our God and Savior Jesus Christ," a translation followed by all other modern translations under consideration (the LB reworks the verse almost beyond recognition, removing entirely "righteousness," but nevertheless has "Jesus Christ our God and Savior").

Once again, we turn to parallel passages for help, and find one in the very next verse.[3] Compare:

2 Peter 1:1   *tou theou hēmōn kai sōtēros Iēsou Xristou*
              of the God of us and (of the) savior Jesus Christ

2 Peter 1:2   *tou theou kai Iēsou tou kuriou hēmōn*
              of the God and (of) Jesus the lord of us

All of the translations we are comparing properly maintain the distinction between "God" and "Jesus, our Lord" in verse 2, while most ignore it in verse 1. But the grammatical structure of the two sentences is identical, making it very doubtful that they should be translated in different ways. In English, we have to have an article before a common noun (*the* savior) and not before a name (Jesus); but that is something about proper English expression, not about the original Greek.

Those who defend the translations that read as if only Jesus is spoken of in both Titus 2:13 and 2 Peter 1:1 attempt to distinguish those two passages from the parallel examples I have given by something called "Sharp's Rule." In 1798, the amateur theologian Granville Sharp published a book in which he argued that when there are two nouns of the same form ("case") joined by "and" (*kai*), only the first of which has the article, the nouns are identified as the same thing. Close examination of this much-used "rule" shows it to be a fiction concocted by a man who had a theological agenda in creating it, namely, to prove that the verses we are examining in this chapter call Jesus "God."[4]

"Sharp's Rule" does not survive close scrutiny. He claimed that the rule did not apply to personal names, only to personal titles. That is why it is cited in connection with Titus 2:13 and not Titus 1:4, with 2 Peter 1:1 and not 1:2. Daniel Wallace has demonstrated that even that claim is too broad, since he found that "Sharp's Rule" doesn't work with plural forms of personal titles. Instead, Wallace finds that a phrase that follows the form article-noun-"and"-noun, when the nouns involved are plurals, can involve two entirely distinct groups, two overlapping groups, two groups of which one is a subset of the other, or two identical groups (Wallace, page 72-78). In other words, there is no evidence that anything significant for the meaning of the words happens merely by being joined by "and" and dropping the second article.

The problem is not with Sharp's honesty or his diligence, but with the premises by which he did his work. He ignored the fact that the Greek language was not confined to the New Testament. The authors of the books of the New Testament did not have their own form of Greek with its own rules. Rather, they were working within a much larger Greek linguistic and literary environment. To be sure that you have identified a "rule" of Greek, you need to look beyond the confines of the New Testament, because within the New Testament a pattern of use may be only a coincidence within the small sample of Greek grammar and syntax found there.

If we turn to the standard work of Greek grammar, that of Smyth, we find no "Sharp's Rule." But we do find several "rules" that may explain the pattern Sharp thought he was seeing in the New Testament. Smyth, section 1143, says: "A single article, used with the first of two or more nouns connected by *and* produces the effect of a single notion." That sounds an awful lot like "Sharp's Rule," doesn't it? But what exactly is meant by "a single notion"? Smyth gives two examples: "the generals and captains (the commanding officers)"; "the largest and smallest ships (the whole fleet)." You can see from these examples that the two nouns combined by "and" are not identical; the individual words do not represent the same thing. Instead, by being combined, they suggest a larger whole. The generals and the captains together make up the more general category of "commanding officers," just as the various sized ships together constitute the fleet as a whole. So the article-noun-"and"-noun construction does combine individual things into larger wholes, but it does not necessarily identify them as one and the same thing. This is further clarified by Smyth in section 1144: "A repeated article lays stress on each word." So when a writer wants to sharply distinguish two things, he or she will use the article with each noun; but when the two things in some way work together or belong to a broader unified whole, the article is left off of the second noun.

Other "rules" established by examining the whole of Greek literature also can account for what we see in Titus and 2 Peter. The absence of the article before "Savior" could just as well be explained by section 1129 of Smyth's grammar: "Words denoting persons, when they are used of a class, may omit the article." Smyth gives the examples "man," "soldier," and "god." "Savior" clearly fits this same description. Or one might consider section 1140: "Several appellatives, treated like proper names, may omit the article." Smyth here uses the example of "king"; the term "Savior" certainly would have the same level of definiteness for a Christian writer.

While we're on the subject of Sharp's attempt to distinguish personal names from personal titles in constructing his rule, it should be pointed out that *ho theos* ("the God") functions as a proper name ("God") in the New Testament. So by a strict reading of "Sharp's Rule," it wouldn't even apply to the verses Sharp hoped to interpret.

Because of this verse's ambiguity in the original Greek, none of the translations we have compared can be rejected outright. They all offer fairly literal translations that can be justified on the basis of the original Greek. The NRSV and TEV offer their readers the two alternatives, and this is the best policy. We have no sure way to judge which translations correctly understand the verse and which ones do not. But with the long overdue dismissal of the phantom of "Sharp's Rule," the position of those who insist "God" and "Savior" must refer to the same being in this verse is decidedly weakened. There is no legitimate way to distinguish the grammar of Titus 2:13 from that of Titus 1:4 and 2 Thessalonians 1:12, just as there is no way to consider 2 Peter 1:1 different in its grammar from 2 Peter 1:2. This is a case where grammar alone will not settle the matter. All we can do is suggest, by analysis of context and comparable passages, the "more likely" and "less likely" translations, and leave the question open for further light.

NOTES

1. Robert Countess, in his book, *The Jehovah's Witnesses' New Testament*, charges that the NW "interpolates the preposition 'of' before 'our Savior" and refers to "of" as an "addition to the text" (Countess, page 69). Such statements totally misrepresent the facts to his readers. The phrase "our Savior" is in the genitive ("of") form, and so "of" is a necessary part of the meaning of the phrase.

In countless other genitive phrases throughout the New Testament, "of" is regularly supplied in English translations with no underlying Greek preposition. In fact, there is no Greek preposition "of"!

2. The KJV is based on a slightly different Greek text which places the possessive pronoun with "Jesus Christ" rather than with "God." Thus the distinction between "God" and "Savior" is retained, as in Titus 2:13.

3. This parallel is pointed out by a footnote in the NW translation.

4. Daniel B. Wallace, who accepts Sharp's rule as having some validity, has this to say about the man whose name it bears: "His strong belief in Christ's deity led him to study the Scriptures in the original in order to defend more ably that precious truth . . . As he studied the Scriptures in the original, he noticed a certain pattern, namely, when the construction article-noun-και-noun involved personal nouns which were singular and not proper names, they always referred to the same person. He noticed further that this rule applied in several texts to the deity of Jesus Christ" (Wallace, page 61). Sharp's book was entitled, *Remarks on the Definitive Article in the Greek Text of the New Testament: Containing Many New Proofs of the Divinity of Christ, from Passages Which Are Wrongly Translated in the Common English Bible.* The "Common English Bible" that Sharp was criticizing was the KJV.

NINE

AN UNCERTAIN THRONE

Hebrews 1:8 is one of those verses where the characteristics of Greek grammar and the tendencies of Greek style give the translator a big headache. In this verse we have a sentence without verbs. When I am grading my students' papers, this is a mistake I frequently must correct. I tell them, "A sentence must have a verb." So how can I admit to them that the Bible has many sentences without verbs? Thankfully, the Bible was composed not in English, but in Greek, and this makes all the difference. In Greek, the verb "is" often is omitted as unnecessary. There are other elements in a Greek sentence, such as noun cases, that usually allow the sentence to be understood even without a simple verb like "is." Since it is implied, it does not need to be said explicitly. When we translate from Greek into English, however, we supply the implied verb, because English is the kind of language where the verb must be there to help put the sentence together. So far, so good.

    The problem in Hebrews 1:8 is that we are not sure where the verb "is" belongs in the sentence, and where it belongs makes a big difference in the meaning of the verse. Take a look at the passage in a lexical ("interlinear") translation:

> *ho thronos sou ho theos eis ton aiōna tou aiōnos*
> the throne of you the god until the age of the age

Let's start to put this sentence together. "The throne of you" means, "your throne." "The god" is the way the Bible indicates "God"; the definite article makes it specifically the one God. "Until the age of the age" is the typical biblical way to say "forever and ever." Now the question is, where does the verb "is" go in this sentence to hold it all together in a coherent statement?

In English, we know exactly where to place a verb: it goes between the subject and the object of the verb, or, in sentences that use the verb "to be," between the subject and the predicate noun or predicate adjective, or some other predicate modifier. The question in Hebrews 1:8 is, what is the subject? Subject nouns in Greek are usually easy to identify because they are in the subject (*nominative*) form, or case. But when the verb is a be-verb, the other nouns in the sentence can also be in the nominative form.

In Hebrews 1:8, we have two nouns in the nominative form: "throne" and "God." The verb "is" might go between these two nouns, as it does in dozens of cases of saying "x is y" in the New Testament. If that is so, then the sentence reads: "Your throne is God, forever and ever." This is the way the sentence is read by the translators of the NW. The NRSV and TEV translators also recognize this as a possible translation of this verse, and so include it in a footnote in their respective translations.

But there is another possible way to translate Hebrews 1:8. The phrase *ho theos* is sometimes used to say "O God" in Greek. In other words, even though the form in which this phrase appears normally and usually marks it as the subject under discussion ("God"), it can also be used for direct address to the subject ("O God").

As Greek spread throughout the ancient world, and simplified into "common" (*koine*) Greek, some very specialized forms of speech dropped out of the language, and more commonly used forms took on more and more work. This happened with the form of speech used in Greek for direct address ("Tell me, John . . ."). If you compare in an interlinear Bible Jesus' cry from the cross in Matthew 27:46 to the same event in Mark 15:34, you will see that Matthew has Jesus address God in the classical, "classy" Greek way (*thee*), while Mark uses the common man's language (*ho theos*). This same substitution of the subject (*nominative*) form of the noun "God" (*ho theos*) for the direct address (*vocative*) form (*thee*) occurs just three other times in the New Testament: in Luke 18:11, Luke 18:13, and, significantly, Hebrews 10:7. In the latter verse, a quote from Psalm 40 includes the following clause, "I have come to do your will, O God." In this verse, "O God" translates *ho theos*. So it is obvious that the author of this book of the Bible can use *ho theos* to mean "O God." At the same time, the same author uses *ho theos* dozens of times to mean "God," the usual meaning of the phrase.

These facts make it very hard for us to know which way to translate this phrase in Hebrews 1:8. Since there are a handful of instances in the New Testament where *ho theos* means "O God," rather than "God," it is *possible* that in Hebrews 1:8 *ho theos* means "O God." But since *ho theos* usually means "God," and there are hundreds of examples of this, it is more *probable* that in Hebrews 1:8 *ho theos* means "God."

But the translators of most of the versions we are comparing have chosen the rarer, less probable way to translate *ho theos*. By taking it to mean "O God," and by putting "is" after the two nouns ("throne" and "God") and before the prepositional phrase "forever and ever," they read the verse as, "Your throne, O God, is forever and ever." The KJV, NASB, NIV, NAB, AB, and LB, choose to translate this way, and do not alert their readers to the uncertainties of the passage. The NRSV and TEV also put this translation into their text, while, as I mentioned, pointing out the translation options in a footnote. In my opinion, the NRSV, TEV, and NW have done the right thing by informing their readers that there are two ways the verse can and has been translated.

Both translations are possible, so none of the translations we are comparing can be rejected as inaccurate. We cannot settle the debate with certainty. But which translation is more probable?

First, on the basis of linguistics, *ho theos* is more likely to mean "God," as it does hundreds of times throughout the New Testament, than "O God," a meaning it has in only three other places in the New Testament. Furthermore, there is no other example in the Bible where the expression "forever" stands alone as a predicate phrase with the verb "to be," as it would if the sentence were read "Your throne is forever." "Forever" always functions as a phrase complementing either an action verb, or a predicate noun or pronoun. Moreover, there is no other way to say "God is your throne" than the way Hebrews 1:8 reads. There is, however, another way to say "Your throne, O God," namely, by using the direct address (*vocative*) form *thee* rather than the subject (*nominative*) form *ho theos*. The test of asking "Is there some other way the author could have expressed x if he or she meant x?" is an important one in translation and interpretation.[1]

Second, on the basis of literary context, we can say that Jesus, who is the subject being discussed in Hebrews 1:8, is not called "God" anywhere else in the Epistle to the Hebrews. In the immediate context of Hebrews 1:7-9, the author is making a contrast between angels and Jesus. Quotes from the Old Testament are used to make this contrast. Verse 7, quoting Psalm 104:4, shows that God talks about the angels as "servants." The contrast is made in verse 8, which says, "But (God says) about the Son . . ." and then quotes the words we are trying to figure out from Psalm 45:6-7. In contrast to the angels who serve, the Son is enthroned. But is God the throne on which the Son rests, or is the Son himself called "God" here?

Fortunately, there is another literary context to help us, namely the original psalm that is being quoted in Hebrews 1:8. Psalm 45 is a hymn in praise of the king of Israel. God is addressed nowhere in this psalm. Instead, we get a lengthy description of the king's ideal life. He is described as shooting arrows, girded with a sword, perfumed, living in ivory-embellished palaces, entertained with lutes, attended by fair princesses, and aroused by their beauty. Can there be any doubt that the life described here is of a very human king? So what does it have to do with Jesus, and why is it quoted as if it is about Jesus?

It's really quite simple: Jesus is the Messiah. The Messiah is the rightful king of Israel. What is said about the king of Israel can be said equally of the Messiah. In fact, the ideal life described here in quite mundane (but not boring!) terms is stated to be the reward given to the king because "you have loved righteousness and hated wickedness." "Therefore," the psalm continues, "God has anointed you with the oil of gladness more than your companions." The psalm is about what God has done for the person spoken to.

Within the Jewish tradition, Psalm 45 has never been taken to call the king "God." The modern translation published by the Jewish Bible Society reads, "Your divine throne is everlasting." The Greek translation of the psalm made before the beginning of Christianity, which reads exactly as the author of Hebrews has quoted it, certainly followed this traditional Jewish understanding of the verse, and its translators thought that by using *ho theos* they were saying "God is your throne," not "Your throne, O God."

It is always possible that the author of Hebrews understood it differently. There are other examples in Hebrews where Old Testament verses are reinterpreted. But these reinterpretations are always made apparent to the reader by slight changes in how the verses are quoted, as in Hebrews 2:6-8. In Hebrews 1:8, the author would have to make some change in phrasing to make the reinterpretation explicit. But no change is made. So even if the author understood *ho theos* here as direct address, he or she has not left us any explicit indication of that.

So we must conclude that the more probable translation is "God is your throne . . .," the translation found in the NW and in the footnotes of the NRSV and TEV. Three giants of modern New Testament scholarship -- Westcott, Moffatt, and Goodspeed -- came to the same conclusion independently. The fact is, if this verse were quoted in the New Testament in reference to anyone else, the translators would have not hesitated to translate it as "God is your throne . . ." It seems likely that it is only because most translations were made by people who already believe that Jesus is God that the less probable way of translating this verse has been preferred. I am not criticizing their belief; I am merely pointing out that such a belief can lead to bias in the choices people make as translators. The issue for the translator is not whether or not Jesus is God, it is whether or not Jesus is called "God" in this biblical passage.

Let me repeat that both ways of translating Hebrews 1:8 are legitimate readings of the original Greek of the verse. There is no basis for proponents of either translation to claim that the other translation is *certainly* wrong. All that can be discussed is which translation is more probable.[2] When the means we have at our disposal (language, context, environment) cannot settle a translation question with certainty, we have to admit to our readers that our choice is based on other factors. Translators should choose the translation they prefer and provide their readers with a note explaining the uncertainty, as well as the reasons for their preference.

NOTES

1. It should be noted that the author of Hebrews is familiar with, and does use, vocative forms of nouns, such as *kurie*, "O Lord," just two verses later, in 1:10. So he or she could have used a vocative form of "God" in 1:8 to make direct address perfectly clear, if that is what was intended.

2. Rolf Furuli, in his book *The Role of Theology and Bias in Bible Translation*, reaches the same conclusion: "Thus, in this passage the theology of the translator is the decisive factor in the translation" (Furuli, page 47).

TEN

TAMPERING WITH TENSES

We are continuing our exploration of problems of grammar involving the verb "to be." If Bible translations are going to communicate meaning to English speakers, they had better speak in English. That seems a minimal requirement and expectation. Despite the many possible approaches to the task of translation, no translator sets out to produce incoherent nonsense. More responsible translators even aim for accurate as well as clear communication. I can easily agree with Robert Bratcher when he states the following:

> At least it can be agreed that any translation, in order to be considered good, should satisfy three requirements: (1) It should handle textual matters in an informed and responsible way. . . . (2) Its exegesis of the original texts should be theologically unbiased . . . (3) Its language should be contemporary, it should conform to normal English usage (Bratcher 1978, pages 115-116).

The readers of Bratcher's "Good News Bible" (TEV) quite naturally assume that it satisfies the three principles laid out by the translator himself. So those same readers must scratch their heads in puzzlement when they come upon the following sentence: "Before Abraham was born,

I Am" (John 8:58). How's that again?

In this verse, the TEV violates the third of Bratcher's own principles (normal English usage) and, as we have found in other cases, the reason for doing so lies in a breech of his second principle (freedom from theological bias). The TEV form of John 8:58 strays from normal English usage in word order and verbal tense complementarity. That is, it puts the subject after the predicate, which is not the normal word order of English sentences, and it mixes a present tense verb with a past tense verb in a totally ungrammatical construction. Most other versions have the same problem.

KJV	Before Abraham was, I am.
NRSV	Before Abraham was, I am.
NASB	Before Abraham was born, I am.
NIV	Before Abraham was born, I am!
TEV	Before Abraham was born, 'I Am'.
AB	Before Abraham was born, I AM.
NAB	Before Abraham came to be, I AM.
NW	Before Abraham came into existence, I have been.
LB	I was in existence before Abraham was ever born!

What is going on here? You may think that there is a particularly difficult or convoluted Greek clause underlying this mess of English. But that is not the case. The Greek reads: *prin Abraam genesthai egō eimi*. What Jesus says here is fine, idiomatic Greek. It can be rendered straightforwardly into English by doing what translators always do with Greek, namely, rearrange the word order into normal English order, and adjust things like verbal tense complementarity into proper English expression. These steps of translation are necessary because Greek and English are not the same language and do not obey the same rules of grammar. Leaving the translation at the stage of a lexical ("interlinear") rendering, which is one way to describe what most translations do here, simply won't work. That is because Greek has more flexibility with word order than English does, and it can mix verbal tenses in a way English cannot.

On the matter of word order, normal English follows the structure we all learned in elementary school: subject + verb + object or predicate phrase. The order of the Greek in John 8:58 is: predicate phrase + subject + verb. So it is the most basic step of translation to move the predicate phrase "before Abraham came to be" (*prin Abraam genesthai*) from the beginning of the sentence to the end, after the subject and verb. Just as we do not say "John I am" or "Hungry I am" or "First in line I am," so it is not proper English to say "Before Abraham came to be I am." Yet all of the translations we are comparing, with the exception of the LB, offer precisely this sort of mangled word order.

On the subject of verbal tenses, there is a proper way to coordinate verb tenses in English that must be followed regardless of the idioms unique to Greek that provide the raw material for a translation. John 8:58 has two verbs, one ("am") in the present tense, and the other ("came to be") in the past (technically, the "aorist") tense. In most sentences where we see a past tense verb and a present tense verb, we would assume that the action of the past verb is earlier in time than the action of the present verb ("John wrote the book that I am reading": "wrote" happened before "am reading"). This is true in most cases in Greek as well as in English. But in John 8:58 this is not the case, and we know it is not the case because the preposition *prin*, "before," coordinates the relationship between the two actions represented by the verbs. This preposition tells us that the action of the verb in the present tense ("am") happened (or began to happen, or was already happening) "before" the action of the verb in the past tense ("came to be").

When verb tenses or any other part of grammar is used in a way outside of usual expectations, we call it an "idiom." Because Greek idioms are different from English idioms, translators do not translate these expressions word-for-word, but rather convey the meaning of the Greek idiom in proper, comprehensible English. At least, that is what translators are supposed to do.

It is ungrammatical English for something referred to with a present "am" to occur earlier in time than something described with a past "came to be." Normally, if we want to refer to an event before one already in the past, we would use a perfect tense: "He had put on his boots before he went out into the snow." In John 8:58, since Jesus' existence is not completed past action, but ongoing, we must use some sort of imperfect verbal form to convey that: "I have been (since) before Abraham came to be." That's as close as we can get to what the Greek says in our own language if we pay attention to all parts of the sentence.[1] Both the LB and the NW offer translations that coordinate the two verbs in John 8:58 according to proper English syntax, and that accurately reflect the meaning of the Greek idiom. The other translations fail to do this.

A quick glance at Smyth's *Greek Grammar* reveals that what we are dealing with in John 8:58 is a well-known Greek idiom. The pertinent entry is section 1885 on verb tenses, which states, "The present, when accompanied by a definite or indefinite expression of past time, is used to express an action begun in the past and continued in the present. The 'progressive perfect' is often used in translation. Thus, . . . *I have been long* (and am still) *wondering*." I think you can see immediately that this entry applies to John 8:58, where the present verb *eimi* is accompanied by an expression of past time, *prin Abraam genesthai*.[2]

It is clear that the translators of the nine versions we are comparing are familiar with this idiomatic aspect of Greek verbs, because they usually translate such expressions accurately into correct English. There are two examples of this in the Gospel according to John itself[3]:

John 14:9   *tosoutō xronō meth' humōn eimi*
              for this much time with you I am

John 15:27   *ap' archēs met' emou este*
              from (the) beginning with me you are

In both of these passages, all of the translations we are comparing translate the present tense form of "to be" ("I am"; "you are") as "have been" because of its relation to an expression of past time ("for this much time"; "from the beginning"). This is exactly the same grammatical construct as found in 8:58, where these same translations (with the exception of the LB and NW) suddenly ignore the larger grammatical construct and have "am."

Of course, all of the translations also put these sentences into proper English word order, whereas with John 8:58 (with the exception of the LB) they leave their translation work incomplete by retaining Greek, not English, order. Orlinsky and Bratcher comment on the idea that "faithfulness in translation demands that the word order of the original be reproduced," in the clearest possible terms: "This, of course, is simply wrong" (Orlinsky and Bratcher, page 251).[4]

Why would translators, whose job it is to make the Bible into comprehensible, good quality English, choose an awkward, ungrammatical rendering instead? Why do Bible translations which in thousands of other verses freely change word order relative to the original Greek, suddenly find a reason to follow exactly the Greek, producing an ungrammatical and syntactically strained sentence, in this instance? Why does Bratcher himself, in the TEV, render John 8:58 as "Before Abraham was born, 'I Am'"? The answer is theological bias.

In the Gospel of John, Jesus uses the words "I am" many times. He says things such as "I am the shepherd" and "I am the vine." He talks in this way so much in the gospel that many interpreters are convinced that there is a particular theme of self-revelation being conveyed in these expressions. Even though this book is not about interpretation, I can say frankly that I agree with these interpreters -- most biblical researchers do. But in the hands of some interpreters, this very reasonable interpretation of Jesus' use of language in the Gospel according to John has grown into a strange, unsubstantiated idea about the words "I am" themselves, independent of the objects and phrases attached to "I am" in Jesus' speech.

On several occasions, Jesus says "I am" without an explicit predicate noun or phrase following the verb (John 4:26; 6:20; 8:24, 28; 13:19; 18:5-6, 8). Most of these verses fit into known idiomatic Greek expressions and make perfect sense in their context. But someone at some point noticed that this perfectly ordinary combination of the first person pronoun "I" and the present tense verb "am" just happens to read the same as what God says when he reveals himself to Moses in English translations of the Old Testament, "I am" (Exodus 3:14). Notice what I'm saying. A literal English rendering of the Greek *ego eimi* as "I am" happens to sound like the King James English rendering of something said by God in the Old Testament.

Actually, "I am" is a very uncertain rendering of the Hebrew expression in Exodus. But those who promote the significance of the parallel between Exodus 3:14 and the expression "I am" in John say that the correspondence between the two is proven by the exact match in how Exodus 3:14 is translated in the Greek translation of the Old Testament (called the Septuagint) that was known to the New Testament authors and the wording used by John. A quick look at the Septuagint, however, shows this claim to be in error.

The Septuagint of Exodus 3:14 has God say *egō eimi ho ōn*, "I am the being," or "I am the one that exists." Plainly, *ego eimi* functions here exactly as it does in the mouth of all speaking characters throughout the Bible, as a first person pronoun subject, followed by the be-verb, to which a predicate noun is attached. God does not say "I am I Am," he says "I am the being." "I am" sets up the title or identification God uses of himself, it is not itself that title. Separating "I am" off as if it were meant to stand alone is an interpretive sleight-of-hand, totally distorting the role the phrase plays in the whole sentence, either in the Greek Septuagint version of Exodus 3:14 or in John 8:58. There is absolutely nothing in the original Greek of John 8:58 to suggest that Jesus is quoting the Old Testament here, contrary to what the TEV tries to suggest by putting quotation marks around "I am." Think about it. If "I am" was a separate quote, there would be no subject or main verb to go with "before Abraham came to be."

Inconsistency in translation is often an indicator of bias. So it is revealing to compare all of the occurrences of *ego eimi* in the Gospel according to John. When *ego eimi* appears with a predicate noun in sentences in John, it is, of course, translated "I am" (the vine, the shepherd, etc.) This is completely accurate because "am" is the only verb and there is no other marker of time in these sentences. But as I mentioned before, there are several cases where *egō eimi* appears without a predicate complement, and so would at first appear to be an independent sentence that reads simply "I am." But closer examination of these cases in context reveal that the predicate complement is implied.

In John 4:26, a Samaritan woman is speaking to Jesus about the prophecies of a coming Messiah. Jesus answers, *egō eimi ho lalōn soi* (word-for-word: I am the one speaking with you). All of the translations we are comparing understand that there is an implied predicate pronoun in this sentence, "I, -- the person speaking with you -- am *he*." In other words, I am the Messiah you are expecting. Jesus is not telling the woman he *is*, that is, that he exists. Nor is he informing her that he is the person speaking with her. She can see both of these facts easily enough. He is saying he is the specific figure she is talking about, the Messiah.

In John 6:20, the disciples are in a boat in the midst of a storm, and Jesus comes walking to them on the water. Since people don't normally walk on water, the disciples naturally think they are seeing a ghost, and are terrified. Jesus says to them, *egō eimi mē phobeisthe* (word-for-word: "I am; do not be afraid"). All of the translations we are comparing recognize an implied predicate pronoun in this sentence: "It is *I*; do not be afraid." Jesus is not telling them that he exists, nor is he walking towards them quoting a biblical phrase. He is telling them that it is he, Jesus, coming to them, so they don't have anything to fear.

In John 8:24, Jesus says to his opponents, "You will die in your sins unless you believe that I am (he)" (*egō eimi*). He is not warning them to believe in his existence; they know he exists well enough, and in fact consider him a nuisance. When he tells them that they must believe that "I am (he)," their response shows the correct meaning of his expression. They ask, "*Who* are you?" Their question only makes sense if *egō eimi* in verse 24 means "I am he." A few lines later, in John 8:28, Jesus answers their question. He refers to the future when they will "lift up the Son of Man," and then, he says, they will understand that "I am (he)" (*egō eimi*). In other words, they will recognize after his crucifixion that he is the Son of Man.[5] Yet the TEV and NAB ignore the context of John 8:28, which identifies *who* Jesus is and completes the meaning of his expression "I am (he)." The TEV has Jesus say "I Am Who I Am" and the NAB has him say "I AM."

In John 13:19, Jesus says that he predicts what will happen so that when it does happen people will believe "I am (he)" (*egō eimi*). Once again, the immediate context fills out the implied identification. In the previous verse, Jesus quotes Psalm 41:9, which speaks of betrayal. Jesus quite obviously is identifying himself as the subject of this Old Testament passage.[6] But once again, the TEV and NAB write into the Bible "I Am Who I Am" and "I AM," as if the two words *egō eimi* had nothing to do with the words around them as part of larger statements by Jesus.

In John 18, Jesus asks the soldiers whom they have come for. When they say they are looking for Jesus of Nazareth, Jesus answers "I am (he)" (*egō eimi*). In other words, "I am Jesus, the one you are looking for." Now when he says this the first time, the soldiers fall back in shock. But there is no reason to think that Jesus has used some sort of verbal spell on them. There is nothing in the words *egō eimi* themselves that have power; it is Jesus who has the power. Nevertheless, the NAB uses "I AM."

The majority of translations recognize these idiomatic uses of "I am," and properly integrate the words into the context of the passages where they appear. Yet when it comes to 8:58, they suddenly forget how to translate. The translators of the TEV and NAB work very hard to intrude into the text a theologically biased interpretation of the words. But their inconsistency in doing so exposes what they were up to. In all of these passages, Jesus says simply "I am" (*egō eimi*); he never says "I am 'I Am'" (*egō eimi egō eimi*), as the TEV explicitly has it. Translating back from English into Greek is one way to see if a translation has been faithful to the original. There is never any indication that Jesus is quoting "I am." Furthermore, none of these passages are even real parallels with John 8:58, because none of them have an explicit predicate phrase. John 8:58 does: "before Abraham came to be."

One passage usually missing from the discussion of the expression "I am" in the Gospel according to John is John 9:9. In this verse, the words *egō eimi* are heard from the mouth not of Jesus, but of a blind man cured by Jesus. He, too, uses the words to say "I am he," the man who before was blind, but have been cured. If anyone needs proof that *egō eimi* need not be a quote from the Old Testament, and is not reserved as a title of God, here it is. Once again, our attention is drawn to inconsistency in how words are handled by biased translators. If *egō eimi* is not a divine self-proclamation in the mouth of the blind man of John 9, then it cannot be such a proclamation in the mouth of Jesus just a few verses earlier. None of the translations we are comparing, of course, have the blind man saying "I am," let alone "I AM." According to the reasoning of those who insist that the phrase must be understood as a declaration of divine identity, and so preserved in its "interlinear" form, the blind man is also God. We'll leave that problem to them. For the rest of us, it is sufficient to see in John 9:9 a clear example of the idiomatic use of the expression *ego eimi* in Greek speech.

In John 8:58, all translations except the LB break the first-person-pronoun + verb ("I am") clause out of its relation to the syntax of the sentence, and place it artificially, and ungrammatically, at the end of the English sentence. These modern translations violate their standard practice of using correct English word order by in this case slavishly following the Greek word order, apparently under the influence of the KJV. Even the TEV, supposedly written in modern idiomatic English does this. All translations except the LB and NW also ignore the true relation between the verbs of the sentence, and produce a sentence that makes no sense in English.[7] On top of this, we see the strange capitalization in the NAB, AB, and TEV. These *changes* in the meaning of the Greek and in the normal procedure for translation point to a bias that has interfered with the work of the translators.

It is Jesus' claim to be superior to Abraham, and to have a superhuman longevity, not a claim to a divine self-designation, that enrages his audience.[8] Jesus' claim here fits perfectly John's understanding of Jesus as God's *logos*, or creative agent at the beginning of time, in John 1. Jesus' argument in 8:58 is that he has seniority over Abraham, and so by the standards of Jewish society, he has greater authority than the patriarch. No one listening to Jesus, and no one reading John in his own time would have picked up on a divine self-identification in the mere expression "I am," which, if you think about, is just about the most common pronoun-verb combination in any language.

    I am not claiming that Jesus' remark in John 8:58 is without theological significance, nor that it has nothing to do with the Old Testament background. Two passages from Isaiah appear to be related in thought. In Isaiah 41:4, God says "I, God, I am first and to (all) futurity." In the Septuagint Greek translation of this verse, the phrase *egō eimi* comes at the end of the sentence. Yet here, as in John 8:58, the verb "am" has a predicate phrase refering to time: "first and to futurity." Another related passage, Isaiah 46:4, shows God saying, "I am, and until you have grown old, I am." *Egō eimi* is used twice in this sentence, once again in relation to a temporal reference. Yet obviously the "I am" is not a name or a title. Instead God declares his ongoing existence in reference to the aging of his audience. In a sense, Jesus appropriates this kind of language for himself in the Gospel of John, and uses it to characterize his close identification with the God who speaks that way in the Old Testament. You can make several different sorts of theological interpretation based upon that fact. But the interpretation should not be forced back into the text of the Bible.

    The LB comes out as the most accurate translation of John 8:58. The translator avoided the lure of bias and the pressure of the KJV tradition. The NW is second best in this case, because it understands the relation between the two verbs correctly, even though the influence of the KJV has led its translators to put the verb improperly at the end of the sentence. The average Bible reader might never guess that there was something wrong with the other translations, and might even assume that the error was to found in the LB and NW. When all you can do is compare the English translations, and count them up like votes, the LB and NW stick out as different in John 8:58. It is natural to assume that the majority are correct and the odd ones at fault. It is only when translations are checked against the original Greek, as they should be, that a fair assessment can be made, and the initial assumption can be seen to be wrong.

NOTES

1. McKay says that the verse "would be most naturally translated 'I have been in existence since before Abraham was born', if it were not for the obsession with the simple words 'I am'" (McKay 1996, page 302).

2. This same idiom is discussed in other grammars under the names "durative present" or "extension from past present" (see Blass and Debrunner, section 322; McKay 1994, pages 41-42).

3. Greg Stafford cites these same examples in his book *Jehovah's Witnesses Defended* (Stafford, page 268).

4. Since the context of this remark is a review of a New Testament passage translated by Kenneth Wuest, and Bratcher is responsible for all comments on New Testaments in the book (Orlinsky handled the Old Testament reviews), we can conclude that Bratcher himself wrote this remark, blissfully unaware that he was indicting his own translation (TEV) of John 8:58.

5. Stafford points out that "Son of Man" is the very likely implied predicate of John 8:28 (Stafford, page 256). He points to a parallel fusion of "I am" with "Son of Man" in Mark 14:62 (Stafford, page 257). He also cites Edwin Freed's reference to John 9:35-37 as expressing the same identification in a slightly different idiom (see Freed, pages 405-406).

6. Stafford correctly identifies the contextual reference here (page 282).

7. Earlier editions of the NASB contained "I have been" as an alternate translation in a footnote, but this has been eliminated in more recent editions.

8. McKay agrees on this point: "the claim to have been in existence for so long is in itself a staggering one, quite enough to provoke the crowd's violent reaction" (McKay 1996, page 302).

ELEVEN

AND THE WORD WAS ... WHAT?

In the previous chapters, you have learned about the great importance for translation of simple things such as the form a word takes, whether it appears with the definite article or not, how it is connected to other words by the use of the verb "to be," and the order in which it is placed relative to other words in a sentence. The knowledge and skills you have picked up in those previous chapters have prepared you to tackle a passage where all of these elements come into play: John 1:1.

To start our exploration of the issues surrounding the translation of this verse, I give John 1:1-2 in the nine translations we are comparing.

KJV: In the beginning was the Word, and the Word was with God, and the Word was God. The same was in the beginning with God.

NASB: In the beginning was the Word, and the Word was with God, and the Word was God. He was in the beginning with God.

NAB: In the beginning was the Word, and the Word was with God, and the Word was God. He was in the beginning with God.

NRSV: In the beginning was the Word, and the Word was with God, and the Word was God. He was in the beginning with God.

NIV: In the beginning was the Word, and the Word was with God, and the Word was God. He was with God in the beginning.

NW: In [the] beginning the Word was, and the Word was with God, and the Word was a god. This one was in [the] beginning with God.

AB: In the beginning [before all time] was the Word (Christ), and the Word was with God, and the Word was God Himself. He was present originally with God.

TEV: Before the world was created, the Word already existed; he was with God, and he was the same as God. From the very beginning the Word was with God.

LB: Before anything else existed, there was Christ, with God. He has always been alive and is himself God.

We will devote our primary attention to the third clause of verse 1: *kai theos ēn ho logos* (word-for-word: "and god was the word"). When we do so, we are confronted with the problem of the missing article before *theos* ("god").

Greek has only a definite article, like our *the*; it does not have an indefinite article, like our *a* or *an*. So, generally speaking, a Greek definite noun will have a form of the definite article (*ho*), which will become "the" in English. A Greek indefinite noun will appear without the definite article, and will be properly rendered in English with "a" or "an." We are not "adding a word" when we translate Greek nouns that do not have the definite article as English nouns with the indefinite article. We are simply obeying the rules of English grammar that tell us that we cannot say "Snoopy is dog," but must say "Snoopy is a dog." For example, in John 1:1c, the clause we are investigating, *ho logos* is "the word," as all translations accurately have it.[1] If it was written simply *logos*, without the definite article *ho*, we would have to translate it as "a word."

Similarly, when we have a form of *ho theos*, as we do in John 1:1b and 1:2, we are dealing with a definite noun that we would initially ("lexically") translate as "the god"[2]; but if it is written simply *theos*, as it is in John 1:1c, it is an indefinite noun that would normally be translated as "a god." To complete our translation into English, we need to take into consideration the fact that English has both a common noun "god" and a proper noun "God." We use the proper noun "God" like a name, without either a definite or indefinite article, even though a name is a definite noun. As a definite noun, "God" corresponds to the Greek *ho theos* (lexically "the god"), which also is used often as the proper noun "God" in both the New Testament and other Greek literature from the same time. So in John 1:1b and 1:2 it is perfectly accurate to drop the "the" from "god" and say that the Word was "with God" (literally "with the god"). But what about the indefinite *theos* in John 1:1c? This does not correspond to the English definite proper noun "God," but to the indefinite noun "a god."

In Greek, if you leave off the article from *theos* in a sentence like the one in John 1:1c, then your readers will assume you mean "a god." The kind of sentence we are dealing with is one with a be-verb, where the predicate noun (*theos*) is in the same noun form (the same "case") as the subject noun (*ho logos*). In this subject ("nominative") form, the definite article is really indispensable for making the noun definite.[3] Its absence makes *theos* quite different than the definite *ho theos*, as different as "a god" is from "God" in English. In other words, John uses the indefinite *theos* in a manner distinct form his use of the definite *ho theos*. This is fairly clear not only from the distinct forms the word takes, but also from the context in which those distinct forms are used. John says on the one hand that the Word "was with" *ho theos*, "God," but on the other hand that the Word "was" *theos*, "a god." It is striking, therefore, that most of the translations we are comparing take no notice of this careful distinction, and translate the different words as if they were exactly the same.

The definite article also can be used in Greek, even when it is not necessary to mark a word's definiteness, to signify that you are still talking about the same thing you were talking about before. Having introduced "God" and "the Word," John would use the definite article to help his readers keep track of the fact that he is still talking about the same God and the same Word. But having mentioned "God" once in 1:1b ("the word was with God"), John does not use the definite article again with *theos* until 1:2 ("this one was with God"), skipping right over the *theos* of 1:1c ("the word was a god"). This middle *theos*, we are left to conclude, is *not* exactly the same thing as the "God" of 1:1b and 1:2.

If John had wanted to say "the Word was God," as so many English translations have it, he could have very easily done so by simply adding the definite article "the" (*ho*) to the word "god" (*theos*), making it "the god" and therefore "God." He could have simply written *ho logos ēn ho theos* (word-for-word: "the word was the god"), or *ho logos ho theos ēn* (word-for-word: "the word the god was"). But he didn't. If John didn't, why do the translators?

The culprit appears to be the King James translators. As I said before, these translators were much more familiar and comfortable with their Latin Vulgate than they were with the Greek New Testament. They were used to understanding passages based on reading them in Latin, and this worked its way into their reading of the same passages in Greek. Latin has no articles, either definite or indefinite. So the definite noun "God" and the indefinite noun "god" look precisely the same in Latin, and in John 1:1-2 one would see three occurrences of what appeared to be the same word, rather than the two distinct forms used in Greek. Whether a Latin noun is definite or indefinite is determined solely by context, and that means it is open to interpretation. The interpretation of John 1:1-2 that is now found in most English translations was well entrenched in the thinking of the King James translators based on a millennium of reading only the Latin, and overpowered their close attention to the more subtle wording of the Greek. After the fact -- after the King James translation was the dominant version and etched in the minds of English-speaking Bible readers -- various arguments were put forward to support the KJV translation of John 1:1c as "the Word was God," and to justify its repetition in more recent, and presumably more accurate translations. But none of these arguments withstands close scrutiny.

Attempted defenses of the traditional translation

Some have argued that since the third clause of John 1:1 is a be-verb sentence that uses an inverted (by English standards) word order, and whose subject and predicate nouns both appear in the "subject" form, John *had to* omit the definite article with "god" because otherwise the reader would not know whether "god" was the subject or belonged to the predicate of the sentence. This is peculiar reasoning. English does not require only the subject of a sentence, and not the predicate noun, to have the definite article, and neither does Greek. In the sentence, "The man in the suit is the president," "the man in the suit" is the subject and "the president" is the predicate noun. We know this even though both nouns are definite.

What English accomplishes with word order, Greek accomplishes with context. We need only glance through the Gospel according to John to find other be-verb sentences where both the subject noun and the predicate noun have the definite article, and in none of these is there a resultant confusion between subject and predicate.[4] In exactly the same way, we know that "the Word" is the subject of the third clause of John 1:1 because in the immediately preceding two clauses "the Word" was the subject under discussion. John can afford the risk of making subject and predicate nouns formally identical because context differentiates them. So there is no validity in the argument that John was forced to omit the definite article from "god" to allow the reader to identify the subject of the clause.

Others have argued that *theos* does not require the definite article to be definite, and that there are examples of article-less ("anarthrous") *theos* used definitely in the New Testament. While this may be true of anarthrous *theos* in the genitive or dative cases, two forms that freely dispense with the article in a number of uses, it is not the case for anarthrous *theos* in the nominative case, the form used in John 1:1c. The nominative case is much more dependent than other Greek cases on the definite article to mark definiteness. There is a very limited range of definitizing elements that may make an anarthrous nominative *theos* definite. These include the presence of an attached possessive pronoun (John 8:54; 2 Corinthians 6:16), the use of the noun in direct address (the "vocative" function, Romans 9:5; 1 Thessalonians 2:5), and the association of the noun with the numeration "one" (1 Corinthians 8:6; Ephesians 4:6; 1 Timothy 2:5). None of these definitizing elements are present in John 1:1c, and it and the remaining eleven examples of anarthrous nominative *theos* in the New Testament are indefinite (Mark 12:27; Luke 20:38; John 1:18; Romans 8:33; 1 Corinthians 8:4; 2 Corinthians 1:3; 2 Corinthians 5:19; Galatians 6:7; Philippians 2:13; 2 Thessalonians 2:4; Revelation 21:7). We will come back to these.

Yet another argument made in defense of the traditional English translation of John 1:1 is based on something called "Colwell's Rule." This is a supposed rule of Greek grammar discovered by the great biblical scholar E. C. Colwell. Colwell introduced his rule in the article, "A Definite Rule for the Use of the Article in the Greek New Testament." Based on a sampling of New Testament passages, Colwell formulated his rule as follows: "A definite predicate nominative has the article when it follows the verb; it does not have the article when it precedes the verb" (Colwell, page 13). There are two problems with using "Colwell's Rule" to argue for the traditional translation of John 1:1. The first problem is that the rule does nothing to establish the definiteness of a noun. The second problem is that the rule is wrong.

"Colwell's Rule" applies to be-verb sentences, where a subject noun and a predicate noun both appear in the nominative ("subject") form. A predicate noun in this form is called a "predicate nominative" because, although it is in the nominative form, it functions as part of the predicate of the sentence. "Colwell's Rule" claims that in Greek, when you have a definite predicate noun in a be-verb sentence (that is, one that normally would have the definite article, *ho*), if you place it before the verb, the definite article is dropped, even though the noun retains its definite meaning. Colwell does not know why the article is dropped when a definite predicate noun is written before the verb, but he claims that it is. If Colwell is right, then "god" could be definite in John 1:1c even though it doesn't have the definite article. "Colwell's Rule" could not *prove* that "god" is a definite noun in John 1:1c, but it could, if valid, open the possibility of it being definite by making the case that there are definite predicate nominatives out there that are missing their articles.

But "Colwell's Rule" is not a valid rule of Greek grammar. You do not have to look very far to find examples of definite predicate nouns that *do not* drop their article when they are placed before the verb, that is, examples that do not obey "Colwell's Rule." In John 6:51, Jesus says *ho artos de hon egō dōsō hē sarx mou estin*, "The bread that I shall give is my flesh" (word-for-word: "the bread now that I shall give the flesh of me is"). The predicate noun "flesh" (*sarx*) is written with the definite article "the" (*hē*) before the verb "is" (*estin*). In John 15:1, Jesus says *ho patēr mou ho geōrgos estin*, "My Father is the farmer" (word-for-word: "the father of me the farmer is"). The predicate noun "farmer" (*geōrgos*) is written with the definite article "the" (*ho*) before the verb "is" (*estin*). In John 20:15, when Mary first encounters the resurrected Jesus, she thinks that *ho kēpouros estin*, "he is the gardener." Again, predicate noun written with the definite article before the verb. And in John 21:7 and 21:12, we see the repeated expression *ho kurios estin*, "It is the Lord," where again the predicate noun is written with the definite article before the verb. So it is obvious, on the basis of the evidence of the Gospel according to John alone, that when Colwell says that, "A definite predicate nominative . . . does not have the article when it precedes the verb," he is wrong.[5]

Colwell himself found fifteen exceptions to his "definite rule" in the New Testament, fifteen predicate nouns that *did* have the definite article even though they were before the verb.[6] In the words of Nigel Turner, though Colwell's Rule "may reflect a general tendency it is not absolute by any means" (Turner, page 184). That's polite understatement. These fifteen exceptions alone show that "Colwell's Rule" is not a "rule" at all.

We've all heard the expression, "the exception that proves the rule." But, generally speaking, exceptions *disprove* rules. The only "exception that proves the rule" is one for which an explanation can be found for why the rule did not apply in that case. But no such explanation is apparent for the exceptions to "Colwell's Rule." Instead, it seems that Colwell was able to come up with his "rule" only by dismissing a large body of evidence that demonstrated that there was no such rule in ancient Greek.

Colwell's mistake, as so often is the case in research, is rooted in a misguided method. He began by collecting all of the predicate nouns in the New Testament that he considered to be definite in meaning, and then, when some of them turned out to look indefinite in Greek, he refused to reconsider his view that they were definite, but instead made up a rule to explain why his subjective understanding of them remained true, even though the known rules of Greek grammar suggested otherwise. Notice that he had already decided that the predicate nouns he was looking at were definite, based on his interpretation of their meaning rather than on the presence or absence of the one sure marker of definiteness in Greek: the article. His predetermination of definiteness made his whole study circular from the start.

Colwell decided that the nouns he was looking at were definite before he even started his research. He was not prepared to change his mind about that. So when nouns he thought were definite showed up without the definite article, he assumed some rule of grammar must cause the article to be dropped. He never even considered the possibility that the article wasn't there because the noun was not definite. It seems that Colwell was misled by how we might say something in English. If a certain expression is definite in English, he assumed it was definite in Greek, regardless of what the grammar suggested. Of course, Colwell knew perfectly well that Greek communicates meaning in different ways than English does. It was an unconscious habit of mind that interfered with his usual capable scholarship in this instance. It was a bias derived from his everyday use of English.

As flawed as the original "Colwell's Rule" is, it has been made worse by misrepresentation down through the years. Notice that, according to Colwell, his "rule" allows him to explain why a noun that you already know (somehow) to be definite turns up sometimes without the definite article. The "rule" does nothing to allow you to determine that a noun is, or is not, definite. Even if "Colwell's Rule" were true, it would at most allow the possibility that an article-less predicate nominative before a verb is definite. It could never prove that the word is definite. But since the rule leaves no way to distinguish between a definite and indefinite predicate nominative before a verb, many have mistaken it as making all pre-verb predicate nominatives definite.

So Bruce Metzger mistakenly writes that "Colwell's Rule" "necessitates the rendering '... and the Word was God'" (Metzger 1953, page 75). Sakae Kubo and Walter F. Specht, in their book *So Many Versions? Twentieth-century English Versions of the Bible*, say "It is true that the Greek does not have the article before 'God' here. However, since in this verse in Greek *theos* (God) is a predicate noun and precedes the verb and subject, it is definite, since a definite predicate noun when it precedes the verb never takes an article in Greek" (Kubo and Specht, page 99). Even Colwell recorded fifteen examples from the New Testament that go against Kubo and Specht's "never." Since many Bible readers rely on the opinions of people like Metzger, Kubo, and Specht, it is easy to understand why the public remains ill-informed about assessing Bible translations.

Understanding John 1:1 accurately

John Harner, in his article, "Qualitative Anarthrous Predicate Nouns: Mark 15:39 and John 1:1," presents a much more careful, systematic analysis of the same type of sentences studied by Colwell. Harner does not predetermine which predicate nouns are definite. Instead, he investigates all predicate nouns that do not have the definite article, and compares those that appear before the verb with those that appear after the verb. Based on his investigation, he concludes that, "anarthrous predicate nouns preceding the verb may function primarily to express the nature or character of the subject, and this qualitative significance may be more important than the question whether the predicate noun itself should be regarded as definite or indefinite" (Harner 1973, page 75). In other words, Greek has a particular way of expressing the nature or character of something that employs predicate nouns before the verb and without the article, just as in John 1:1. The nature or character of *ho logos* ("the Word") is *theos* ("divine").

In my opinion, Harner successfully makes the case that predicate nouns without the article placed before the verb tend to have a qualitative function. In other words, such nouns describe or define the character of the subject of the sentence. But Harner fails to demonstrate that this is *always* the function of pre-verb predicate nominatives, or that this is a function that is not found in predicate nominatives placed *after* a verb.[7] In other words, I think that Harner has detected an important use of anarthrous predicate nominatives, but not one that in any way depends upon the position of the noun relative to the verb.

Generally speaking, the function of indefinite predicate nouns, before or after the verb, is to identify the class or category to which the subject belongs. Sometimes the emphasis is on identity or membership, and sometimes it is on character or quality. I think one function easily slips into the other, and that they really cannot be distinguished in any meaningful way. In any case, English indefinite phrases are more akin to Harner's qualitative meaning than are definite phrases, and Harner himself frequently dismisses the definite translation of passages conveying qualitative meaning as impossible.

John uses this kind of sentence fifty-three times. From this sample, Harner contends that there are forty cases where the qualitative sense of the word is more important to the meaning than either its definiteness or indefiniteness. In most of these cases, however, a translator will be forced to choose whether to use "the" or "a." It simply cannot be avoided. Harner does his best not to directly challenge "Colwell's Rule," but in the final analysis one must do so in order to communicate the qualitative sense Harner argues for to an English-speaking audience. If "the" is used with these predicate nouns, the qualitative sense will be lost. The use of "a" conveys that qualitative sense.

For example, in John 4:19 we must translate "You are a prophet," not "You are the prophet." In John 8:48 it is "You are a Samaritan," not "You are the Samaritan." In John 9:24 the translation is "This man is a sinner," not "This man is the sinner." In John 12:6 it must be "He was a thief," not "He was the thief." Notice that this is not a case of how we say things in English dictating the meaning of the Greek, but a matter of choosing the English that best communicates what the Greek means. So, for example, in English we can say "You are *a* disciple of that man," or

"You are *the* disciple of that man"; but the Greek of John 9:28 uses the indefinite, and so should we. "The disciple" would be an identification; "a disciple" is a characterization, and that's what Harner means by the "qualitative" function of such an expression.

Harner states that the anarthrous predicate noun before the verb cannot be definite in John 1:14; 2:9; 3:4; 3:6 (twice); 4:9; 6:63; 7:12; 8:31; 8:44 (twice); 8:48; 9:8; 9:24-31 (5times); 10:1; 10:8; 10:33-34 (twice); 12:6; 12:36; 18:26; 18:35. The very last verse in this long list is a good place for us to start in exploring sentences structured like John 1:1c and the meaning they are meant to convey. The setting is Pilate's exchange with Jesus. In John 18, verse 35, Pilate asks, "Am I a Jew (*egō Ioudaios eimi*)?" The predicate noun here appears before the verb and without the article, as it does in John 1:1c, and clearly is indefinite in meaning, "a Jew." Two verses later, he asks Jesus, "Are you a king (*basileus ei su*)?" Here is the exact same syntax as John 1:1 -- the predicate noun precedes the verb, the subject follows it, and the predicate noun lacks the definite article. Yet Pilate is asking if Jesus is "a king," not "the king." Jesus' answer in the same verse uses the same basic construction: "You say that I am a king (*su legeis hoti basileus eimi*)." As the story continues, the opponents of Jesus provide, through John's report, a basic lesson in the distinction between definite and indefinite constructions in Greek. Seeing the placard placed over the crucified Jesus, they tell Pilate: "Do not write '*The* king of the Jews,' but that this one said, 'I am *a* king of the Jews'" (John 19:21). They try to distance Jesus from the royal title by two moves: first by making it clear that it is merely a claim, and second by changing the title itself from "the king" (*ho basileus*) to "a king" (*basileus* without the article, before the be-verb).

There are several other examples skipped by Harner. In John 6:20 we see a sentence set up exactly like John 1:1c which even has *ho logos* (here meaning simply "the saying" or "the teaching") as the subject: *sklēros estin ho logos houtos*, "This word is a hard one (word-for-word: a hard one is the word this)." Notice how closely this resembles John 1:1c. The subject is *ho logos*, with the article, following the be-verb, just as in John 1:1c. The predicate noun precedes the verb, and lacks the article, just as in John 1:1c. In meaning, the predicate noun is indefinite. We know this both from its lack of a definite article, and from the larger contextual meaning of the sentence. The word Jesus has spoken is not the one-and-only difficult saying he ever uttered, but is one of them. In other words, it is *a* hard saying. So, in the same fashion, in John 1:1, the

Word is not the one-and-only God, but is *a* god, or divine being. I know that sounds strange and even seems impossible coming from the pen of a Christian writer. But the fact remains that that is what John wrote. His purpose in doing so was, at least in part, to avoid the notion that God the Father himself incarnated as Christ. The one who incarnated was somehow distinct from "God," while still being "a god."

John 4:24 provides another example of the same construction as John 1:1c, with the sole exception that the be-verb is omitted as unecessary: *pneuma ho theos*, "God (is) a spirit." Greek writers frequently omit the be-verb for succinctness, as John does here. If we supply the implied verb, we would have *pneuma estin ho theos* or *pneuma ho theos estin*. In either case, the subject is marked with the article, and the predicate noun appears before the verb without the article in a clearly *indefinite* sense. That "spirit" is indefinite here is confirmed by the context. In Jesus' address to the Samaritan woman, the meaning "God is *the* spirit" makes no sense at all, since there has been no identification or explanation of what "the spirit" could possibly be. Instead, he is using "spirit" to characterize God, to describe him as a spirit rather than a material being.

The properly indefinite translation "God is a spirit" is given by the KJV, AB, and NW. Both the KJV and the AB cloud matters by capitalizing Spirit as if it is a proper noun (the NAB does also). The NRSV, NIV, and NASB have "God is spirit," which seems to use "spirit" in the sense of a substance (like saying "The jar is pewter"). The latter meaning is in agreement with the indefinite sense found in the KJV, AB, and NW, and that agreement is confirmed by the fact that the NRSV, NIV and NASB do not capitalize "spirit." The NAB and TEV have "God is Spirit," capitalizing "spirit" as if it is a proper noun in this sentence, which it is not. To be a proper noun, the Greek word "spirit" would need to have the definite article, which it does not in John 4:24. The NAB and TEV translators make the same mistake in John 4:24 that they do in John 1:1, namely, changing a characterization into an identification.

This brings us back to John 1:1. Harner points out that if John had wanted to say "The Word was God," he could have written *ho logos ēn ho theos*. But he didn't. If he wanted to say "The Word was a god," he could have written *ho logos ēn theos*. But he didn't. Instead John took the anarthrous predicate noun and placed it before the verb, which to Harner suggests that John was not interested in definiteness or indefiniteness, but in character and quality. Nevertheless, Harner concludes, "There is no basis for regarding the predicate *theos* as definite," and "In John 1:1 I think that the qualitative force of the predicate is so prominent that the noun cannot be regarded as definite" (Harner 1973, pages 85 and 87). So, although Harner tries very hard to be deferential to Colwell and to not set up his article as a refutation of "Colwell's Rule," he recognizes in the end that the qualitative character of this kind of sentence precludes the definiteness of the noun. If Harner is right, then Colwell cannot be, and vice versa.

Harner rejects outright the renderings "the Word was God" (KJV, NASB, NAB, NRSV, NIV) and "He was the same as God" (TEV) as inaccurate translations of John 1:1c (Harner, page 87). He gives qualified approval to the translation "the Word was divine," at the same time offering other suggestions. I am comfortable with this translation as well, since it communicates in an English idiom what the original text says in a Greek idiom. What Harner calls the "qualitative" function of Greek predicate nouns, and what I call the Greek "expression of class" amounts basically to the same thing. A person who writes a sentence in this way is telling us that the subject belongs to the class or category represented by the predicate noun ("The car is a Volkswagen"). In English, we often accomplish the same thing by using what we call "predicate adjectives." We can say "John is a smart person," or we can say "John is smart." The latter is an example of a predicate adjective, and you can see that it means exactly the same thing as saying "John is a smart person." Both sentences place John in the category of smart persons, but one does it by using a noun phrase ("a smart person") and the other does it by using an adjective ("smart"). So if the meaning of "the Word was a god," or "the Word was a divine being" is that the Word belongs to the category of divine beings, then we could translate the phrase as "the Word was divine."[8] The meaning is the same in either case, and is summed up well by Harner as "*ho logos* ... had the nature of *theos*" (Harner, page 87).

When you compare the key clause of John 1:1 in the nine translations, you find that all but one of these translations give the word "god" a definite sense, even though the Greek word *theos* lacks the article necessary to make it definite. Surprisingly, only one, the NW, adheres to the literal meaning of the Greek, and translates "a god."

The translators of the KJV, NRSV, NIV, NAB, NASB, AB, TEV and LB all approached the text of John 1:1 already believing certain things about the Word, certain creedal simplifications of John's characterization of the Word, and made sure that the translation came out in accordance with their beliefs. Their bias was strengthened by the cultural dominance of the familiar KJV translation which, ringing in their ears, caused them to see "God" where John was speaking more subtly of "a god" or "a divine being." Ironically, some of these same scholars are quick to charge the NW translation with "doctrinal bias" for translating the verse literally, free of KJV influence, following the most obvious sense of the Greek.[9] It may very well be that the NW translators came to the task of translating John 1:1 with as much bias as the other translators did. It just so happens that their bias corresponds in this case to a more accurate translation of the Greek.

How can there be "a god" in the Bible?

The objection might be made that in the context of the Bible, there is only one God, and therefore any reference to *theos* must be to the one true God. But rather than assume limits on how the biblical authors used a word like *theos*, it is a better idea to actually look into the question and find out the facts.

The noun *theos* ("god") in the nominative ("subject") form is used two-hundred-ninety-eight times in the New Testament. In two-hundred-seventy-four of those occurrences, the definite article is used. The definite article specifies that the reference is to "the god," that is, "God," with three exceptions. In 2 Corinthians 4:4, Paul refers to "the god of this age," meaning Satan. In Philippians 3:19, he speaks of those for whom "the god is the belly" (one could arguably translate this as "God is the belly"). Acts 14:11 speaks of "the gods" in the plural, referring to the pantheon of Greco-Roman paganism. The exceptions show that "god" can be used in the New Testament as part of the jargon of the times in which it was written. The people around the early Christians spoke of "gods," and the New Testament authors used this language to communicate important ideas.

The large percentage of *theos* with the definite article compared to without the definite article is not particularly surprising. The New Testament is all about God, so naturally he is spoken about much more than any other "god." The large number also suggests that, despite all the variety of style and expression found among the books of the New Testament, there is a standard way to refer to God, namely, *ho theos*. This is true if "God" comes before or after the verb, whether it is first or last in the sentence. Variation in word order does not have much impact on this standard way to refer to God.

In only twenty-four of the two-hundred-ninety-eight uses of *theos* in the New Testament is the article absent. We will look at a selection of these to see why "a god" is used in the New Testament for particular purposes. In the examples that follow, the purpose for using "a god" is the same as in John 1:1, to characterize or categorize the subject of the sentence. The fact that the subject of most of these sentences is the being Christians call by the name "God" (but also "Lord," "Father," etc.) should not be allowed to obscure the fact that the writer is describing this being as a particular type of "god," or as playing the role of a "god" for someone, using the indefinite of quality, character, or class.

Luke 20:38 reads: "But he is not a god of the dead" (*theos de ouk estin nekrōn*). Notice that in this verse *theos* is before the verb (*estin*), just as it is in John 1:1. The article is missing not because of "Colwell's Rule," but because *theos* is indefinite. The implied question is: What kind of god is the Christian god? The answer is: He is not a god of the dead, but a god of the living. The word "god" is indefinite because it is speaking of a category to which the subject belongs. Because categories are indefinite, *theos* is written here without the article. The proper translation is "a god." The indefiniteness of "god" is proved by the parallel passage in Mark 12:27 (*ouk estin theos nekrōn*), where *theos* follows the verb, rather than preceding it as it does in Luke 20:38. In such a position, anarthrous *theos* must be indefinite.

How do our nine translations handle these two passages? In both passages the NW translates "a God." The KJV, similarly, has "a God" in Luke 20:28, but inconsistently "the God" in Mark 12:27. The NASB, NIV, AB, and TEV have "the God" (the LB is too transformed to compare) in both passages. The NRSV and NAB avoid the article entirely by using "He is God not of the dead" (NRSV) or "He is not God of the dead" (NAB). The NW is the most accurate translation of these two verses because it consistently adheres to the indefinite construction of the Greek, although it falls short of absolute accuracy by capitalizing "God" when it is not used as a proper noun. The other translations are less accurate than the NW because they obscure the descriptive, categorical use of the indefinite.

In 2 Corinthians 1:3, Paul refers to the Christian god (the being called "God") as "a god of every consolation" (*theos pasēs paraklēseōs*). He is characterizing the subject, and so uses the indefinite form of *theos* in the predicate. The question is once again: What kind of god is the Christian god? He is a god of every consolation. The KJV, NIV, NRSV,

AB, TEV, and NW have "the God." The NASB and NAB avoid using any article. The LB rewrites the passage entirely. None of the translations accurately convey the indefinite sense. It is possible that the translators were misled in this case by "Sharp's Rule."

In Revelation 21:7, God promises, "I will be a god to him, and he will be a son to me" (*esomai autō theos kai autos estai moi huios*). Since "god" (and "son") is a predicate nominative and follows the verb, it *must* be indefinite. God is characterizing the kind of relationship he will have with the one of whom he is speaking. How will that person relate to God? He will act towards him as to "a god" (in other words, will act toward him with worship and service). God, likewise, will act towards that one as towards "a son." Characterization is achieved through categorization, and "god" and "son" function here as such categories. Therefore, they are indefinite. All of the translations we are comparing are less than satisfactory. The KJV, NASB, NIV, NAB, TEV, LB, and NW read, "I will (NAB, NW: shall) be his God." The NRSV uses "their God" to avoid the male pronoun. The AB has "I will be God to him," which is a bit closer to the Greek, but still misses the indefinite expression.

In Philippians 2:13, Paul states, "For it is a god who is working in you" (*theos gar estin ho energōn en humin*). The implied question is: What sort of thing is working in/among us? Paul's answer is that it is not a human force, or a demonic one, but a divine one. He is stating the character of the experience, the category to which the agency acting in these peoples' lives belongs. Therefore the indefinite is used. But all of the translations miss this. The KJV, NASB, NIV, NRSV, and AB say, "It is God . . ." The NAB, TEV, LB, and NW have, "God is . . ."

The actions of the "Antichrist" in 2 Thessalonians culminate in chapter 2, verse 4, when he seats himself in the Temple and puts forward the claim "that he is a god" (*hoti estin theos*). The noun "god" is an anarthrous predicate nominative following the verb, and so can *only* be indefinite. The Antichrist claims (falsely) to belong to the "god" category of beings. The NW and NAB accurately translate "a god." The other translations erroneously translate "God."

Despite the failure of English translations to get these passages right, I hope you can see how the expression "a god" finds a home in the New Testament. One can speak of a class or category of things called "god." In his grammar, Smyth specifically cites "god" as an example of a noun that omits the article when used of a class (section 1129: "Words denoting persons, when they are used of a class, may omit the article.").

There are different types of "god" -- for example, a god of the living as opposed to a god of the dead. One can talk of someone being in the role of "a god" to someone else. In John 10:34, Jesus even quotes a passage from the Old Testament in which God tells the recipients of his commandments, "You are gods" (*theoi este*). The term clearly is used broadly, both of "true" gods and of "false" gods, and even of individuals who may be entitled to some characteristic associated with the popular notion of a "god," while not necessarily being fully "divine" by a stricter standard. This is all theoretical speech, the rhetoric of explanation used by the authors of the New Testament to help their readers understand new ideas.

Both Greek and English put the word "god" to dual use, sometimes as an indefinite common noun and sometimes as a definite proper noun. But while the Greek-speaking authors of the New Testament were very careful to keep the two uses always distinct through the use or non-use of the definite article, English-speaking translators of the Bible have hopelessly muddled the distinct uses by neglect of the indefinite article and careless use of the capital "G." These Christian translators, like their Jewish and Muslim counterparts, are used to thinking of only one member of the "god" category, and so "God" and "god" are interchangeable to them in most speech contexts. But the biblical authors could not assume such thinking in their readers, and so made careful use of the general category "god" as well as of the specific being "God" to explain to their readers important matters of belief. John 1:1c is one of the most significant examples of this explanatory effort, because it deals with the very crucial issue of how Christ can be so central to the Christian faith without violating the Christian commitment to monotheism.

What is the Word?
At the risk of lapsing into interpretation, I do not wish to leave the reader totally out to sea about the thinking and use of language that stands behind the accurate translation of John 1:1. Both the larger literary context of John 1:1, and its cultural environment, help us to understand John's language and so ensure and make sense of accurate translation. Only by not attending to John's overall characterization of Christ and his highly nuanced use of language is it possible to arrive at something as inaccurate as "the Word was God." The reader must keep in mind that when John says "God" he means "God the Father." The heavy concentration of "Father" and "Son" language in the gospel helps us to understand this.

In the immediate literary context, we see how carefully John differentiates between the Word and God (the Father). The Word is "with" or "near" God (the Father) (John 1:1-2). The Word becomes flesh and is seen; God (the Father) cannot be seen (John 1:18).

Some early Christians maintained their monotheism by believing that the one God simply took on a human form and came to earth -- in effect, God the Father was born and crucified as Jesus. They are entitled to their belief, but it cannot be derived legitimately from the Gospel according to John. John is not describing something like the Hindu concept of an *avatar*, such as when the god Vishnu is thought to periodically take a mortal form to accomplish things on earth. John is careful to say that what incarnates is the *logos*, something that was "with," "near," and "in the bosom" of God (the Father).

What then is the *logos* ("Word")? John says it was the agent through which God (the Father) made the world. He starts his gospel "In the beginning..." to remind us of Genesis 1. How does God create in Genesis? He speaks words that make things come into existence. So the Word is God's creative power and plan and activity. It is not God (the Father) himself, but it is not really something separate from God either. It occupies a kind of ambiguous status. That is why a monotheist like John can get away with calling it "a god" or "divine" without becoming a polytheist. This divine thing or being acts, takes on a kind of distinct identity, and in "becoming flesh" brings God's will and plan right down face to face with humans.

I am in basic agreement with Harner that *theos* in John 1:1 is used qualitatively. I think the best translation would be: "And the Word was divine." Goodspeed and Moffatt came to the same conclusion long ago. By placing *theos* first in a be-verb sentence, without the article, John is trying to stress that the Word has a divine character, or belongs to the class of divine things, however that is to be worked out technically. This divine Word proceeds to "become flesh" in the form of Jesus Christ.

John stresses this point because many of his readers were of the opinion that Jesus was *merely* the Messiah, that is, a specially chosen human being, exactly what the Jews expected their Messiah to be. Whatever the other New Testament authors intended, it was and is still possible to read their language about Christ in this more limited way. In the other three canonical gospels, for example, Jesus could be understood as a remarkable man "adopted" as God's son at the moment of baptism. The miraculous birth reported by Matthew and Luke was typical of ancient heroes, both in the Bible and outside of it, and would not in itself have promoted Jesus to divine status in the minds of the gospel readers. Paul could be read in a similar way, since he often emphasized that Jesus' obedient death and triumphant resurrection in some way justified his status as God's son (Romans 1:4; Philippians 2:9).

Throughout the Gospel according to John, the author takes pains to clarify the identity of Christ, to explain that only one who descends from heaven is able to ascend there, as Jesus does. John is leading his readers to what he regards as a new, more complete understanding of Jesus, and he has to work so hard at it, and choose his language so carefully, because it is something John is telling them for the first time. Starting from the accepted notion that Jesus is God's "son," John lays out a very careful elaboration of the common character, will, and nature that may be assumed between a father and a son. And if the father's nature is "divine," will not the son's be also?

When one says "the Word was divine" a qualitative statement is being made, as Harner suggests. The Word has the character appropriate to a divine being, in other words, it is assigned to the god category. Of course, once you make the move of saying the Word belongs to that category, you have to count up how many gods Christians are willing to have, and start to do some philosophical hair-splitting about what exactly you mean by "god." As Christians chewed on this problem in the decades and centuries after John, some of them developed the idea of the Trinity, and you can see how a line can be drawn from John 1:1 to the later Trinity explanation as a logical development. But John himself has not formulated a Trinity concept in his gospel. Instead, he uses more fluid, ambiguous, mystical language of oneness, without letting himself get held down to technical definitions.

To many modern Christians, living in their safe, homogenous world of like-minded believers, the issue seems straightforward. There is the one God, and on the other side of a great gulf are all of the creatures. But in John's world, the god-category was not as sharply distinguished as it is for modern Christians, and there were all kinds of beings occupying the gray area between God and mortals. There were various angels and demi-gods to consider. Not that the New Testament writers and other early Christians accepted the exact same definition of these categories as their non-Christian contemporaries and potential converts did. But in reaching out to this audience, one had to start with shared language and concepts, and build a new understanding from there. Indeed, in Paul's letters and the anonymous Letter to the Hebrews, these other beings are a big concern, as the Christian writers argue for Christ's superiority over them. Whatever these biblical authors knew to be true, they had to communicate it within the concepts of their audience as much as possible. You can move readers to new understandings and insights, but to do so you have to make contact at some point with something they already know or believe to be true. That is the challenge particularly of religious communication.

One being on the borderline between God and the rest of creation in ancient thinking was the *logos*, believed by certain Jews and Greeks alike to be the creative, ordering energy, thought, or speech by which the universe is made and sustained. John picks this already known concept as the key to explaining Jesus' super-human status and character. It was a brilliant choice, because the relation of the *logos* to God, according to those who discussed the concept among both Christian and non-Christian thinkers, is as close as can be without simply disappearing into God, and yet not so distinct as to alienate those committed to monotheism (for example, Philo, the Jewish philosopher from Alexandria who was a contemporary of Jesus and Paul). Christians still disagree about how to interpret John's language, and how to make it fit precise physical and philosophical categories of being. Some even question whether trying to make it fit something so technically precise is a worthwhile endeavor. But wherever these lines of interpretation go, it was John who took the first crucial step towards understanding Jesus to have a divine quality within him, which John identified with the ordering principle, the *logos*, of God.

A failure to grasp the nuance of John's thought can be seen in how several translations inappropriately introduce the male pronoun "he" into John 1:1-2. In John 1:1 both the TEV and LB use the pronoun "he" for "the Word" at some point to reduce the redundancy of John saying "the Word" three times. A similar substitution of "he" can be seen in John 1:2 in the NASB, NIV, NRSV, NAB, and the AB. In this case, "he" replaces *houtos*, "this one." By using "he" instead of "this one," all of these translations suggest that "the Word" is a male of some sort. The AB and the LB seem to reveal the erroneous thinking behind this translation choice, when they simply substitute "Christ" for "the Word." But the Word is not Christ in the Gospel according to John. The Word is a divine being intimately associated with God that at a point in time "becomes flesh," and only then, when the Word is flesh, can one say we are dealing with Christ.[10] The Word, as we have seen, is not really a "he." It is a divine being or agency that transcends human qualities. It becomes (or becomes a part of) a "he" by "becoming flesh" as, or in, Jesus Christ. Only the KJV and NW accurately maintain John's careful, non-personal language for the Word in this phase of its existence, before it "becomes flesh" and, in the process, becomes a "he."

I have no doubt that the wording of John 1:1 is careful and deliberate in its every detail. John was doing a very tricky thing: trying to express Jesus' exalted status without violating monotheism. This has been a challenging task throughout Christian history, and John was the first person to tackle it. I think we owe it to him, therefore, to stick as closely to his words as we can, and not contort them into something else.

Summing Up
Grammatically, John 1:1 is not a difficult verse to translate. It follows familiar, ordinary structures of Greek expression. A lexical ("interlinear") translation of the controversial clause would read: "And a god was the Word." A minimal literal ("formal equivalence") translation would rearrange the word order to match proper English expression: "And the Word was a god." The preponderance of evidence, from Greek grammar, from literary context, and from cultural environment, supports this translation, of which "the Word was divine" would be a slightly more polished variant carrying the same basic meaning. Both of these renderings are superior to the traditional translation which goes against these three key factors that guide accurate translation. The NASB, NIV, NRSV, and NAB follow the translation concocted by the KJV translators. This translation awaits a proper defense, since no obvious one emerges from Greek grammar, the literary context of John, or the cultural environment in which John is writing.

The AB, TEV, and LB are even further away form the original Greek than the KJV tradition. The AB reads, "the Word was God Himself." The LB, similarly, has "He . . . is himself God." There is no word in the original Greek of John 1:1 corresponding to "himself." The TEV offers, "he was the same as God." We find nothing in the original Greek from which "the same" could be derived. So these translators are even more cavalier with the Bible than the others. They seek to introduce elements that support their views about the relation of God to the Word. Ironically, by missing the basic fact that when John writes "God" ("The God") he means "God the Father," these translators dissolve the very Trinity they think they are supporting by translating in a way that eliminates the distinctiveness of the Word from God the Father -- a distinctiveness that John very carefully worked into his gospel alongside of statements suggesting intimacy and unity.

Bias has shaped most of these translations much more than has accurate attention to the wording of the Bible. The NW translation of John 1:1 is superior to that of the other eight translations we are comparing. I do not think it is the best possible translation for a modern English reader; but at least it breaks with the KJV tradition followed by all the others, and it does so in the right direction by paying attention to how Greek grammar and syntax actually work. No translation of John 1:1 that I can imagine is going to be perfectly clear and obvious in its meaning. John is subtle, and we do him no service by reducing his subtlety to crude simplicities. All that we can ask is that a translation be an accurate starting point for exposition and interpretation. Only the NW achieves that, as provocative as it sounds to the modern reader. The other translations cut off the exploration of the verse's meaning before it has even begun.

NOTES

1. Actually, "word" is a very inadequate translation of *logos* and, like many elements of the KJV translation that have dominated the English translation tradition, owes much more to the Latin *verbum* of the Vulgate than it does to the original Greek *logos*. I will have more to say about the meaning of *logos* later in this chapter.

2. The form used in John 1:1b and 1:2 is the "accusative" *ton theon*, which is the form used when a noun is the object of a preposition such as *pros* ("with" or "near").

3. Greek nouns change their form depending on how they are used in a sentence, and these distinct forms are called noun cases. The necessity of the definite article as a marker of definiteness varies from one noun case to another. If you wanted to say "of God," you would use the genitive ("of") form of the noun, which is *theou* rather than *theos*. In its genitive form, a definite noun doesn't necessarily need the article.

4. John 1:4: "The life was the light of humans." Both the subject and the object have the definite article, yet we know that "the life" is the subject because in the immediately preceding clause John was talking about "the life," not "the light." Compare John 6:63: "The spirit is the life-maker"; John 6:51: "The bread that I shall give is my flesh (word-for-word: the bread that I shall give the flesh of me is)"; John 15:1: "My father is the farmer (word-for-word: the father of me the farmer is)."

5. Based on the exceptions in the Gospel of John, Harner concludes: "The fact that John sometimes uses this type of clause supports the view that he did not necessarily regard an anarthrous predicate as definite simply because it precedes the verb" (Harner 1973, pages 82-83, note 19).

6. Luke 4:41; John 1:21; 6:51; 15:1; Romans 4:13; 1 Corinthians 9:1 and 2; 11:3; 11:25; 2 Corinthians 1:12; 3:2; 3:17; 2 Peter 1:17; Revelation 19:8; 20:14

7. Examples of pre-verb anarthrous predicate nominatives that do not have a qualitative function include John 9:16 ("And there was a schism among them."), and 1 Corinthians 8:4 ("There is no god except one."). Examples of anarthrous predicate nominatives after the verb with a qualitative function include Mark 9:35; Luke 20:33; John 4:18; John 18:13; Acts 10:36; 2 Thessalonians 2:4.

8. Another example from John would be 7:12: *agathos estin*. This sentence consists of an anarthrous predicate nominative before the be-verb, with a subject implied in the form of the verb, and can be translated either as "He is a good person," or "He is good."

9. An example of this is Orlinsky and Bratcher, page 210. Bratcher was the principal translator of the TEV.

10. What I have just explained is not some novel interpretation of the passage. It is, in fact, part of the orthodox, mainstream understanding within Christianity, what is known as the "Two-Nature Christology." The "Two-Nature" doctrine is not the only possible way to understand what John means by the Word becoming flesh. But that doctrine is in agreement with John in the idea that Jesus Christ does not pre-exist with God, rather the Word does.

TWELVE

THE SPIRIT WRIT LARGE

In the New Testament, we find the phrase "holy spirit" a total of eighty-seven times. The New Testament writers use this expression to speak about a definite, single entity that plays a dominant and multifaceted role in the life of the Christian community. It is obviously a key concept of the Bible. The terminology of the phrase "holy spirit," like all of the language employed in the New Testament, is drawn from a larger cultural context which helps modern translators and readers to understand the implicit and explicit significance of the concept.

The books of the New Testament were written by and for people who were much more accustomed to speak of "spirits" than we are today. The vocabulary of "spirit" was used broadly, and covered just about everything that occurred beyond the realm of the physical senses. Of course, we still speak of "spiritual" things, and still have expressions such as "the human spirit." But the relative rarity of such expressions in our daily speech skews our understanding of the biblical language of "spirit." Because we have effectively narrowed the range of "spirit" in our thinking, when compared to that of the New Testament world, we tend to run together in our mind the distinct things called "spirit" in the New Testament. This tendency collaborates with the historical development of Christian theology, which has over the centuries elaborated the idea of the Holy Spirit, and consolidated many references to "spirit" in the New

Testament within this idea. Later Christian theology also applied the technical status of a "person" on the Holy Spirit, which has lead modern translators and readers to think of the Holy Spirit in human terms as a "who," even a "he," rather than as an "it" that transcends human measures of personhood.

As a result of these conditions, many modern translators read the Holy Spirit into passages where it does not actually appear, verses where "spirit" is used to refer to other "spiritual" things. At the same time, they confine the Holy Spirit within human concepts of personhood by altering the meaning of Greek pronouns from neuter to masculine. The real danger here is that the Holy Spirit as it is actually found in the New Testament will be misunderstood and distorted by adding to it qualities it does not have and attributing to it acts that the biblical authors actually ascribe to other kinds of "spirit." It is essential that the New Testament texts be read with an understanding of their own manner of expression. It is the duty of translators to convey to modern readers the exact way in which the New Testament speaks of the Holy Spirit and other spirits, and not to distort the texts by reading into them biased interpretations rooted in our later position in history.

"The holy spirit"
In the eighty-seven occurrences of the phrase "holy spirit," it appears forty-two times with the definite article[1] and forty-five times without the definite article. As we have seen, the lack of a definite article with a noun normally means that it should be translated indefinitely ("a holy spirit"). But under certain grammatical conditions, the article may not be necessary to establish the definiteness of the "holy spirit." For example, in section 1128 of Smyth's grammar, we read, "The article is very often omitted in phrases containing a preposition." In other words, the absence of the definite article with a noun following a preposition is a regular feature of Greek grammar, and does not *necessarily* mean that the noun is indefinite.

The phrase "holy spirit" occurs in a prepositional phrase twenty-one times in the New Testament.[2] The article generally is not used in these phrases, and the few times it is can be explained by other rules of Greek grammar and syntax. In these examples, Smyth's "rule" that the article may be omitted from a noun preceded by a preposition without necessarily making the noun indefinite seems to apply. So we cannot assume that the lack of an article in these passages means that "holy spirit" is indefinite in them. It is more probable that the definite entity, "the holy spirit," is meant.

"Holy spirit" also appears in verbal phrases where characteristics of the verb may cause the article to be dropped. The expression "filled with holy spirit" occurs fourteen times in the New Testament.[3] The verb "fill" has objects in the genitive form, a form which does not need the article to establish definiteness as much as the nominative or accusative forms do.[4] The lack of the article in these cases does not necessarily make the expression indefinite.

So, even though in the eighty-seven occurrences of "holy spirit" it appears forty-five times without the definite article, we have found reason in thirty-two of those instances to accept a possible definite sense to the phrase. That leaves thirteen occurrences of "holy spirit" without the definite article.

In six of these remaining cases, because the phrase "holy spirit" is in the genitive ("of") or dative ("to") form, which can omit the article without *necessarily* becoming indefinite, we cannot say whether "holy spirit" is more likely to be definite or indefinite: Romans 15:13; 1 Thessalonians 1:6; Titus 3:5; Hebrews 2:4; 6:4; 1 Peter 1:12. In all six of these verses, the NW translates "holy spirit" indefinitely, while the other translations have "the holy spirit." Either translation is possible.

"a holy spirit"

We are left with seven cases where we can be fairly sure that "holy spirit" is used indefinitely. Most of these cases can be explained by the requirements of the narratives in which they appear. By playing with indefiniteness, the New Testament authors were able to convey the novelty of the "holy spirit" as it began to become known to people touched by the Christian mission.

Acts 8:15: . . . that they might receive a holy spirit (*pneuma hagion*).

Because the phrase is in the accusative form, the absence of the article suggests indefiniteness. The NW translation ("to get holy spirit") is indefinite in meaning, even though the indefinite article is not used. In this, as in the following cases, the NW seems to be employing the form of English expression used of material or substance ("The jar is pewter"), where the indefinite article is not used, just as several translations do in John 4:24 (mentioned in chapter eleven).[5] All other translations use the definite article in Acts 8:15, even though it is not found in the original

Greek.

Acts 8:17-19: Then they placed their hands upon them and they received a holy spirit (*pneuma hagion*). And when Simon saw that through the placement of the hands of the apostles the spirit (*to pneuma*) is given, he offered them money, saying, 'Give to me also this authority, so that on whomever I might place my hands they might receive a holy spirit (*pneuma hagion*).[6]

The missing article here makes the phrase indefinite. Here, too, the NW follows the Greek in not making "holy spirit" definite ("receive holy spirit"), although it doesn't actually use the indefinite article. The other translations again add the definite article.

Acts 10:38: Jesus of Nazareth, how God anointed him with/by a holy spirit (*pneumati hagiōi*) and power.

"Holy spirit" is coordinated with "power," and both terms are indefinite here. The NW has, accordingly, "anointed him with holy spirit." The other translations ignore the original Greek and add "the" to "holy spirit."

Acts 19:2: And he said to them, 'Did you receive a holy spirit (*pneuma hagion elabete*) when you believed? And they (said) to him, 'We have not even heard if there is a holy spirit (*pneuma hagion*).'

In this example, the first sentence involves "holy spirit" in the accusative form. The absence of the article suggests indefiniteness here. This suspicion is confirmed by the second occurrence of "holy spirit," this time with the verb "is," a combination (similar to that discussed in chapter eleven) that leaves no room for doubt that "holy spirit" is meant to be indefinite. So the NW has "receive holy spirit" and "a holy spirit." The other translations obey the rules of Greek grammar in the second sentence, and all print "a Holy Spirit." By having both the indefinite article and capitalized "Holy Spirit," they are entangled in a contradiction. How can the definite, singular "Holy Spirit" be indefinite? None of these translators seem to have noticed the contradiction built into their translations. In the first sentence they all add the definite article.

Luke 2:25: And a holy spirit was upon him (*kai pneuma ēn hagion ep'auton*).

As the subject of the verb "was," "spirit" would normally have the definite article. Therefore, the fact that it does not shows that the author wanted it to be understood in the generic, indefinite sense. The NW prints accordingly "and holy spirit was upon him." The other translations ignore the rules of Greek grammar and add the article "the."

Luke 11:13: The Father from heaven will give a holy spirit to those who ask him (*ho patēr ex ouranou dōsei pneuma hagion tois aitousin auton*).

If Luke meant a specific "holy spirit," he would have been obligated to use the definite article here. He does not. So the NW translates "will give holy spirit." The other translations add "the" without justification in the original Greek.

John 20:22: And when he had said this, he breathed on them and said to them, 'Receive a holy spirit (*labete pneuma hagion*).'

We would fully expect "holy spirit" to be definite here, but the Greek grammar does not cooperate. With an object in the accusative form, we are constrained to take "holy spirit" indefinitely. All translations other than the NW, of course, make it definite despite this grammatical obstacle.

According to the normal rules of Greek grammar, the most obvious translation of the phrases in these seven passages would be "a holy spirit." None of the translations we are comparing give that reading. Another possible way to translate these phrases would be the article-less English indefinite of substance: "holy spirit." This is the way the NW translators handle them. The other translation teams make a habit of changing the wording "a holy spirit" or "holy spirit" into "the Holy Spirit," apparently so uncomfortable with the indefiniteness of the expression that they sometimes stumble into the nonsensical "a Holy Spirit."

Which spirit?

English has three relative pronouns. The personal relative pronoun "who/whom" is used in reference to people. The impersonal relative pronoun "which" is used in reference to everything else: objects, animals, and so on. It is also used for forces, abstract principles, and so forth. The relative pronoun "that" is used in certain kinds of expressions in place of either "who/whom" or "which." In other words, "that" is a neutral relative pronoun that does not in itself indicate whether what is referred to is personal or impersonal.

Greek also has three relative pronouns.[7] But they do not directly correspond with the three English ones. Greek nouns have something called "gender." That is, some nouns are "masculine," some are "feminine," and some are "neuter." Greek has three forms of pronoun to match these three kinds of nouns. The pronoun *hos* is used of people and things the name of which is a "masculine" noun. The pronoun *hē*, likewise, is used of people and things named with a "feminine" noun. Finally, the pronoun *ho* is used of anything to which a "neuter" noun corresponds.

Now it turns out that both "masculine" and "feminine" Greek nouns can be used for impersonal things as well as persons. But "neuter" nouns are used only for impersonal things, such as objects, animals, forces, abstract principles, and so on. The same holds true for "masculine," "feminine," and "neuter" pronouns. Greek tends to use personal pronouns more than English does. Some things that would be handled with "which" in English, because they are not persons, are referred to with the equivalent of "who/whom" in Greek because the nouns that name them are either "masculine" or "feminine." But even though the "personal" category is larger in Greek than in English, the "Holy Spirit" is referred to by a "neuter" noun in Greek. Consequently, it is never spoken of with personal pronouns in Greek. It is a "which," not a "who." It is an "it," not a "he."

This is a case, then, where the importance of the principle of following the primary, ordinary, generally recognized meaning of the Greek when translating becomes clear. To take a word that everywhere else would be translated "which" or "that," and arbitrarily change it to "who" or "whom" when it happens to be used of "the holy spirit," is a kind of special pleading. In other words, it is a biased way to translate. And because this arbitrary change cannot be justified linguistically, it is also inaccurate.

In Acts 5:32 it is said, "We are witnesses of these things, and (so is) the holy spirit, which (*ho*) God has given to those who obey him." The NW has "which," the NAB uses "that." Both are accurate renderings of the relative pronoun *ho*. But the KJV, NASB, NIV, NRSV, and AB all change the word to "whom," the TEV and LB to "who," guided in this choice solely by a theological bias about the nature or character of the "Holy Spirit" that overrides accurate translation.

In Ephesians 4:30, Paul writes, "And do not cause grief to the holy spirit of God, by which you are sealed for a day of redemption." How do our translators handle the relative pronoun "which" in the phrase *en hōi*? The NRSV, NAB, and NW translate literally "with which"; the KJV offers "whereby." But the NASB, NIV, and AB change the expression to "by/with whom." The LB has "he is the one who." The TEV restructures the sentence to avoid the relative pronoun.

In 1 Corinthians 6:19, Paul asks "Don't you know that your body is a temple of the holy spirit in you, which you have from God?" The Greek relative pronoun is used here at the beginning of the clause "which you have from God." It appears in the genitive ("of") form because it refers back to "of the holy spirit," which is also in the genitive form. Both the personal, masculine relative pronoun *hos* ("who/whom") and the impersonal, neuter relative pronoun *ho* ("which") become *hou* in the genitive form, and that is the form that appears in 1 Corinthians 6:19: *hou*. For translators to decide whether to translate *hou* as "who/whom" or "which," they have to see whether the antecedent (the noun it refers back to) is masculine or neuter. The antecedent in this verse is *to hagion pneuma*, which is neuter. Therefore, the relative pronoun *hou* should be translated "which."

The KJV, NRSV, and NW, following sound rules of translation, print "which." The NASB, NIV, NAB, TEV, and AB use "who" or "whom" instead (the AB even capitalizes "Who"). There is no linguistic justification for doing this. Instead, these translators have allowed their bias towards a personal understanding of the "Holy Spirit" to override accurate translation. Some of them touch up the verse in other ways for the same reason. Paul says "the holy spirit in you." The NASB and NIV change this to "who is in you." Both the AB and TEV further personify by translating the Greek "in you" as "who lives inside/within you." The LB similarly adds "he lives within you." All of these changes are due to theological bias, since they have no foundation whatsoever in the Greek words of the biblical text.

In John 14:26, Jesus says, "But the defender (*paraklētos*) -- the holy spirit, which the Father will send in my name -- that one will teach you everything." Here a relative pronoun and a demonstrative pronoun are involved in the sentence. The demonstrative pronoun "that one" (*ekeinos*) refers back to the word "defender" (*paraklētos*), a masculine noun meaning a defense attorney or supporter, a role thought appropriate only for males in the male-dominated society in which the Greek language was formed. Since Greek grammar requires gender agreement between a pronoun and the noun it refers back to, "that one" is in the masculine form, like "defender." The relative pronoun "which" (*ho*) refers back to the phrase "holy spirit," which as always appears in the neuter form. So, the neuter pronoun "which" (*ho*) is used rather than the masculine form (*hos*).

In accordance with these details of the verse, the KJV and NW accurately have "which." Another legitimate option is to avoid making an issue of whether the "holy spirit" is an it or a s/he. So the NAB uses the universal relative pronoun "that," and the LB rephrases to avoid the relative pronoun altogether. But the NASB, NIV, NRSV, AB, and TEV employ the personal form "whom," which deliberately goes against the neuter gender of the original Greek. Their only reason for doing so is a theological bias in favor of their own belief in a personalized "Holy Spirit."

A similarly biased choice is made with respect to the demonstrative pronoun "that one." Demonstratives have the sole function of pointing to something. In themselves they carry no information other than identifying what previously mentioned thing is being talked about again. We see an accurate literal handling of this part of Greek speech in the NW's "that one"; but this comes across a bit stilted in English. The NIV and NRSV avoid this awkwardness by constructing the sentence in such a way as to make the demonstrative unnecessary. On the other hand, the KJV, NASB, NAB, AB, TEV, and LB change "that one" to "he" (the NASB and AB even capitalize "He"), adding a personalizing (and masculinizing) sense to the "holy spirit." In chapter six, I already discussed cases like this where a demonstrative pronoun should only be translated with "he" when the immediate context points to a specific male person as being the subject under discussion. In John 14:26, the subject under discussion is the -- neuter -- "holy spirit." Therefore, the use of the pronoun "he" is inappropriate here.

As always, it is not the theology of the translators to which I object, but the habit of imposing that theology on the biblical text. Their theological interpretation of the character of the Holy Spirit may be right. But it can only be right if it is based on an unbiased reading of the Bible, which is supposedly the authoritative source. With regard to the use of the relative pronoun when it refers to the "holy spirit," I would suggest using "that." Since this English relative pronoun is used of both persons and things, its use in translations of the New Testament would not foreclose the issue of the character of the "holy spirit," but would allow both personal and impersonal interpretations of it. The grammatical gender of the phrase suggests an impersonal interpretation, but the question cannot be settled by that fact alone. I think the evidence of the literary context is complex enough that we should replicate the Bible's own ambiguity about the "holy spirit" in English translations.

"Holy Spirit" or "holy spirit"?
At the time when the books of the New Testament were written, Greek writing did not distinguish between capital and small letters. The early biblical manuscripts are written entirely in what by later standards would be called capital letters. The original Greek manuscripts can give us no guidance about capitalization.

Therefore, the capitalization of certain words in the Bible is entirely a matter of convention, habit and tradition. The King James translators chose to capitalize certain words, such as personal names, formal titles, especially those used of God and Jesus, and a few theologically significant concepts, such as "Holy Ghost." Most modern translations simply have chosen to follow the standard set by the KJV. Some have expanded upon it, by capitalizing pronouns that refer to God or Jesus (the NASB and AB do this). Most have adopted the form "Holy Spirit" in place of the KJV's "Holy Ghost". The NAB translators departed from this tradition by deciding not to capitalize the adjective "holy" in the expression "holy Spirit." The NW has broken entirely with the KJV tradition by never capitalizing "holy spirit" or "spirit."

Since the original Greek does not dictate capitalization, one cannot fault these various capitalization programs. It is as perfectly legitimate to print "holy spirit" as it is to print "Holy Spirit." One can only demand consistency in the application of capitalization. Since the KJV program followed by most modern translations capitalizes "Spirit" only when a reference to the "Holy Spirit" is understood, any appearance of a capitalized "Spirit" implies "Holy Spirit." An issue of accuracy, therefore, is whether the original Greek suggests that the "Holy Spirit" is meant when the word "spirit" appears. The decision to capitalize "Spirit" when the reference is thought to be to the "Holy Spirit" gives license to the biased insertion of the "Holy Spirit" into dozens of passages of the Bible where it does not belong.

More than one spirit

The Greek word translated as "spirit" is *pneuma*, the most basic meaning of which is "wind," the movement of air. Wind is a force that we can feel, but cannot see or even really touch. So this was a good word to be applied to all areas of human experience that are not external and visible. Jesus makes use of this core meaning of the word in John 3:8: "The wind (*to pneuma*) blows where it wills, and you hear the sound of it, but do not know from where it comes and where it goes. So is everyone who has been born from the spirit (*tou pneumatos*)." It is quite clear that Jesus is making a spiritual point with a natural, mundane analogy. Jesus draws upon Nicodemus' experience of nature to help him understand what he is trying to tell him. Because the word *pneuma* means "wind" as well as "spirit" (the same is true of the Hebrew and/or Aramaic word Jesus might have employed in an actual conversation with Nicodemus), his analogy between the behavior of the wind and the behavior of one "born from spirit" works very well. Notice that it is impossible to translate *pneuma* the same way in both places in John 3:8 without losing the meaning of what Jesus is saying. You cannot just choose one definition out of the dictionary and use it every single time to translate a term. Context shifts the possible meaning of a term, and must be carefully considered when making a translation. All of the translations we are comparing translate the word as "wind" in the first occurrence, and "spirit" in the second. Most modern readers of these Bibles, however, have no idea how Jesus' explanation works in the original Greek, where the connection between "wind" and "spirit" is obvious. The NRSV and the NW add helpful footnotes to explain the connection.

All of the translations we are comparing show that their translators recognized the multiple uses of "spirit" in the New Testament. They all have several occurrences of "spirit" without capitalization. Among the many uses of "spirit" to be found in the New Testament are the following:

A. The breath or life-giving spirit, that which animates the body, for example:

James 2:26   For just as the body without a spirit (*chōris pneumatos*) is dead, so also faith without deeds is dead.
Matthew 27:50   And Jesus cried out again in a loud voice and gave up the

John 19:30	spirit (*to pneuma*). He bowed the head (and) delivered the spirit (*to pneuma*).

B. A person's individual spirit, his or her character and personality, one's private thoughts,[8] for example:

Matthew 26:41	The spirit (*to pneuma*) is willing, but the flesh is weak.
Luke 1:80	And the child grew and became strong in spirit (*ekrataiouto pneumati*).
John 11:33	He groaned in the spirit (*tō̄i pneumati*), and was disturbed.
John 13:21:	Jesus was disturbed in the spirit (*tō̄i pneumati*).

C. The spiritual domain of activity, the realm that transcends material reality, for example:

1 Peter 4:6	... so that they not only might be judged as humans are in flesh, but also might live as God does in spirit (*pneumati*).

In all the examples given above, the translations we are comparing accurately reflect the distinct meanings of "spirit" in the three categories. The formal equivalence translations use "spirit" without capitalization, and the dynamic equivalence translations frequently substitute phrases that convey the same idea without even using the word "spirit." But it is not difficult to find examples where each of the same translations show a misunderstanding of how the word "spirit" is being used. These misunderstandings are encouraged by theological bias that tends to read the Holy Spirit into the text.

Misunderstood references to "breath" or "life-spirit"

Because we don't use language of a "life-spirit" every day, and because the tendency of modern Christians is to think of only the one, "holy" spirit whenever "spirit" is mentioned, modern translators sometimes misunderstand that a New testament author is employing this idea of the individual's life-giving spirit. For example:

John 6:63:	The spirit (*to pneuma*) is that which gives life (*to zō̄iopoioun*); the flesh does not benefit anything. The words that I have spoken to you are spirit (*pneuma*) and life (*zōē*).

Starting with the basic idea that the breath/spirit is what gives life to a body, Jesus equates "spirit" with "life," and goes on to equate both of these with his words. His words are for the hearer like what "breath" and "life" are for the lifeless body. Jesus makes his point by an analogy that builds on the general understanding of "spirit" or breath as life-giving. The basic, unspecialized meaning of "spirit" in this verse is accurately translated by the KJV, NRSV, NAB, and NW, none of which capitalize "spirit."

The NASB, NIV, and AB, however, by capitalizing "Spirit" in the first part of the passage, show a misunderstanding of how "spirit" is being used by Jesus, and import into the passage the "Holy Spirit." The NASB and AB translators further alter the meaning of the original to suit their theology when they use the personal pronouns "who" to refer to the spirit, even though the original Greek uses the neuter ("it") article in the phrase "that which gives life" (*to zōopoioun*).

The TEV completely rewrites the verse, giving it a totally different meaning: "What gives life is God's Spirit; man's power is of no use at all. The words I have spoken to you bring God's life-giving Spirit." By this wording, the translator not only has introduced the "Holy Spirit" into a passage that has nothing to do with it, but also has interpreted Jesus' meaning in line with his own evangelical views about salvation, which may or may not be correct, but are not to be found in this verse. Jesus says that his words bring life; he says nothing specifically here about the role of the Holy Spirit in that process, nor that his words "bring" it.

The LB also changes the meaning of the verse: "Only the Holy Spirit gives eternal life. Those born only once, with physical birth, will never receive this gift. But now I have told you how to get this true spiritual gift." Where does the translator get all this? Not from the original words of the Gospel of John![9]

Misunderstood references to a person's own individual spirit
The habit of thinking of the Holy Spirit as the primary spirit presence in the New Testament causes some modern translators to substitute it for an individual's own personal spirit in passages they do not accurately understand.

> Romans 12:10-11: Those who are affectionate with brotherly love for each other, those who give preference in honor to each other, not lacking in zeal, fervent in the spirit (*tōi pneumati zeontes*),

serving the Lord.

Paul is describing the qualities he wants his readers to possess and develop. The verb *zeō* means to boil or bubble up. When used of a person, "boiling" means effervescent, energized, active. The English word "zest" comes from the related Greek noun (*zesis*) and adjective (*zestos*). So the phrase Paul uses here means to have a zestful character. The article functions as a possessive: "fervent in their spirit."

Several translations are literal: "fervent in spirit" (KJV, NASB, NAB); "ardent in spirit" (NRSV). The TEV, fulfilling in this case its stated intention of offering more modern, meaningful clarifications of culture-specific Greek expressions, proposes, "with a heart full of devotion."; the LB similarly offers the helpful "serve the Lord enthusiastically." The NIV suggests "keep your spiritual fervor," for which technically we would need a genitive rather than a dative form, but is in the general area of meaning. The NW and AB, however, bring the "Holy Spirit" into the verse by the translation "aglow with the Spirit." Even though the NW doesn't capitalize "spirit" as the AB does, this wording can only mean the same as it does in the AB. The AB also offers the variant: "burning with the Spirit." The translators of these two versions have not grasped that Paul is using "spirit" to speak of a person's own character and attitude.

Colossians 1:8:   . . . who also informed us of your love in spirit (*en pneumati*).

"Spirit" is used here, as it often is, to refer to the set of attitudes or personality traits a person has. The "spirits" of the Colossian Christians were characterized by love. On this foundation, Paul intends to build an accurate knowledge of the Christian faith, which he feels is still somewhat deficient among the Colossians. This is pretty straightforward stuff. Yet modern translations go out of their way to confuse things.

Most formulate something called "love in the Spirit" (KJV, NASB, NIV, NRSV, NAB, AB). I have to admit that I have no idea what that means. Does it mean that they love the Spirit? Or do they love in the Spirit, but not in other ways? Or do they experience love when possessed by the Spirit? So for help with this concept, I turn to the paraphrases. The TEV makes this sense of it: "He has told us of the love that the Spirit has given you." The LB, similarly, offers: "And he is the one who has told us about the great love for others which the Holy Spirit has given you." These are gallant attempts to make sense of *the other English translations*, but unfortunately they take great liberties with the original Greek, which has nothing in it to suggest that the "spirit" referred to has given anything. The love mentioned is *in* spirit, not given by it. The NW tries something completely different: "who also disclosed to us your love in a spiritual way." Is their love "in a spiritual way," or is the disclosure somehow delivered "in a spiritual way"? The translation is unclear, and in either case misses the mark.

Ephesians 6:18: By means of every prayer and petition, praying always in spirit (*en pneumati*)...

Paul is encouraging his audience to be in a constant state of prayer. He certainly does not mean that they should stop everything else in their lives and make vocal prayers unceasingly until they drop over from exhaustion and starvation. He is talking about prayerfulness within, mental prayers, made "in your spirit," not out loud.

The NW follows Paul's intent here: "carry on prayer on every occasion in spirit." The other major translations, through a bias that tempts their translators to see the specific "Holy Spirit" in most occurrences of the word "spirit," concoct something called "praying in the Spirit." The KJV, NASB, NIV, NRSV, NAB, and AB all use this interpretive form of the phrase, adding the definite article and a capital "S." The TEV goes further in this biased direction, by translating "Pray on every occasion as the Spirit leads." This is a highly interpretive rendering, following the tendency of the TEV to make the spirit the active subject of every passage where it appears, in line with the beliefs of the translator rather than the meaning of the Greek. The LB, similarly, provides the spirit with personality that is lacking in the original: "Pray all the time. Ask God for anything in line with the Holy Spirit's wishes." To be fully open with its readers, the LB should mark its additions: "in [line with the Holy] Spirit['s wishes]."

1 Corinthians 14:2: For the one who speaks in tongues is not speaking to people, but to God; for no one understands [literally, "hears"] (him), rather he speaks mysteries in spirit (*pneumati*).

Several translations understand that since Paul uses the phrase "in spirit" to refer to what goes on inside a person, it can have that meaning in this verse. The meaning of things spoken "in tongues" is locked up inside the speaker, and not revealed to those who can only hear the sounds. To help readers understand Paul's meaning that the "spirit" is the hidden inner realm of the human, the NASB and NIV add the possessive pronoun "his" to "spirit." The KJV and NAB leave the wording literal "in spirit" or "in the spirit."

The NIV translators seem to have argued among themselves about Paul's meaning, for a footnote gives the alternative "by the Spirit." The NRSV has "speaking mysteries in the Spirit." The AB chooses "in the Spirit he utters secret truths." The NW reads "speaks sacred secrets by the spirit." The TEV opts for "speaking secret truths by the power of the Spirit." And the LB offers the awkward "speaking by the power of the Spirit but it will all be a secret." So four translations capitalize "Spirit," implying the "Holy Spirit." The NW translation is ambiguous, since it gives agency to "the spirit," but does not capitalize "Spirit," so that we do not know if the word is meant to refer to person's own spirit or the "holy spirit."

While the above verse in isolation is somewhat ambiguous about what is meant by "spirit," the literary context proves that the spirit involved is one's own personal spirit. A few verses down the page, Paul comments further:

I Cor. 14:14-16:   If I pray in a tongue, my spirit (*to pneuma mou*) prays, but my mind is unfruitful. What is it then? I will pray in/by/with the spirit (*tōi pneumati*), and I will pray also in/by/with the mind; I will sing in/by/with the spirit (*tōi pneumati*) and I will sing also in/by/with the mind. Otherwise, if you say a blessing (only) in/by/with spirit (*pneumati*), how will the one occupying the place of the uninstructed speak the 'Amen' upon your thanksgiving, since he or she does not know what you are saying?"

As in 14:2, Paul treats speaking "in spirit" as something incomprehensible to an audience. What he adds here is the detail that what he means by "spirit" is a person's own spirit. In verse 14 he specifically says that when speaking in a tongue, his own spirit ("my spirit") is the one speaking, while his mind is unable to understand what the words mean. He then goes on to argue that useful prayer and song in the church is that produced by the spirit and mind working together, that is, a person's spiritual intuition must be connected to his or her conscious understanding.

In his references to "the spirit" (as well as "mind") in verse 15, then, Paul means the same as "my spirit" (and "my mind") in verse 14. When he switches to advice to his readers in verse 16, he means "your spirit." The definite article serves in both verses in place of the possessive pronoun. The NIV, AB, and TEV appropriately translate using "my" in verse 15, and the NIV and AB use "your" in verse 16. The KJV, NASB, NRSV, and NAB stick to the more woodenly literal "the." All of these translations accurately convey Paul's use of "spirit" here as meaning an individual's own spirit. The NW goes astray in this case. It has "my [gift of the] spirit" in verse 14, "the [gift of the] spirit" in verse 15, and "a [gift of the] spirit" in verse 16. This is not what Paul means, and the NW has slipped the "Holy Spirit" into the passage illegitimately. The parallelism with "mind" should have made it clear that the "Holy Spirit" is not meant here.

Misunderstood references to a spiritual domain of activity and reality
The habit of reading the Holy Spirit into references to spirit also finds its way into passages where "spirit" is used to refer to a level of reality.

1 Peter 3:18-19: Christ suffered once for sins, the righteous one for the unrighteous, so that he might lead you to God, put to death in flesh, but animated in spirit (*pneumati*), in which also he went and preached to the spirits (*tois pneumasin*) in prison.

The death of Jesus "in flesh" is contrasted to his ongoing existence "in spirit." In the latter state, he is said to have preached to imprisoned "spirits," which must be similarly disembodied dead, or else other kinds of spirit-beings. You could argue whether the expressions "in flesh" and "in spirit" refer to states of being (Jesus was put to death in his fleshly existence, and exists afterwards in spirit) or to the agents of "putting to death" or "giving life" (Jesus is put to death by flesh and given life by spirit). It would certainly have made sense to Peter's original audience for him to speak about someone being animated *by* spirit, since that is a basic role that the *pneuma* plays in ancient thought. But since the idea that Jesus was put to death *by* flesh is otherwise unknown, and since the two phrases are in exact parallel, it is most likely that "flesh" and "spirit" refer to physical and spiritual states of existence. This is supported also by verse 19, which begins with "in which," referring back to "in spirit," most easily understood as the state in which he visited the imprisoned spirits.

The NASB, NRSV, AB, and NW have "made alive in the spirit," while the NAB offers "brought to life in the spirit." The TEV has the equally acceptable "made alive spiritually," and the LB "his spirit lived on." All of these translations demonstrate their recognition that "in spirit" can refer to a state of existence. "In the spirit" can be accurately translated here as "in his spirit." On the other hand, the KJV has "quickened by the Spirit," and the NIV "made alive by the Spirit." Both break the parallelism between "flesh" and "spirit" and must be considered less likely to accurately reflect the meaning of the original Greek. The NIV translators also change the opening of verse 19 to "through whom" to support their introduction of the "Holy Spirit" (the NIV actually has the correct treatment of the passage in a footnote: "Or alive in the spirit, through which").

1 Timothy 3:16: He who was manifested in flesh, justified in spirit (*en pneumati*) . . .

The expression "justified in spirit" could mean either that his character ("spirit") was justified (in which case "spirit" has the basic meaning of a component of a person's identity), or that justification occurred in spiritual reality as opposed to the physical human court that condemned him. The NRSV adheres to Paul's language without tampering with its meaning ("vindicated in spirit"); so too does the NW ("declared righteous in spirit"). There is no reason to think that the "Holy Spirit" is involved in this passage. Was Christ justified in or by the Holy Spirit? The parallel that is drawn with "in flesh" rules such a reading out, unless someone wants to argue that Christ was manifested *by* the flesh, as if "the flesh" was some sort of entity. Nevertheless, we find "justified in the Spirit" (KJV), "vindicated in the Spirit" (NASB, NAB, AB), "vindicated by the Spirit" (NIV, NRSV footnote), "shown to be right by the Spirit" (TEV). The LB presents an interesting case, since on grammar alone it follows Paul exactly, agreeing with the NRSV and NW: "was proved spotless and pure in his Spirit." But by capitalizing "Spirit" it implies, despite the "his," not the personal "spirit" or character of Jesus in his human dimension, but the "Holy Spirit."

Ephesians 2:20-22: . . . Christ Jesus, by whom (the) whole assembled dwelling grows into a holy temple in (the) Lord, by whom also you are being constructed into a habitation of God in spirit (*en pneumati*).

This is the end of an elaborate simile in which Paul compares the Christian community to a building, with the apostles and prophets as the foundation, and Christ as the cornerstone. This language is symbolic and imaginative, not literal, of course. The Christian community is not literally a building. But it is like a building in that in can be inhabited. Just as gods were imagined to inhabit their temples in the Greco-Roman world, and God was imagined to inhabit the Jewish temple in Jerusalem, so God is described by Paul as inhabiting the metaphorical temple of the Christian community. This presence of God does not manifest itself physically, in the external realm of the senses, but spiritually, in the realm of the invisible. Thus, says Paul, you are becoming a habitation of God "in spirit." It is in the spiritual dimension that the individuals of the Christian community, even the widely scattered Christian communities, are knitted together like the blocks of a building; and it is within this physically invisible but spiritually real "building" that God is present, not as a statue or an ark or a visibly manifest form, but spiritually.

The NRSV translates Paul's meaning accurately as "in whom you also are built together spiritually into a dwelling place of God." A footnote gives the alternative "in the Spirit." Predictably, the other translations turn the phrase "in spirit" into a technical, literal reference to the "Holy Spirit." The NASB has "a dwelling of God in the Spirit," the NAB "a dwelling place of God in the Spirit," and the AB "a fixed abode of God in the Spirit." Without the capital "S" these translations seem fairly literal; but by adding the capital "S," they imply the "Holy Spirit," changing the meaning of the passage.

Since the Greek preposition *en* can mean "by" as well as "in," other translations see the "spirit" as the means, instrument, or agent by which God dwells in the community, or else by which the community is formed into a dwelling for God (although Paul actually says that Jesus performs this function). So the KJV translates "an habitation of God through the Spirit." The NIV reads, a little more freely, "a dwelling in which God lives by his Spirit"; and the TEV, similarly, has "a place where God lives through his Spirit." The NW understands the verse as "a place for God to inhabit by spirit," which while not capitalizing "spirit" still understands it as the means or agent of God's habitation, rather than the dimension of that habitation's reality. The LB totally reworks the verse, replacing the centrality of Jesus in it by the "Spirit": "And you also are joined with him and with each other by the Spirit, and are part of this dwelling place of God."

John 4:23-24: But an hour is coming, and now is, when the true worshipers shall worship the Father in spirit and truth (*en pneumati kai alētheiai*) . . . God (is) a spirit (*pneuma ho theos*), and the ones who worship him must worship him in spirit and truth (*en pneumati kai alētheiai*).

To worship "in spirit" seems to mean to worship "spiritually," just as to worship "in truth," means to worship "truly." There is no apparent reference to the "Holy Spirit," and this is understood by the KJV, NASB, NIV, NRSV, AB, and NW. Yet the NAB capitalizes "Spirit" in both occurrences of the expression "in spirit."

The TEV creates an elaborate personification out of the word "spirit," and reads here: "But the time is coming and is already here, when by the power of God's Spirit people will worship the Father as he really is . . . God is Spirit, and only by the power of his Spirit can people worship him as he really is." First of all, the passage says nothing about worshipping "by the power" of spirit, let alone by the power of "God's Spirit." Second, if "in truth" is understood as "as he really is," then similarly "in spirit" should be treated as having to do with the *mode* of worship, something done "in a spiritual way." The TEV's inconsistencies are all based in the theological bias of the translator, which has caused him to ignore the meaning of Jesus' words and substitute in their place a meaning in which he is more interested.

The LB, although extremely paraphrastic, starts out with the right understanding of the phrase "in spirit": "For it's not where we worship that counts, but how we worship -- is our worship spiritual and real?" But then, inevitably, something is added: "Do we have the Holy Spirit's help? For God is Spirit, and we must have his help to worship as we should." The original passage says nothing about either the Holy Spirit's or God's help. It says how one must worship for it to be acceptable or appropriate to the worship of God. The LB has completely changed the meaning of the passage. I have already discussed the clause "God (is) a spirit" in chapter eleven.

Inspired spirits

It is part of the thought-world of the New Testament, as it was of the society and culture in which it was written, to believe that external spirits can enter into a human being and take over the thoughts and behaviors of the individual. This idea, of course, is essential to the whole concept of the Holy Spirit. But that does not mean that the Holy Spirit is necessarily involved every time one speaks of an inspiring spirit. Needless to say, all of the negative, "evil," "unclean," or "foul" spirits mentioned in the New Testament are the very antithesis of the Holy Spirit. But even on the positive side of these phenomena, the category of spirit is more complex in the New Testament than it has become in later Christian interpretation.

According to 1 Corinthians 15:45, Jesus becomes a "life-giving spirit," an image that draws on the same basic meaning of *pneuma* we have seen underlying all applications of the word. Other examples of spirits with important positive attributes are: "the spirit of truth" (John 14:17; John 15:26; John 16:13; 1 John 4:6), in other words, the force that enables Christians to know rightly; "the spirit of life" (Romans 8:2; Revelation 11:11), in other words, the force that preserves Christians through death towards the promise of immortality; "the spirit of grace" (Hebrews 10:29), in other words, the force of God's generosity that enables Christians to live free of their past sinfulness; "the spirit of glory" (1 Peter 4:14), in other words, the force that points towards the manifestation of God in final triumph.

As I have mentioned, the trend in the history of Christian theology has been to consolidate all of these references to spirit within the concept of the Holy Spirit. But it would be rash to impose the result of this interpretive development onto the source documents of the Christian faith. One cannot assume that every positive spiritual force mentioned in the Bible is the Holy Spirit.

Perhaps the best known example of this kind of positive bestowed spirit is that given to prophets enabling them to know things others do not, something for which we still use the word "inspiration," that is, having something blown into you.

Rev. 22:6: the Lord, the God of the spirits of the prophets (*ho kurios ho theos tōn pneumatōn tōn prophētōn*)

With God as their source, these spirits are certainly positive. The "spirits" spoken of are the individual inspirations which prompted the prophets to speak. The NW translators have opted for a dynamic equivalence approach to this verse: "the God of the inspired expressions of the prophets." This is an accurate dynamic equivalent of what the Greek has, but shifts the emphasis ever so slightly from the spirits to what the spirits produce. The LB works along the same lines in offering "God, who tells his prophets what the future holds"; but "what the future holds" somewhat oversimplifies what prophets speak about. Other translations are rather straightforward and literal, showing a recognition of "spirit" being used as the multiple individual bestowals of inspiration God gives. But the translator of the TEV apparently was troubled by the suggestion that there are multiple spirits rather than one single Spirit. So he substituted "God, who gives his Spirit to the prophets," misleadingly introducing the "Holy Spirit" where it does not belong.

Of course, the claim to be a prophet, or to be inspired by the positive sort of spirit, can be made by anyone. The Bible wisely counsels that such claims be examined and tested. This important subject is taken up in 1 John 4:1-6, and this passage provides another example of how the Bible's own language of inspiring spirits is disturbing to some modern translators.

Since the KJV translation of 1 John 4:1-3, and 6 has been followed closely by the NASB, NIV, NAB, NRSV, and AB, I will give just the KJV:

> Beloved, believe not every spirit (*panti pneumati*), but try the spirits (*ta pneumata*) whether they are of God . . . Hereby know ye the Spirit of God (*to pneuma tou theou*): Every spirit (*pan pneuma*) that confesses that Jesus Christ is come in the flesh is of God: and every spirit (*pan pneuma*) that confesseth not that Jesus Christ is come of the flesh is not of God: and this is that *spirit* of antichrist . . . Hereby know we the spirit of truth (*to pneuma tēs alētheias*), and the spirit of error (*to pneuma tēs planēs*).

The key to an accurate translation is the sentence "Every spirit that . . . is of God." John clearly is speaking of many individual inspirations ("every spirit"), and categorizing them as either "of God" or "of antichrist." John says, test the spirits to see if they are from God. He then switches to the singular simply because he now takes up the individual case: this is how you know that the spirit under consideration is of or from God. This is a quite ordinary rhetorical shift, and should not lead us in this particular passage to read the singular Holy Spirit in a passage that speaks of spirits -- even of spirits of or from God -- in the plural. There is certainly nothing wrong with a Christian reader who believes that the Holy Spirit is at the root of all individual "spirits" of inspiration to apply this passage to his or her broader understanding of exactly how God inspires people. Such an added interpretation comes out of the Bible, and does not have to be written into the Bible illegitimately.

Yet all of the translations that follow the KJV slip the Holy Spirit into the text by capitalizing "Spirit of God." There is every reason to believe in this context that "the spirit of God" is a typical Greek genitive construction with the genitive phrase "of God" functioning like an adjective, with the result that the phrase should be read "divine spirit." This same "divine spirit" is then identified with "the spirit of truth," that is (using the same genitive construction) "true spirit" (also capitalized by the NIV and AB), as opposed to the spirit "of antichrist" or "of error." Because the passage speaks of "every spirit that confesses . . . Christ," in the plural, the singular (Holy) Spirit does not fit the context.

The NW gets around the problem of the plural expression of the passage, rightly or wrongly, by using the dynamic equivalent "inspired expressions," so as not to imply a multitude of spirits, but rather a multitude of what one spirit inspires:

> Beloved ones, do not believe every inspired expression [note: Lit., "spirit"], but test the inspired expressions [note: Or, "test the spirits." Lit., "be you proving the spirits."] to see whether they originate with God . . . You gain the knowledge of the inspired expression from God by this: Every inspired expression that confesses Jesus Christ as having come in the flesh originates with God, but every inspired expression that does not confess Jesus does not originate with God. Furthermore, this is the antichrist's [inspired expression] which you have heard was coming . . . This is how we take note of the inspired expression of truth and the inspired expression of error.

The LB follows a similar tactic by employing the term "message" instead of "spirit":

> Dearly loved friends, don't always believe everything you hear just because someone says it is a message from God: test it first to see if it really is . . . and the way to find out if their message is from the Holy Spirit is to ask: Does it really agree that Jesus Christ, God's Son, actually became man with a human body? If so, then the message is from God. If not, the message is not from God . . . That is another way to know whether a message is really from God . . .

Both the NW and the LB transfer the reference of these verses from inspiration itself to the vocal expression of inspiration. To a certain degree, this shift is accurate (as a dynamic equivalent) because John is indeed talking about people speaking at the prompting of inspiration. John even applies a verbal test: it is the content of what is said that determines the character of the inspiration. On the other hand, John chooses to focus on the inspiration itself by the language of "spirits" he uses, and translators should be careful of shifting emphasis to a different place than that of the biblical text itself. The shift involved in these two versions causes the reader to lose track of the belief in "spirits" which was fundamental to the New Testament writers and to the people around them.

Finally, we have the TEV, which we have seen being the most aggressive in reworking passages that refer to "spirit" in an effort to make them conform to the translator's beliefs about the role of the Holy Spirit. The same tendency holds true for the TEV handling of this passage:

> My dear friends, do not believe all who claim to have the Spirit, but test them to find out if the spirit they have comes from God . . . This is how you will be able to know whether it is God's Spirit: anyone who acknowledges that Jesus Christ came as a human being has the Spirit who comes from God. But anyone who denies this about Jesus does not have the Spirit from God. The spirit that he has is from the Enemy of Christ . . . This, then, is how we can tell the difference between the Spirit of truth and the spirit of error.

In the TEV, every positive reference to a spirit becomes "Spirit," implying the one and only Holy Spirit, no less than five times. It furthers this false specification of the spirit by changing John's wording dramatically, so that "do not trust every spirit" becomes "do not believe all who claim to have the Spirit." There is nothing in John's wording to suggest that people are claiming to have "the Spirit"; rather, he is instructing people how to distinguish one kind of spirit people display from another. The TEV goes even further away from the Greek by personifying the spirit as a "who" even though "every spirit" is expressed in the Greek neuter, so that it is clearly treated as an "it," not a "who." This, too, moves the passage closer to the translator's preconceptions about what the Holy Spirit should be in the Bible.

The TEV engages in extremely tendentious interpretation by reading "anyone who acknowledges that Jesus Christ came as a human being has the Spirit who comes from God." This change conforms to the translator's evangelical beliefs about determinism and the necessity of the Holy Spirit to enable people to believe in Christ.[10] Regardless of whether this particular brand of Christianity is right or wrong, it should not be worked into the text of the Bible where it is not to be found in the original wording of the biblical authors.

But the TEV does not stop there. It transforms a focused discussion of judging between different kinds of inspiration into a sweeping judgment of the people of the earth. The spirits of inspiration with which John is concerned become in the TEV "anyone," inspired or not. The TEV goes on ominously to say, "But anyone who denies this about Jesus does not have the Spirit from God. The spirit that he has is from the Enemy of Christ." By departing from the sense of the original Greek and over-generalizing the subject of the sentences, the TEV makes John say, in effect, that anyone who does not confess Jesus is possessed by the devil. The TEV's translator has been at the very least careless in his handling of this passage and, in my opinion, has displayed a lack of integrity in his role as a mediator of the biblical text to the reader.

Conclusion

As long as this chapter is, I have covered only a fraction of the occurrences of "spirit" in the New Testament. But I hope I have demonstrated that close attention to grammar, syntax, literary context, and cultural environment is necessary to figure out exactly how the word is used in a specific verse. Sometimes, even with all of this information, we cannot be sure. But the most important thing in all cases is to be cautious about oversimplifying "spirit" and assuming that the word always refers to the "holy spirit."

In our survey of the use of "spirit" in the New Testament, we

THE SPIRIT WRIT LARGE

have found no translation that heeds grammar, syntax, literary context, and cultural environment with complete consistency. The translators of all of the versions we are comparing allowed theological bias to interfere with their accuracy. At one point or another, they all imported the "Holy Spirit" into passages where "spirit" is being used in a different sense. The TEV and LB are easily the worst in this department, offering free interpretation in place of translation. The NIV is not far behind in this offense. I am sure we are all pleased to know the opinions of the editors of these versions concerning the role of the Holy Spirit in the Bible. But these opinions should not masquerade as Bible translations.

NOTES

1. The definite expression translated "the holy spirit" in English Bibles appears in two distinct forms in the original Greek. There are thirty occurrences of *to pneuma to hagion* (Matthew 12:32; Mark 3:29; 12:36; 13:11; Luke 2:26; 3:22; 10:21; John 14:26; Acts 1:16; 2:33; 5:3; 5:32; 7:51; 10:44; 10:47; 11:15; 13:2; 15:8; 15:28; 19:6; 20:23; 20:28; 21:11; 28:25; Ephesians 1:13; 4:30; 1 Thessalonians 4:8; Hebrews 3:7; 9:8; 10:15), and twelve of *to pneuma hagion* or *to hagion pneuma* (Matthew 28:19; Luke 12:10; 12:12; Acts 1:8; 2:38; 4:31; 9:31; 10:45; 13:4; 16:6; 1 Corinthians 6:19; 2 Corinthians 13:13 [in some Bibles, 13:14]). There is no significant difference in meaning between these two forms of the expression, and no reason to distinguish them in English. We can observe these two forms used interchangeably, and with no apparent shift in meaning, in the parallel passages Matthew 12:32, Mark 3:29, and Luke 12:10.

2. Matthew 1:18; 1:20; 3:11; Mark 1:8; Luke 3:16; John 1:33; Acts 1:2; 1:5; 11:16; 13:4; 16:6; Romans 5:5; 9:1; 14:17; 15:16; 1 Corinthians 12:3; 2 Corinthians 6:6; 1 Thessalonians 1:5; 2 Timothy 1:14; Jude 20; and 2 Peter 1:21.

3. Luke 1:15; 1:35; 1:41; 1:67; 4:1; Acts 2:4; 4:8; 4:31; 6:5; 7:55; 9:17; 11:24; 13:9; 13:52.

4. In only one case (Acts 4:31) is the article used, and this can be explained as a case where the adjective "holy" has been placed in a position where the added article helps to link it clearly to the noun "spirit" for the reader.

5. My thanks to David Brakke for clarifying this usage for me (personal communication).

6. The use of the article in verse 18 is to be expected in this passage, because it serves to convey "the spirit just mentioned," "that spirit."

7. Technically, it has three forms of the same pronoun, just as "who" and "which" are technically two forms of the same pronoun in English.

8. The New Testament is full of occurrences of "spirit" with the possessive pronoun that reflect this idea of an individual's personal spirit: "my spirit" (Matthew 12:18; Luke 1:47; 23:46; Acts 2:17-18; 7:59; Romans 1:9; 1 Corinthians 5:4; 14:14; 16:18; 2 Corinthians 2:13), "your spirit" (1 Corinthians 6:20; Galatians 6:18; 1 Thessalonians 5:23; 2 Timothy 4:22; Philemon 25), "his spirit" (Mark 2:8; Mark 8:12; Acts 17:16; Romans 8:11 [twice]; 1 Corinthians 2:10; 2 Corinthians 7:13; Ephesians 3:16; 1 John 4:13), "her spirit" (Luke 8:55), "our spirit" (Romans 8:16).

9. The translator of the LB reveals that he is not even looking at the original Greek when he adds a footnote to the first part of the verse that says, "Literally, 'It is the Spirit who quickens.'" "Quickens" is not a literal translation of $z\bar{o}opoie\bar{o}$, but it just happens to be how the KJV translates the word, which is where the LB gets it.

10. What the translator actually has done is read an *interpretation* of another verse, 1 Corinthians 12:3 (which actually uses the indefinite "a holy spirit"), into 1 John 4. By running the two passages together in his mind, and conforming them to a particular evangelical reading, he weaves his beliefs into the text of the Bible in multiple places, making his beliefs seem well-supported.

THIRTEEN

A FINAL WORD

In the early part of this book, as I introduced the various translations we would be comparing, I raised questions about the kind of assumptions we might tend to bring to our exploration of accuracy and bias in Bible translating. It is natural, I think, for people to assume that translations produced by individuals, or by members of a single religious group, would be more prone to bias than translations made by large teams of translators representing a broad spectrum of belief. By providing some details about the origins of the various translations, I made it clear that every translation has been created by vested interests, and that none of the translations represent the ideal of a scholarly, neutral project.

In some ways, our natural assumptions have been proven correct. The TEV, LB, and AB, all mostly the work of single authors, have been shown over and over again to be extremely tendentious, interpretive, and biased translations. But so has the NIV, the work of a quite large team of translators representing many different denominations. Even the NRSV, which deserves credit for reaching out to a very broad spectrum of interests, has turned out to have quite a few blind spots of its own.

But our assumptions also have been challenged. Translations produced by single denominations can and do defy our expectations of bias. Let's review the outcome of our investigation.

In chapter Four, we saw that the NW and NAB handle the Greek word *proskuneō* most consistently, accurately translating it as "give homage" or "do obeisance" rather than switching to "worship" when Jesus is the recipient of the gesture.

In chapter Five, the NW was shown to have the most accurate translation of *harpagmos*, offering "seizure" consistent with its handling of other words derived from the verb *harpazō*. The NAB and NASB offer the acceptable "grasp." None of these three translations deviate from the accurate meaning of *morphē* ("form"). But the other translators altered one or other of these words to make the passage more palatable to their views.

In chapter Six, the NAB and NRSV (with the TEV not too far behind) emerged as the most conscientious translations when it comes to avoiding the inherent male bias of many habits of English, allowing the more gender-neutral characteristics of the original Greek to come through. They even go a bit further to remove some of male bias to be found also in Greek, when such removal does not alter the basic meaning of a passage.

In chapter Seven, it could be seen that the NW, NAB, KJV, and NASB refrain from adding material to Colossians 1:15-20 that changes its meaning or interprets its ambiguities. The other translations, which (along with the NAB) do not indicate additions to the text in any way, slip interpretations and glosses into the text.

In chapters Eight and Nine, no translation could be judged inaccurate, since either way of translating the passages is possible. But the weight of probability in chapter Nine favored the NW's way of handling the verse discussed there.

In chapter Ten, it was revealed that only the NW and LB render the verbal expression *egō eimi* into a coherent part of its larger context in John 8:58, accurately following the Greek idiom. The other translations distort the obvious sense of the verb under the influence of an unfortunate interpretive mistake.

In chapter Eleven, I demonstrated at length that only the NW adheres exactly to the literal meaning of the Greek clause *theos ēn ho logos* in John 1:1. The other translations have followed an interpretive tradition that ignores the nuance in John's choice of expression.

In chapter Twelve, no translation emerged with a perfectly consistent and accurate handling of the many uses and nuances of "spirit" and "holy spirit." The NW scored highest in using correct impersonal forms of the relative and demonstrative pronouns consistently with the neuter noun "holy spirit," and in adhering to the indefinite expression "holy spirit" in those few instances when it was used by the biblical authors. Avoidance of reading the "holy spirit" into passages where "spirit" is used in other ways was managed best, if imperfectly, by the NW, NAB, NRSV, NASB, and KJV.

While it is difficult to quantify this sort of analysis, it can be said that the NW emerges as the most accurate of the translations compared. Holding a close second to the NW in its accuracy, judging by the passages we have looked at, is the NAB. Both of these are translations produced by single denominations of Christianity. Despite their distinctive doctrinal commitments, the translators managed to produce works relatively more accurate and less biased than the translations produced by multi-denominational teams, as well as those produced by single individuals.

I have pondered why these two translations, of all those considered, turned out to be the least biased. I don't know the answer for certain. The reason might be different in each case. But, at the risk of greatly oversimplifying things, I think one common element the two denominations behind these translations share is their freedom from what I call the Protestant's Burden. By coining this phrase, I don't mean to be critical of Protestantism. After all, without Protestantism, we might never have had that demand for direct access to the Bible that restarted the whole enterprise of Bible translation after it had been suppressed by the Catholic Church. I use this expression simply to make an observation about one aspect of Protestantism that puts added pressure on translators from its ranks.

You see, Protestant forms of Christianity, following the motto of *sola scriptura*, insist that all legitimate Christian beliefs (and practices) must be found in, or at least based on, the Bible. That's a very clear and admirable principle. The problem is that Protestant Christianity was not born in a historical vacuum, and does not go back directly to the time that the Bible was written. Protestantism was and is a *reformation* of an already fully developed form of Christianity: Catholicism. When the Protestant Reformation occurred just five hundred years ago, it did not re-invent Christianity from scratch, but carried over many of the doctrines that had developed within Catholicism over the course of the previous thousand years and more. In this sense, one might argue that the Protestant Reformation is incomplete, that it did not fully realize the high ideals that were set for it.

For the doctrines that Protestantism inherited to be considered true, they had to be found in the Bible. And precisely because they were considered true already, there was and is tremendous pressure to read those truths back into the Bible, whether or not they are actually there. Translation and interpretation are seen as working hand in hand, and as practically indistinguishable, because Protestant Christians don't like to imagine themselves building too much beyond what the Bible spells out for itself. So even if most if not all of the ideas and concepts held by modern Protestant Christians can be found, at least implied, somewhere in the Bible, there is a pressure (conscious or unconscious) to build up those ideas and concepts within the biblical text, to paraphrase or expand on what the Bible does say in the direction of what modern readers want and need it to say.

Catholicism, while generally committed to the idea that what the Church believes can be proven by and is grounded in the Bible, maintains the view that Christian doctrine was developed, or brought to more precise clarity on key points, by the work of theologians over time. It is not necessary, from the Catholic point of view, to find every doctrine or practice explicitly spelled out in the Bible. If it is, so much the better. But if it is not, the authority of the Catholic Church as an institution is sufficient in itself to establish it as true. So there is, in principle, greater liberty to let the Bible say as much as it does, without the pressure to read into it all the other things Christians believe to be true.

I am neither commending nor condemning the Catholic position on the complementarity of scripture and tradition. I merely point to it as a possible explanation for what I observe in the Catholic translation of the New Testament. The distinction between translation and interpretation is more strongly maintained here, because the Catholic Church accepts the idea that beliefs and practices transmitted by the Church independent of the Bible work with what the Bible reveals to form a greater whole. This may be a contributing reason why the NAB is a relatively less biased translation than many of the versions produced even by large interdenominational Protestant translation teams.

The Jehovah's Witnesses, on the other hand, are more similar to the Protestants in their view that the Bible alone must be the source of truth in its every detail. So you might expect translators from this sect to labor under the Protestant Burden. But they do not for the simple reason that the Jehovah's Witness movement was and is a more radical break with the dominant Christian tradition of the previous millennium than most kinds of Protestantism. This movement has, unlike the Protestant

Reformation, really sought to re-invent Christianity from scratch. Whether you regard that as a good or a bad thing, you can probably understand that it resulted in the Jehovah's Witnesses approaching the Bible with a kind of innocence, and building their system of belief and practice from the raw material of the Bible without predetermining what was to be found there. Some critics, of course, would say that the results of this process can be naive. But for Bible translation, at least, it has meant a fresh approach to the text, with far less presumption than that found in many of the Protestant translations.

Since the Jehovah's Witnesses are well outside of the Christian mainstream, the impression among the general public, and among several important biblical scholars, is that the differences of the NW from other translations are due to the peculiar ideas and biases of the Witnesses. I have identified a handful of examples of bias in the NW, where in my opinion accuracy was impaired by the commitments of the translators. But the biases of the NW translators do not account for most of the differences of the NW from the other translations. Most of the differences are due to the greater accuracy of the NW as a literal, conservative translation of the original expressions of the New Testament writers.

The NW and NAB are not bias free, and they are not perfect translations. But they are remarkably good translations, better by far than the deeply flawed TEV, certainly better as a translation than the LB and AB, which are not really translations at all, consistently better than the heavily biased NIV, often better than the compromised NRSV.

I could only consider a small number of samples in this book. Another set of samples might yield some different configuration of results. But the selection of passages has not been arbitrary. It has been driven mostly by an idea of where one is most likely to find bias, namely, those passages which are frequently cited as having great theological importance, the verses that are claimed as key foundations for the commitments of belief held by the very people making the translations. Choosing precisely those passages where theology has most at stake might seem deliberately provocative and controversial. But that is exactly where bias is most likely to interfere with translation. Biblical passages that make statements about the nature and character of Jesus or the Holy Spirit are much more likely to have beliefs read into them than are passages that mention what Jesus and his disciples had for lunch.

Granting that the more theologically significant passages are the most likely place for bias to have its way, we still must try to put our finger on what is wrong with the approach generally taken by Bible translators. As I said at the beginning of this book, the people who take up the task are often those who are least suited to it because they are not trained or practiced in bracketing their own personal beliefs from their work. The results of the survey in this book suggest a pervasive problem, which I think can be best characterized as a crude handling of the relation of scripture to theology. By confusing translation with interpretation, Bible translators tend to ignore both the historical situatedness of Christian scripture and the process of theological development that necessarily occurs as the ideas expressed appropriately in the language and culture of one time are explored in ever new contexts of understanding.

Theological interpretation is a process of building a system of belief out of the individual testimonies of recognized religious authorities, such as the writers of the New Testament. Distinct scriptural statements, each with its own unique point and emphasis, are brought together selectively and strategically in order to yield a creedal position on some aspect of the faith. Christians generally believe that the chorus of voices in the Bible provide a kind of mutual supplement that ultimately produces Truth between them. If that is true, then if even one of the pieces is out of place, if even one of the voices is misconstrued, the interpretive path would be skewed away from Truth. That is why the translator's task must be to accurately situate each crucial piece in the place of meaning it has according to all of the evidence of what the biblical writer intended. The evidence of that intention is entirely contained in the language of the writer, understood within the literary and cultural context of its use. There is no other means by which a modern person can have any idea of what the Bible teaches.

In science, we recognize that an investigation can only have a valid outcome if the observations and results are honestly recorded, unshaped by desired outcomes. It is illegitimate to decide beforehand what results you will accept from an experiment. Likewise, in Bible translation, the only legitimate results are those that are based on neutral, sound, academically rigorous methods, not those prejudiced by a desired conclusion. As I have said, bias can be a tricky thing, and by definition is overlooked by those who are affected by it. In science, bias is combated by making every piece of data available, every step of reasoning plain, every conclusion testable by other scientists who are free to look at the same evidence and repeat the investigation for themselves. The same approach is necessary in the work of translation, and the task of mutual assessment and criticism is an essential part of getting to valid, accurate, unbiased results.

I was lead to many of the passages discussed in this book by hearing accusations of bias made against one or more translations, and going to look for myself. Ironically, these charges of bias were often leveled against the translations that turned out to have things right. As I said at the beginning of this book, people can see the differences between Bible translations, but have no means to judge between them. In that situation, they typically resort to the traditional text (the KJV) or to a consensus among translations whose individual accuracy is not part of their inquiry. This is a flawed methodology, like judging a new scientific result by the conclusions of a previous generation of researchers. Assessment can only be made in the details, in the data on which a conclusion is based, not by dismissing something because it differs from what someone else concluded. No English Bible can serve as the "standard" for judging the quality of Bible translation. All of them have biases and shortcomings of their own, and we can only make progress in our understanding of the Bible by constantly going back to the data, to the text, and making sure that a mistake has not been made.

The translators of the versions we have been comparing thought they were doing the right thing. They honestly believed that the way they translated the passages we have discussed was the most accurate reading of their meaning. That's the tricky thing about bias, it sneaks in and interferes with your work without your knowledge of it. And that is precisely the reason we need to examine these translations closely, check them against the original Greek, and draw attention to how biases may have produced inaccurate translations. Once we are alerted to these problems, we can go back and try to do a better job next time. There is no reason why all of these translations can't be constantly improved by this process of examination and critique. I hope they will be.

Yes, I have biases of my own, and I struggle to be aware of them. One bias that is present in this book is my bias in favor of history. When I read a passage from the New Testament, I am biased in favor of its 1st century meaning, rather than the meanings that might be claimed for it by 21st century interests. I show favoritism towards the original expressions of the New Testament authors, who took on the seemingly impossible task of finding the right words to convey a totally new set of ideas and values to an audience previously unexposed to them. I relish the rich potential and complex meshing of voices in these explorations of truth, which various later, narrowing interpretations tried (and continue to try) to organize, systematize, and contain within the tidy confines of dogma. That's my bias.

But I maintain that the sort of historical bias I am expressing is what Bible translation should be all about. The later Christian writers, of the 4th, 12th, or 20th century, have their own voice. They wrote their own works, explored their own truth, often by commenting on the Bible. There are riches here, too, believe me. But why repeat these ideas and insights in the biblical text by anachronistically reading them into it? What do we gain by that? And what, on the other hand, do we lose by divorcing the Bible from the context in which it was born? Why make the Bible less by making it an echoing voice of later, and by no means universally accepted doctrine? Why make it a prop for the creeds of later centuries, of later interpretations, rather than a world-changing event in its own right? And what does that sort of imposition on the Bible say about the "truth" of those who would commit it? To me, it expresses a lack of courage, a fear that the Bible does not back up their "truth" enough. To let the Bible have its say, regardless of how well or poorly that say conforms to expectations or accepted forms of modern Christianity is an exercise in courage or, to use another word for it, faith.

APPENDIX

THE USE OF "JEHOVAH" IN THE NW

Having concluded that the NW is one of the most accurate English translations of the New Testament currently available, I would be remiss if I did not mention one peculiarity of this translation that by most conventions of translation would be considered an inaccuracy, however little this inaccuracy changes the meaning of most of the verses where it appears. I am referring to the use of "Jehovah" in the NW New Testament. "Jehovah" (or "Yahweh" or some other reconstruction of the divine name consisting of the four consonants YHWH) is the personal name of God used more than six thousand times in the original Hebrew of the Old Testament. But the name never appears in any Greek manuscript of any book of the New Testament. So, to introduce the name "Jehovah" into the New Testament, as the NW does two-hundred-thirty-seven times, is not accurate translation by the most basic principle of accuracy: adherence to the original Greek text.

    Of course, "Jehovah" also appears throughout the NW Old Testament. In this case, the NW is the only accurate translation of the nine we are comparing, since all of the other translations replace the personal name of God, in over six thousand passages, with the euphemistic title "Lord" (given by many of these translations in all capitals, as "LORD," which my students invariably misunderstand as some sort of emphasis). YHWH does appear in the original Hebrew of these passages, and the only accurate translation is one that renders that name into some pronouncible form. The NW rightly does this; the others do not. As a result, the NW has "Jehovah" consistently in both its Old and New Testaments, while the other translations consistently have "Lord" in both their Old and New Testaments. Both practices violate accuracy in favor of denominationally preferred expressions for God.

This problem arises because the Bible itself is not consistent in the way all of these translators want it to be. The Old Testament authors regularly use "Jehovah" as God's personal name, and the New Testament authors never do so. To cover over this inconsistency, translators *harmonize* the two testaments, that is, they make them read the same even though originally they do not. To harmonize the Bible is to change one part to make it match another. This is not a legitimate part of the translator's task.

From "Jehovah" to "Lord" and back again
In ancient Judaism, the Biblical commandment not to profane God's name developed into a taboo against pronouncing it aloud except in very special circumstances. In ordinary reading from the Bible, therefore, it became customary to substitute the euphemistic title *adonai*, "lord," whenever one came to YHWH in the biblical text. This development restricting the pronunciation of YHWH in turn caused the text of the Bible itself to be modified. It became common practice to mark the biblical text wherever YHWH appeared in a way that reminded the reader not to pronounce the name, but to substitute "Lord."

The oldest manuscripts of books of the Old Testament that we possess, from the collection known as the "Dead Sea Scrolls" found at Qumran in Israel, show that this handling of the divine name was already in practice among the Jews two centuries before the New Testament was written. In the nearly complete Isaiah scroll from Qumran, for example, *adonai*, "Lord," is written in tiny letters above YHWH. In fact, many of these oldest manuscripts of the Old Testament use a very old form of Hebrew letters, different from those used in the rest of the text, when writing YHWH. This conservative rendering of the divine name shows that the name was, in effect, "frozen" in the text, set apart from the portions to be read aloud. This state of affairs continued when the Old Testament was translated into Greek for the use of Greek-speaking Jews.

We know of several manuscripts of this translation, known as the *Septuagint*[1], which contains YHWH written in archaic Hebrew letters (or crude imitations of them[2]), just like those used in Hebrew manuscripts.[3] Eventually, the practice of copying the Hebrew letters YHWH was dropped in favor of simply writing *kurios*, "Lord."[4]

All of the books now contained in the New Testament were written originally in Greek. Even when the authors of these books quote the Old Testament, they do so in Greek. Since "Jehovah" or "Yahweh" is not found in the original Greek New Testament, even when passages from the Old Testament that contain YHWH are quoted, it would seem that the New Testament authors followed the general Jewish custom of not using God's personal name. Even if these authors were using copies of the Greek Septuagint that preserved the divine name in archaic Hebrew letters, they were careful in their own writings to substitute the accepted euphemism "Lord" (*kurios*).

This makes perfect sense, since the New Testament authors were writing works that would be read aloud in Christian communities. Many of these Christian communities contained Gentiles as well as Jews, and these Gentiles would be mystified by the peculiar practices around the name of God. In the interests of reaching the broadest possible audience with their message, the New Testament authors used universal titles such as "God" and "Lord," rather than the specifically Jewish name for God, which Jews themselves did not want spoken aloud, anyway. How do I know all this? Because the Greek manuscripts of the New Testament -- *all* of them -- use *kurios*, the Greek word for "lord," in every single place where an Old Testament verse that contains YHWH in the original Hebrew is quoted.

When all of the manuscript evidence agrees, it takes very strong reasons to suggest that the original *autographs* (the very first manuscript of a book written by the author himself) read differently. To suggest such a reading not supported by the manuscript evidence is called making a *conjectural emendation*. It is an *emendation* because you are repairing, "mending," a text you believe is defective. It is *conjectural* because it is a hypothesis, a "conjecture" that can only be proven if at some future time evidence is found that supports it. Until that time, it is by definition unproven.

The editors of the NW are making a conjectural emendation when they replace *kurios*, which would be translated "Lord," with "Jehovah." In an appendix to the NW, they state that their restoration of "Jehovah" in the New Testament is based upon (1) a supposition concerning how Jesus and his disciples would have handled the divine name, (2) the evidence of the "J texts," and (3) the necessity of consistency between Old and New Testaments. These are three very different reasons for the editorial decision. The first two may be handled here quite briefly, while the third requires more detailed examination.

The first basis for using "Jehovah" is a matter of theological interpretation. It is an assumption about how individuals would have acted in accordance with values the editors believe they held. I am in no position to judge this theological interpretation; it is more appropriate in discussing an interpretation of a particular passage than in debating its translation. I might simply note that this first line of reasoning used by the editors of the NW provides a sweeping principle that the name of God was used by the early Christians; it does not and cannot establish that the name of God was used in particular verses of the New Testament (since the editors readily acknowledge that "Lord" appears legitimately in many passages of the Bible).

The second basis for using "Jehovah" relies upon a set of texts that similarly employ a form of "Jehovah" in particular passages of the New Testament. The NW cites various texts of this sort, referred to with a "J" followed by a number, in support of its own practice. These "J texts" are mostly other translations of the Bible or translation aids of various kinds.[5] Most are printed Hebrew translations of the Greek, or of the Latin Vulgate, made in the last five centuries for the use of Jewish converts to Christianity.[6] But the fact that their missionary translators chose to use the Jewish name for God in some passages of the New Testament does not constitute any sort of evidence about the original form of those passages.

What the NW editors are actually doing in these notes is citing *other translations*. It is similar to notes that can be found in some modern translations citing the wording used by the KJV, or the occasional reference to the Latin Vulgate found in the notes of the NAB or NRSV. This kind of citation of another translation does not *prove* anything; it merely indicates how the choice of the translator is similar to that made by another translator at some time. It supports the choice without decidedly settling the translation issue.[7]

Since one-hundred-sixty-seven of the occurrences of "Jehovah" in the NW New Testament are based solely upon these "J texts," and the "J texts" offer evidence only about other translations, not about the original Greek New Testament, the use of "Jehovah" is not sufficiently justified in these verses. The editors of the NW can still retain the notes indicating that other translations introduce "Jehovah" here (as an indication of the biblical author's likely reference), while using "Lord" in the text itself, in accordance with the reading of all known Greek manuscripts. But that leaves seventy occurrences of "Jehovah," supported by the third basis given by the NW editors, to be considered.

New Testament quotations of the Old Testament

The New Testament quotes the Old Testament quite often, and many of the quoted passages in their original Hebrew version have the name of God. A precise quotation of these passages, it stands to reason, would incorporate the name of God, and not replace it with a substitution such as *kurios*. The editors of the NW reason that if New Testament writers quote the Old Testament they will, of course, quote it accurately. If the original Hebrew of the Old Testament passage contains YHWH, an accurate quote of it would also include that name. So there appears to be a serious discrepancy between New Testament quotes of the Old Testament and the original Old Testament sources of those quotes when the former reads "Lord" while the latter has "Jehovah."

But it is not the job of translators to fix or correct the content of the biblical text. So when it comes to New Testament quotes of the Old Testament, we are constrained to translate what the New Testament author has given, even if it shows some discrepancy when compared to the original Old Testament passage. To do otherwise runs the risk of undoing something important that the New Testament authors wished to convey by the way they quote the Old Testament.

In a small number of cases, it seems to be likely that a New Testament author is consciously changing the referent of the Old Testament passage from Jehovah, as the Jewish tradition understood him, to Jesus Christ in the role the Christian tradition understands him to have. This shift of reference is made easier by the Jewish custom of substituting the broad and potentially ambiguous title "Lord" for God's personal name. In other words, once an Old Testament passage was read as referring to "the Lord," rather than specifically "Jehovah," it was possible to apply what the passage said to Jesus, to whom Christians also applied the title "Lord." With this fact in mind, modern translators must be careful not to undo the work of the author by "restoring" God's name in a place where a New Testament author may not intend it.[8]

The editors of the NW have chosen instead to follow the original

Hebrew of the Old Testament verse being quoted in the New Testament. On that basis they can make a case for seventy occurrences of "Jehovah" that currently appear in the NW New Testament. But their decision presents certain problems that they have not dealt with fully.

There are actually *seventy-eight* passages where a New Testament author rather directly quotes an Old Testament passage in which YHWH appears in the original Hebrew. In the following table, I give all seventy-eight verses, marking with an asterisk the eight cases where the NW translators inconsistently chose not to put "Jehovah" into their translation.

> Matthew 3:3; 4:4; 4:7; 4:10; 5:33; 21:9; 21:42; 22:37; 22:44; 23:39.
> Mark 1:3; 11:9; 12:11; 12:29 (twice); 12:30; 12:36.
> Luke 2:23; 3:4; 4:8; 4:12; 4:18; 4:19; 10:27; 13:35; 19:38; 20:37[9]; 20:42.
> John 1:23; 6:45; 12:13; 12:38.[10]
> Acts 2:20; 2:21; 2:25; 2:34; 3:22; 4:26; 7:49; 15:17.[11]
> Romans 4:3; 4:8; 9:28; 9:29; 10:13; 11:2*; 11:8*; 11:34; 14:11; 15:11.
> 1 Corinthians 1:31; 2:16; 3:20; 10:21[12]; 10:26.
> 2 Corinthians 10:17.
> Galatians 1:15*; 3:6
> 2 Thessalonians 1:9*.
> Hebrews 2:13; 7:21; 8:8; 8:9; 8:10; 8:11; 9:20*; 10:16; 10:30; 12:5; 12:6; 13:6.
> James 2:23[13]
> 1 Peter 2:3*; 3:12 (twice); 3:15*; 4:14.
> Revelation 4:8.[14]

If the exact preservation of Old Testament passages when they are quoted in the New Testament is a principle to which the NW editors want to give priority, then the seventy-eight verses listed in the table above is where they can put "Jehovah" in their New Testament text according to that principle.[15]

But in five of the verses in the list above, the NW has "God" rather than either "Jehovah" or "Lord" (Romans 11:2; 11:8; Galatians 1:15; Hebrews 9:20; 1 Peter 4:14).[16] I cannot say why the NW editors abandoned their principle of conjectural emendation in these five cases; it makes no difference in the meaning of the text.[17] Then there are three more verses where, by the principles applied by the NW editors, "Jehovah" should be used, and yet is not: 2 Thessalonians 1:9; 1 Peter 2:3;

and 1 Peter 3:15. These three passages present a serious problem for the NW translators and their principle of using "Jehovah" based on Old Testament passages with YHWH. The fact that they do not, and apparently *cannot*, have "Jehovah" in these three passages underscores the problem with the whole idea of using "Jehovah" in the New Testament.

Take 2 Thessalonians 1:9, for example. Here Paul quotes Isaiah 2:21, which includes YHWH in the Hebrew version and "Lord" in the Septuagint. There is no reason for the NW not to have "Jehovah" here according to its own principles. But in the context of 2 Thessalonians 1, Jesus is the primary subject. "Lord" in verse 9 could be taken as a reference to Jesus (not necessarily so, but it is usually read that way). This may be an instance of a New Testament author reapplying an Old Testament passage about YHWH to Jesus because the word "Lord" is ambiguous in its reference. In such a circumstance, the NW editors shy away from using "Jehovah."

Likewise, in 1 Peter 2:3 and 3:15, the NW translators have deviated from the principles by which they would normally use "Jehovah," and they have done so quite obviously because of bias.[18] In both passages, by taking advantage of the ambiguity of the Greek *kurios* ("Lord"), Peter reapplies to Jesus an Old Testament statement that was originally about YHWH.

The inconsistency of the NW translators in not using "Jehovah" in 2 Thessalonians 1:9, 1 Peter 2:3, and 1 Peter 3:15 shows that interpretation rather than a principle of translation is involved in deciding where to use "Jehovah." If the NW translators stick consistently to using "Jehovah" whenever an Old Testament passage containing God's personal name is quoted in the New Testament, that is a translation principle of a sort (whether one agrees with it or not). But if in such cases they sometimes use "Jehovah" and sometimes revert to "Lord," then they are interpreting the reference of the biblical author. Once we recognize that interpretation is involved, and see three examples where this interpretation has led the translators not to use "Jehovah," we must wonder if they have been correct to use it in all seventy of those other occurrences. Couldn't there be other passages among them where, as apparently in 2 Thessalonians 1:9, 1 Peter 2:3, and 1 Peter 3:15, the reference of the verse has been redirected to Jesus? By moving beyond translation of the Greek to an interpretation, the translator ventures from the bedrock of the text to the shifting sands of opinion -- and that's a risky move to make.

For that very reason, interpretation is best left to commentaries on the Bible, or to notes in a Bible translation. It is certainly right and proper for a note to inform the reader that the original Hebrew of the verse being quoted has YHWH; and the Jehovah's Witnesses are perfectly entitled to believe what they do about the importance of God's name among Jesus and his disciples. But "restoring" that name in the New Testament itself is unnecessary for either purpose. For the NW to gain wider acceptance and prove its worth over its competitors, its translators will have to rethink the handling of these verses, and they may find that that rethinking needs to extend to the use of "Jehovah" in the New Testament at all.

Conclusions

The main problem, as the editors of the NW see it, is the ambiguity surrounding the use of "lord" in the New Testament. This rather generic title is used not only of God, but also of Jesus and other figures in the books of the New Testament.[19] The editors of the NW point out that the ambiguity leads to confusion between God and Jesus and leaves the reader uncertain as to whom a passage refers. Carefully distinguishing God from Jesus by using the name Jehovah for the former, the NW resolves ambiguity in a way that keeps these two personages distinct and aids in the formulation of theology and christology by showing which entity is responsible for which activities in the thinking of the biblical authors.

These are reasonable points, but fundamentally matters of *interpretation* rather than translation. The clarification that the NW editors seek to bring to the Bible can only be a matter of translation if it is based upon something in the original Greek text. Since there is nothing in that original Greek text as it is known to us in the surviving manuscripts to provide the basis for the desired clarification, it cannot legitimately be made in the English translation itself.

This is one case, therefore, where the NW departs from its usual conservative treatment of the Greek text in its translation and introduces an innovation into the translation. To use "Jehovah" where the original Greek reads *kurios* is no more legitimate than using "Lord" where the original Hebrew reads YHWH. The latter practice, you will recall, occurs in over six thousand instances with no justification whatsoever in the Old Testament translations of the KJV, NASB, NIV, NRSV, NAB, AB, TEV, and LB. The NW does not improve the situation by engaging in the same sort of harmonizing practice in the New Testament as these other translations indulge in in the Old Testament.

Every single translation that we have compared deviates from the biblical text, one way or another, in the "Jehovah"/"Lord" passages of the Old and New Testament. Past efforts by some translations, such as the Jerusalem Bible and the New English Bible, to follow the text accurately in these passages, have not been well-received by the uninformed public conditioned by the KJV. But popular opinion is not a valid regulator of biblical accuracy. We must adhere to the standards of accurate translation, and we must apply those standards equally to all. If by those standards we say that the NW should not substitute "Jehovah" for "Lord" in the New Testament, then by those same standards we must say that the KJV, NASB, NIV, NRSV, NAB, AB, LB, and TEV should not subsitute "Lord" for "Jehovah" or "Yahweh" in the Old Testament.

The zeal of the NW editors to restore and preserve the name of God against an obvious trend towards expunging it in modern translations of the Bible, while comendable in itself, has carried them too far, and into a harmonizing practice of their own. I personally do not agree with that practice, and think that identifications of "Lord" with "Jehovah" should be placed in footnotes. At the very least, use of "Jehovah" should be confined in the NW New Testament to the seventy-eight occasions where an Old Testament passage containing "Jehovah" is being quoted. I leave it to the NW editors to resolve the problem of the three verses where their principle of "emendation" does not seem to work.

Most of the New Testament authors were Jews by birth and heritage, and all belonged to a Christianity still closely tied to its Jewish roots. While Christianity went on to distance itself from its Jewish mother, and to universalize its mission and its rhetoric, it is important to remember how much the New Testament thought-world is a Jewish one, and how much the authors build on Old Testament antecedents in their thought and expression. It is one of the dangers of modernizing and paraphrasing translations that they tend to strip away the distinct references to the culture that produced the New Testament. The God of the New Testament writers is the Jehovah (YHWH) of the Jewish biblical tradition, however much re-characterized in Jesus' representation of him. The name of Jesus himself incorporates this name of God. These facts remain true, even if the New Testament authors communicate them in language that avoids, for whatever reason, the personal name Jehovah.

It may be that some day a Greek manuscript of some portion of the New Testament will be found, let's say a particularly early one, that has the Hebrew letters YHWH in some of the verses listed above. When that happens, when evidence is at hand, biblical researchers will have to give due consideration to the views held by the NW editors. Until that day, translators must follow the manuscript tradition as it is currently known, even if some of its characteristics appear to us puzzling, perhaps even inconsistent with what we believe. Anything translators want to add to clarify the meaning of ambiguous passages, such as those where "Lord" might refer to either God or the Son of God, can and should be put into footnotes, while keeping the Bible itself in the words given to us.

NOTES

1. This name refers to the number seventy, because that is how many translators were said to have worked on it. For this same reason, scholars often refer to the Septuagint with the Roman numeral LXX.

2. Based on the stiff, awkward, and inconsistent forms of the Hebrew letters used for YHWH in the Greek Minor Prophets Scroll from Nahal Hever, for example, the manuscript's editor concludes: "Both scribes 'drew' rather than wrote the letters from an imprecise model" (Tov 1990, 13). This evidence suggests a situation in which Septuagint Greek versions of the Old Testament were being copied by scribes who did not read Hebrew. They drew imitations of the letters YHWH as best they could. Neither these scribes nor the people who read from the manuscripts they produced would be able to "read" the letters YHWH. Instead, when using these Greek Old Testament manuscripts with YHWH, they would have taken the four strange, "sacred" letters as a signal for saying "Lord."

3. Examples of this are the Greek Minor Prophets Scroll from Nahal Hever (8HevXIIgr; Rahlfs 943), Papyrus Fouad 266 (Rahlfs 848), and Papyrus Oxyrhynchus 3522; see Tov 1990, 12-13. The oldest of these manuscripts dates to the late 1st century BCE. But regardless of their date, all such manuscripts necessarily depend on a prototype made at the stage when the translation from Hebrew to Greek was first being made. The same practice was followed by the chief rival to the Septuagint, the Greek translation of Aquila (Tov 1990, 13).

4. The transition from the practice of preserving YHWH in archaic Hebrew letters to replacing it with the Greek *kurios* can be seen in Papyrus Oxyrhynchus 656 (Rahlfs 905). In the text of Genesis preserved in this manuscript, the original scribe left blank spaces for YHWH exactly like the scribe of PFouad 266 did. But later another scribe, instead of writing YHWH into those spaces, wrote *kurios* (Tov 1990, page 12).

5. J20 is Moulton and Geden's *Concordance to the Greek Testament*; J21, J24, J25, and J27 are all translations of part or the whole of the New Testament into modern languages.

6. This is true of J1, J3-19, J22-23, and J26 (and of J28 which appears in the more recent German edition of the NW).

7. The one actual manuscript among the "J texts," J2, is a copy of a 14th century work by a Jewish writer which includes a Hebrew translation of the Gospel according to Matthew. The source and date of this translation are uncertain. It may be derived from a Latin translation, or even from an Arabic translation of a Latin translation, and so highly derivative. With the value of J2 thus undetermined, it is not prudent to place too much weight upon its evidence, particularly since it is not even a Greek manuscript of the New Testament.

8. Bruce Metzger, "The Jehovah's Witnesses and Jesus Christ: A Biblical and Theological Appraisal," *Theology Today* 1953, 73-74, gives some examples of this: Isaiah 60:19 quoted in Luke 2:32; Isaiah 6:1-10 alluded to in John 12:37-41; Psalm 23:1 and Isaiah 40:10-11 (God as shepherd) reapplied in John 10:11; Joel 2:32 quoted in Romans 10:13.

9. Neither Stafford nor Countess accept this verse as a direct quote from the Old Testament with YHWH. But it is a fairly direct quote of Exodus 3:6 and 3:15; in the latter verse YHWH is used as God's name.

10. In the NW translation of John 12:38 the second "Jehovah" is based in an Old Testament quote with YHWH. The first "Jehovah" of John 12:38, however, is based on a "Lord" (*kurios*) in the Greek Old Testament which has no corresponding YHWH in the Hebrew text.

11. Of the two occurrences of "Jehovah" in the NW version of Acts 15:17, the first has no basis in the original Hebrew of the Old Testament quote.

12. There are two occurrences of "Jehovah" in the NW's translation of 1 Corinthians 10:21. The first "Jehovah" has no basis in any Old Testament passage. The second is part of the phrase "the table of Jehovah." Such a phrase does appear in Malachi 1:12. Assuming that Paul is making an allusion to that Old Testament passage, this second "Jehovah" is justified according to the NW's principle.

13. In James 2:23 the first "Jehovah" of the NW translation is based upon YHWH in the original Hebrew of the Old Testament quote. The second "Jehovah" is used in place of God saying "my" in both the Hebrew and Greek Old Testament texts.

14. Neither Stafford nor Countess accept this verse as a direct quote of Isaiah 6:3.

15. My list excludes 1 Peter 1:24-25, which is accepted by both Stafford and Countess as a quote of an Old Testament passage with YHWH. The passage quoted is Isaiah 40:6-8. But Peter does not quote all of verses 6-8. He quotes only 6b-7a and 8b. The repetition of the same words in 7a and 8a might explain the jump. It's a typical scribal mistake. But in any case, Peter skips exactly that part of the passage (verse 8a) in which YHWH occurs. The quoted portion includes 8b where both the original Hebrew and the Septuagint Greek have "God," not YHWH. My list also excludes some passages accepted by Stafford, but excluded by Countess (Matthew 27:10; Romans 11:3; 12:19; 1 Corinthians 10:22; and 14:21). I also exclude Jude 9, which is not actually a quote from Zechariah 3:2, as the NW editors and Stafford believe it to be (it is actually a quote from a book outside of the biblical canon, *The Assumption of Moses*). My list also excludes two passages accepted by Countess, but not by Stafford (2 Timothy 2:19 and 1 Peter 1:25).

16. In Countess' analysis of these NW passages (Countess, Table III, on page 103), he overlooks 1 Peter 4:14 and Galatians 1:15. Countess claims that Hebrews 12:29 should be considered here as well. But in Hebrews 12:29, the New Testament author has given an abbreviated quote of Deuteronomy 4:24, and the word "Lord" (YHWH) of the original "The Lord thy God" seems to have been omitted from the quote.

17. But I can say that these five passages are part of a larger set of eleven cases where a New Testament author has used "God" in agreement with the Septuagint in a quote where the original Hebrew has not "God" but "Jehovah" (the other six

are Matthew 4:4; John 6:45; Romans 4:3; Galatians 3:6; Hebrews 2:13; James 2:23). Such examples support the idea that the New Testament authors were using Septuagint manuscripts with *theos* and *kurios* already substituted for YHWH.

18. Countess has an accurate treatment of the problem of these verses on pages 34-37 of his book.

19. "Lord" is used quite frequently in reference to others beside God and Jesus, for example twenty-nine times in Matthew alone: Mt. 6:24; 10:24-25; 13:27; 15:27 (plural); 18:25-27, 31-32, 34; 20:8; 21:30; 21:40; 24:45-46, 48, 50; 25:18-24, 26; 27:63. For comparison, "Lord" is used nineteen times for God and thirty-one times for Jesus in Matthew.

BIBLIOGRAPHY

Bratcher, Robert G.

1978 "One Bible in Many Translations," *Interpretation* 32: 115-129.

1990/1 "Translating for the Reader," *Theology Today* 47: 290-298.

Burdick, Donald W.

1975 "Bible Translation: Why, What, and How?" *Seminary Review* 21: 3-7.

Colwell, E. C.

1933 "A Definite Rule for the Use of the Article in the Greek New Testament," *Journal of Biblical Literature* 52: 12-21.

Countess, Robert

1982 *The Jehovah's Witnesses' New Testament.* Phillipsburg: Presbyterian and Reformed Publishing.

Dana, H. E. and Mantey, Julius R.

1927 *A Manual Grammar of the Greek New Testament.* Toronto:

Macmillan Company.

Freed, E. D.

1965 *Old Testament Quotations in the Gospel of John.* Leiden: E. J. Brill.

Furuli, Rolf

1999 *The Role of Theology and Bias in Bible Translation.* Huntington Beach: Elihu books.

Goodspeed, Edgar

1927 *The Bible -- An American Translation* (New Testament). Chicago: University of Chicago Press.

Harner, Philip B.

1970 *The 'I AM' of the Fourth Gospel: A Study of Johannine Usage and Thought.* Philadelphia: Fortress Press.

1973 "Qualitative Anarthrous Predicate Nouns: Mark 15:39 and John 1:1," *Journal of Biblical Literature* 92: 75-87.

Hoover, R. W.

1971 "The Harpagmos Enigma: A Philological Solution," *Harvard Theological Review* 64: 95-119.

Jackson, Don

1984 "The Theology of the NIV," *Restoration Quarterly* 27: 208-220.

Kubo, Sakae and Walter F. Specht

1983 *So Many Versions? Twentieth-century English Versions of the Bible.* Grand Rapids: Zondervan.

Lewis, Jack P.

1981   *The English Bible/From KJV to NIV: A History and Evaluation.* Grand Rapids: Baker Book House.

McKay, K. L.

1994   *A New Syntax of the Verb in New Testament Greek.* New York: Peter Lang.

1996   "'I am' in John's Gospel," *Expository Times* 107: 302-303.

Metzger, Bruce

1953   "The Jehovah's Witnesses and Jesus Christ: A Biblical and Theological Appraisal," *Theology Today* 10: 65-85.

1992   "Recent Translations: A Survey and Evaluation," *Southwestern Journal of Theology* 34.2: 5-12.

1993   "English Translations of the Bible, Today and Tomorrow," *Bibliotheca Sacra* 150: 397-414.

Moffatt, James

1926   *A New Translation of the Bible.* New York: Harper & Brothers.

Moule, C. F. D.

1963   *An Idiom-Book of New Testament Greek.* Cambridge: Cambridge University Press.

Nichols, A. H.

1988   "Explicitness in Translation and the Westernization of Scripture," *Reformed Theological Review* 47: 78-88.

Nida, Eugene and Charles Taber

1969   *The Theory and Practice of Translation*. Leiden: E. J. Brill.

O'Neill, J. C.

1988   "Hoover on *Harpagmos* Reviewed, with a Modest Proposal Concerning Philippians 2:6," *Harvard Theological Review* 81: 445-449.

Orlinsky, Harry M. And Robert G. Bratcher

1991   *A History of Bible Translation and the North American Contribution*. Atlanta: Scholars Press.

Ray, Vernon

1982   "The Formal vs Dynamic Equivalent Principle in New Testament Translation," *Restoration Quarterly* 25: 46-56.

Smyth, Herbert Weir

1920   *Greek Grammar*. Cambridge: Harvard University Press.

Stafford, Greg

2000   *Jehovah's Witnesses Defended: An Answer to Scholars and Critics* (2nd ed.). Huntington Beach: Elihu Books.

Strauss, Mark L.

1998   *Distorting Scripture? The Challenge of Bible Translation & Gender Accuracy*. Downer's Grove: InterVarsity Press.

Tov, Emanuel

1990   *The Minor Prophets Scroll from Nahal Hever (8HevXIIgr)* (Discoveries in the Judaean Desert VIII). Oxford: Clarendon Press.

Turner, Nigel

1963   *A Grammar of New Testament Greek, vol.3 Syntax.* Edinburgh: T & T Clark.

Waddell, W. D.

1944   "The Tetragram in the LXX," *Journal of Theological Studies* 45: 158-161.

Wallace, Daniel B.

1983   "The Semantic Range of the Article-Noun-Kai-Noun Plural Construction in the New Testament," *Grace Theological Journal* 4: 59-84.

Wanamaker, C. E.

1987   "Philippians 2.6-11: Son of God or Adamic Christology?" *New Testament Studies* 33: 179-193.

Worth, Roland H.

1992   Bible Translations: A History through Source Documents. Jefferson: McFarland & Co.

Youngblood, Carolyn Johnson

1978   "The *New International Version* Translation Project: Its Conception and Implementation," *Journal of the Evangelical Theological Society* 21: 239-249.

INDEX

Subjects and Persons
accuracy, definition of, xi-xiv
accusative form (case), 133n2
Amplified Bible, 21, 23-24, 35, 38, etc.
bias, definition of, xii-xiii, 9-10, 165-167
Bratcher, Robert G., 18-19, 32, 37, 76, 103, 112n4
Burdick, Donald W., 49n1
capitalization, 143-157
Colwell's Rule, 117-120, 123
conjectural emendation, 171
Countess, Robert, 95n1, 179nn9, 14, 15, 180nn16, 18
dative form (case), 117, 137
dynamic equivalence translation, 17-22, 24-26, 35, 37
etymology, 12, 14, 63n2
formal equivalence translation, 13-17, 24-26, 28, 31-32, 35, 131
Freed, E. D., 112n5
Furuli, Rolf, 54, 102 n1
gender-inclusive language, 31-32, 34, 63-73
genitive form (case), 117, 133n3, 137, 141
Good News Bible, *see* Today's English Version
Goodspeed, Edgar J., 101, 128
Harner, Philip B., 120-124, 129, 133n5
Holy Spirit, 135-158
Hoover, R. W., 63n3

"I am," 103-111
implicit meaning, 75-87
interlinear, 11-13, 104, 131
Jehovah, 39, 169-177, 179nn10, 11, 12, 13, 180n17
J-texts, 172, 178nn5, 6, 7
King James Version, xi-xii, 7-8, 15-17, 21, 27-30, 35-36, 40n3, 42, etc.
Kubo, Sakae and Walter F. Specht, 120
lexical translation, 11-13, 104, 131
literal translation, *see* formal equivalence
Living Bible, 23-24, 35-38, 40n10, etc.
Lockman Foundation, 34-5, 39
manuscripts, Bible, 2-5, 8-9, 28
McKay, K. L., 112nn1, 2, 8
Metzger, Bruce, 31-32, 36, 38, 120, 179n8
Moffatt, James, 101, 128
Nestle-Aland, 8-9, 31, 34-35, 38
New American Bible, xiii, 15, 20-22, 32-33, etc.
New American Standard Bible, 15-17, 21, 34-36, 38-39, 40n6, etc.
New International Version, xiii, 15, 19-22, 32-33, 40n5, etc.
New King James Bible, 30, 39
New Revised Standard Version, 15, 19-22, 27, 30-32, 39, etc.
New World Translation, xiii, 15-17, 38, etc.
Nichols, A. H., 17, 75
Nida, Eugene, 37
Nida, Eugene and Charles Taber, 14-15, 85
nominative form (case), 98, 115-132
O'Neill, J. C., 63n3
Orlinsky, Harry M. and Robert G. Bratcher, 36, 106, 134n10
paraphrase, 22-24, 36, 83
Sharp's Rule, 92-94, 95n4
Siewert, Frances E., 35
Smyth, Herbert Weir, 93, 106, 127, 136
sola scriptura, vi, 163
Stafford, Greg, 112nn3, 5, 6, 179nn9, 14, 15
Taylor, Kenneth N., 36-37, 40n10
Today's English Version, 19-22, 32, 37-38, etc.
Tov, Emanuel, 178nn2, 3, 4
Turner, Nigel, 118
United Bible Societies, 8-9, 31, 34, 38

verb tense, 40n6, 103-111
vocative form (case), 98, 117
Wallace, Daniel B., 92, 95n4
Wanamaker, C. E., 60, 63n4
Westcott, B. F., 101
Westcott & Hort, 8, 35, 38
YHWH, 169-177, 179nn10, 13, 15, 180nn16, 17
Youngblood, Carolyn Johnson, 32-3

Greek terms
agapē, 28
anēr, 64-65
anthrōpos, 66-68
dikaios, 29
doulos, 28
egō eimi, 103-111, 162
episēmos, 72
exousia, 29
gunē, 64-65
hagiasmos, 21, 29
harpagmos 53-62, 162
hē, 140-141
ho (article), 69-71, 74n2, 114-132
ho (pronoun), 140
ho theos 94, 98-99, 114-132; *see also* theos
hos, 140-141
houtos, 69-71, 131
ktasthai, 21
kurios, 169-177, 179n10, 180nn16, 19
logizomai, 29
logos, 114-132, 133n1
morphē, 53, 162
oudeis, 68-69
pan, 83-84
paraklētos, 141-142
pneuma, 143-158
porneia, 16, 22
proskuneō, 41-48, 161-162
psuchē, 29

theos, 114-132, 180n17; *see also* ho theos
zeō, 146
zōiopoieō, 160n9

Biblical Citations

Exodus
3:6   179n9
3:14   107-108
3:15   179n9

Deuteronomy
4:24   180n16

Psalms
23:1   179n8
40   98
40:10f. 179n8
45:6-7 100
104:4   100

Isaiah
6:1-10 179nn8, 14
40:6ff. 179n15
41:4   111
46:4   111
60:19   179n8

Joel
2:32   179n8

Micah
1:12   179n12

Zechariah
3:2   179n15

Matthew
1:18   159n2
1:20   159n2

Matthew
2:1f.   44-45
2:8   44-45
2:11   44-45
3:3   174
3:11   159n2
4:4   66, 174, 180n17
4:7   174
4:10   174
5:18   40n7
5:33   174
6:1   66
6:14   66, 68
6:24   180n19
7:15   58 Table 5.3
10:24f. 180n19
10:33   66
11:12   56 Table 5.1
11:27   68
12:18   159n8
12:31   66
12:32   159n1
13:19   56 Table 5.1
13:27   180n19
14:33   45-46
15:27   180n19
17:21   40nn2, 6
18:11   40nn2, 6
18:25ff. 42-43, 180n19
18:31f. 180n19
18:34   180n19
20:8   180n19
21:9   174
21:30   180n19
21:40   180n19

INDEX

Matthew
21:42	174
22:37	174
22:44	174
23:14	40n2
23:25	59 Table 5.4
23:39	174
24:13	70
24:45f.	180n19
24:48	180n19
24:50	180n19
25:18ff.	180n19
25:26	180n19
26:41	144
27:10	179n15
27:46	98
27:50	144
27:63	180n19
28:9	46
28:16f.	47-48
28:19	159n1

Mark
1:3	174
1:8	159n2
2:8	159n8
2:27	66
3:29	159n1
6:20	40n11
6:22	40n11
7:16	40n2
8:12	159n8
9:35	133n7
9:44	40n2
9:46	40n2
11:9	174
11:26	40n2
12:11	174
12:27	117, 125-126

Mark
12:29	174
12:30	174
12:36	159n1, 174
13:11	159n1
13:13	70
13:30	40n7
13:32	68
14:62	112n5
15:18f.	43-44
15:28	40nn2, 6
15:34	98
16:9-20	40n4

Luke
1:15	159n3
1:35	159n3
1:41	159n3
1:47	159n8
1:67	159n3
1:80	144
2:14	66
2:23	174
2:25	138
2:26	159n1
2:32	179n8
3:4	174
3:16	159n2
3:22	159n1
4:8	174
4:11	159n3
4:12	174
4:18	174
4:19	174
4:41	133n6
8:55	159n8
9:48	70
10:21	159n1
10:27	174

Luke		John	
11:13	139	3:8	143-144
11:39	59 Table 5.4	3:13	69
11:42	84	4:9	121
12:10	159n1	4:18	133n7
12:12	159n1	4:19	121
12:39	40n4	4:23f.	152
13:35	174	4:24	122, 137
17:36	40n2	4:26	108
18:11	58 Table 5.3, 98	5:3f.	40n6
18:13	98	5:4	40n2
19:38	174	6:15	56 Table 5.1
20:33	133n7	6:20	108, 122
20:37	174	6:45	174, 180n17
20:38	117, 125-126	6:51	118, 133nn4, 6
20:42	174	6:63	121, 133n4, 145
21:19	40n11	7:12	121, 134n9
21:29	84	7:53ff.	40n4
22:19f.	40n4	8:15	69
22:43f.	40n4	8:24	108-109
23:17	40n2	8:28	109
23:46	159n8	8:31	121
24:47a	40n4	8:44	121
		8:48	121
John		8:54	117
1:1f.	113-132, 162	8:58	103-111, 162
1:2	70	9:8	121
1:4	67, 133n4	9:9	110
1:14	121	9:16	133n7
1:18	69, 117	9:24ff.	121
1:21	133n6	9:35ff.	112n5
1:23	174	10:1	121
1:33	159n2	10:8	121
1:43	40n6	10:11	179n8
2:9	121	10:12	56 Table 5.1
2:22	71	10:28f.	56 Table 5.1
3:2	69	10:33f.	121
3:4	121	10:34	127
3:6	121	11:33	144

INDEX

John	
12:6	121
12:13	174
12:14	40n7
12:36	121
12:37ff.	179n8
12:38	174, 179n10
13:19	109
13:21	144
14:9	106
14:17	153
14:26	141, 159n1
15:1	118, 133nn4, 6
15:26	153
15:27	106
16:13	153
18	109
18:13	133n7
18:26	121
18:35	121
19:21	122
19:30	144
20:15	118
20:22	139
21:7	118
21:12	118

Acts	
1:2	159n2
1:5	159n2
1:8	159n1
1:11	65
1:16	159n1
2:4	159n3
2:5	65
2:14	65
2:17f.	159n8
2:20	174
2:21	174

Acts	
2:22	65
2:25	174
2:33	159n1
2:34	174
2:38	159n1
3:12	65
3:22	174
4:8	159n3
4:26	174
4:31	159nn1, 3, 4
5:3	159n1
5:32	140, 159 n1
5:35	65
6:5	159n3
7:46	40n11
7:49	174
7:51	159n1
7:55	159n3
7:59	159n8
8:15	137
8:17ff.	138
8:37	40nn2, 6
8:39	57 Table 5.2
9:5-6	40n3
9:17	159n3
9:31	159n1
10:19	40n11
10:36	133n7
10:38	138
10:44	159n1
10:45	159n1
10:47	159n1
11:15	159n1
11:16	159n2
11:29	159n3
12:25	40n11
13:2	159n1
13:4	159n1

Acts		Romans	
13:14	159n2	8:9	70
13:16	65	8:11	159n8
13:19	159n3	8:16	159n8
13:52	159n3	8:28	40n11
14:6ff.	40n6	8:33	117
14:11	125	9:1	159n2
15:8	159n1	9:5	117
15:17	174, 179n11	9:28	174
15:28	159n1	9:29	174
15:34	40n2	10:13	174, 179n8
16:16	159nn1, 2	11:2	174
17:16	159n8	11:3	179n15
17:22	65	11:8	174
19:2	138	11:34	174
19:6	159n1	12:10f.	146
19:35	65	12:18	67
20:23	159n1	12:19	179n15
20:28	159n1	14:11	174
21:11	159n1	14:17	159n2
21:28	65	15:11	174
23:10	57 Table 5.2	15:13	137
24:7	40n2	15:16	159n2
28:25	159n1	16:7	71-72
28:29	40n2	16:24	40nn2, 6

Romans		1 Corinthians	
1:4	129	1:31	174
1:9	159n8	2:10	159n8
2:9	67	2:16	174
2:16	67	3:20	174
3:28	67	5:4	159n8
4:3	174, 180n17	5:10f.	58 Table 5.3
4:8	174	6:10	58 Table 5.3
4:13	133n6	6:19	141, 159n1
5:5	159n2	6:20	159n8
5:12	67	8:4	117, 133n7
7:6	40n3	8:6	117
8:2	153	9:1f.	133n6

INDEX

1 Corinthians
10:21   174, 179n12
10:22   179n15
10:26   174
11:3   133n6
11:25   133n6
12:3   159n2, 160 n10
13:3   40n11
14:2   148
14:14   159n8
14:14ff. 149
14:21   179n15
15   84
15:45   153
16:18   159n8

2 Corinthians
1:3   117, 126
1:12   133n6
2:13   159n8
3:2   133n6
3:17   133n6
4:4   125
5:16   69
5:19   117
6:6   159n2
6:16   117
7:12   69
7:13   159n8
8:7   40n11
10:17   174
13:13f. 159n1

Galatians
1:15   174, 180n16
3:6   174, 180n17
3:11   69
6:7   117
6:18   159n8

Ephesians
1:13   159n1
2:20ff. 151
3:16   159n8
4:6   117
4:30   140, 159n1
6:18   147

Philippians
2:5ff. 51-62
2:9   129
2:13   117, 126-127
3:19   125
4:2   72

Colossians
1:8   147
1:15ff. 77-87, 162
1:28   67
2:9   88n3

1 Thessalonians
1:5   159n2
1:6   137
2:5   117
4:3-6   13, 15-16, 19-20, 23-24
4:8   159n1
5:23   159n8

2 Thessalonians
1:9   174-175
1:12   91, 94
2:4   117, 127, 133n7

1 Timothy
2:5   117
3:16   150
4:10   67

2 Timothy
1:14	159n2
2:8	40n8
2:19	179n15
4:22	159n8

Titus
1:4	90-91, 94
2:11	67
2:13	89-94
3:5	137

Philemon
25	159n8

Hebrews
1:8	97-101
2:4	137
2:6ff.	100
2:13	174, 180n17
3:7	159n1
4:2	40n11
6:4	137
7:21	174
8:8ff.	174
9:8	159n1
9:18	40n8
9:20	174
10:7	98
10:15	159n1
10:16	174
10:29	153
10:30	174
10:34	59 Table 5.4
12:5	174
12:6	174
12:29	180n16
13:6	174

James
1:8	65
1:12	65
1:20	65
1:23	65, 70
2:23	174, 179n13, 180 n17
2:26	144
3:2	65

1 Peter
1:12	137
1:24f.	179n15
2:3	174-175
3:12	174
3:15	174-175
3:18f.	149-150
3:20	40n3
4:6	145
4:14	153, 174, 180n16

2 Peter
1:1	91-94
1:2	92, 94
1:17	133n6
1:21	159n2
3:10	40n11

Jude
5	40n11
9	179n15
20	159n2
23	57 Table 5.2

1 John
3:17	85
4	160n10
4:1ff.	154
4:6	153
4:13	159n8

2 John
9   71

Revelation
1:9   40n3
1:11   40n3
2:3   40n3
2:20   40n3
2:24   40n3
3:2   40n3
3:9   43
4:8   174
5:10   40n3
5:14   40n3
11:11 153
12:5   57 Table 5.2
14:3   40n11
15:3   40n3
16:5   40n3
17:8   40n3
17:16 40n3
18:2   40n3
19:8   133n6
20:14 133n6
Revelation
21:3   40n11
21:7   117, 126
22:6   154

ABOUT THE AUTHOR

Jason David BeDuhn is an associate professor of religious studies at Northern Arizona University, in Flagstaff. He holds a B.A. in Religious Studies from the University of Illinois, Urbana, an M.T.S. in New Testament and Christian Origins from Harvard Divinity School, and a Ph.D. in the Comparative Study of Religions from Indiana University, Bloomington. He is the author of many articles in the areas of Biblical Studies and Manichaean Studies, and of the book, *The Manichaean Body: In Discipline and Ritual* (Baltimore: The Johns Hopkins University Press, 2000), winner of the "Best First Book" prize from the American Academy of Religion.

Printed in Great Britain
by Amazon